The Socioeconomic Impact
of Resource Development

Social Impact Assessment Series
C. P. Wolf, General Editor

The Socioeconomic Impact of Resource Development:
Methods for Assessment
F. Larry Leistritz and Steven H. Murdock

Large-scale industrial and energy-development projects are profoundly affecting the social and economic climate of rural areas across the nation, creating a need for extensive planning information, both to prepare for the effects of such developments and to meet state and federal environmental impact assessment requirements. This book examines alternative methods of modeling the economic, demographic, public service, fiscal, and social impacts of major development projects. The authors provide a synthesis of the conceptual bases, estimation techniques, data requirements, and types of output available, focusing on models that address multiple impact dimensions and produce information at the county and subcounty levels. They also look at the kind of data each model produces in each impact category.

Dr. F. Larry Leistritz is professor of agricultural economics and director of sponsored programs at North Dakota State University. In a study begun in 1973, he conducted extensive research on economic and fiscal impacts of resource development projects. Dr. Steven H. Murdock is associate professor of rural sociology at Texas A&M University.

C. P. Wolf, *general editor of the Social Impact Assessment Series, is research professor of social sciences at the Polytechnic Institute of New York. He was previously associated with the Environmental Psychology Program at the City University of New York and was a AAAS congressional fellow in the U.S. Office of Technology Assessment. Dr. Wolf also worked as a sociologist with the U.S. Army Engineer Institute for Water Resources and is the editor of <u>Social Impact Assessment,</u> a monthly professional newsletter.*

The Socioeconomic Impact of Resource Development: Methods for Assessment

F. Larry Leistritz
and Steven H. Murdock

Westview Press / Boulder, Colorado

Social Impact Assessment Series

Copyright © 1981 by Westview Press, Inc.

Published in 1981 in the United States of America by
     Westview Press, Inc.
     5500 Central Avenue
     Boulder, Colorado 80301
     Frederick A. Praeger, Publisher

Library of Congress Cataloging in Publication Data
Leistritz, F. Larry.
     The socioeconomic impact of resource development.
     (Social impact assessment series;no. 6)
     Bibliography: p.
     Includes index.
     1. Economic development--Social aspects. 2. Economic development
projects--Evaluation. I. Murdock, Steven H. II. Title. III. Series.
HD82.L344   338.9   81-2026
ISBN 0-89158-978-3   AACR2

82-6788

Composition for this book was provided by the authors
Printed and bound in the United States of America

TO OUR PARENTS

ELSIE M. AND KENNETH E. LEISTRITZ

AND

LOIS M. AND RAY H. MURDOCK

Contents

Tables and Figures

Preface

Large-scale resource and industrial developments are
having profound effects on many rural areas across the nation.
Increased energy resource development in many of the Western
states; water developments in the Northwest and Southwest; and
growth in rural manufacturing, particularly in the South, are
only some of the types of development impacting rural areas.
These developments may bring increased employment opportunities
and renewed economic and demographic growth to the affected
areas, but extensive planning information is required to prepare for these projects and to meet federal and state environmental impact assessment and siting requirements. As a result,
decision makers in cooperation with social scientists are increasingly called upon to undertake assessments of the social,
economic, demographic, public service, and fiscal changes resulting from resource developments.

Impact is often an ambiguous term, frequently with negative connotations, denoting change of some kind. For the
purposes of this work, we define impact as the phenomenon of
rapid change in established economic, demographic, and social
structures, usually geographically localized, caused by large-
scale, precipitous growth or decline in an area's economic
base. While the impacts of large-scale development projects
can be described in generic fashion, the nature of these effects also can be expected to differ substantially depending
on the characteristics of the project and of the site area.
Thus, the impact of a given project will differ depending on
whether the site area is rural or urban, sparsely or densely
populated, and whether its economic base is agricultural or
industrial. The impacts of a project also are likely to be
different for individual locales within the general area of
project influence. These factors increase the complexity of
impact assessment.

To make these assessments, a number of conceptual and
methodological approaches of both a qualitative and quantitative nature have been developed. These methods range from relatively simple techniques for extrapolating various social and

economic indicators, in which the interrelations between dimensions are only casually examined, to very complex computerized models in which model dimensions are systematically interrelated and integrated. Whatever their complexity, each of these methods represents an attempt to project the likely impacts of resource and industrial developments for such indicators of social and economic change as: business volume, income, employment, population, public service demands and service delivery, public costs and revenues, and community perceptions. The scope of such methods and their increasing complexity have placed increasing demands on decision and policy makers and social science analysts alike.

The demands on decision makers are extensive. If they desire to become familiar with socioeconomic impact assessment techniques to more effectively administer their programs and monitor the completion of impact assessments, they must be willing to undertake an extensive effort to master a broad base of information from such fields as demography, regional economics, sociology, and fiscal analysis. Because this information is found in a large number of individual sources which are often difficult to obtain and whose interpretation often requires a rather extensive background in a given subject matter area, decision makers face a formidable task. As a result, decision makers are often forced to rely on assessments that use methods and assumptions unfamiliar to them.

For social science analysts, particularly those who have little prior knowledge of impact assessment techniques, the task is nearly as formidable. Although they may have obtained basic conceptual and methodological training in an individual discipline, making socioeconomic impact assessments will require obtaining basic knowledge in several other disciplines, will require knowledge of the processes of economic and social change and of impact assessment procedures, and will require gaining familiarity with the pragmatic needs of decision makers and the public -- the clients in the assessment process.

For both decision makers and professional social scientists, then, there is a critical need for a single source that can provide information on the conceptual, methodological, and pragmatic considerations related to socioeconomic impact assessment methods. This work is an attempt to address this need. Specifically it attempts to: (1) describe the conceptual and methodological approaches and specific techniques for assessing the major economic, demographic, public service, fiscal, and social impacts of resource development and the patterns of interrelationship among these impact categories; (2) delineate the policy considerations and information needs related to each type of impact; and (3) present the state-of-the-art of impact assessment for projecting each of the types of impacts and their integration.

The work is thus intended to address the needs of both public and private sector decision makers who desire a single source reference on impact assessment techniques. Impact researchers and scholars who require not only knowledge of the assessment techniques used in their own disciplines, but those in related disciplines as well, and who require a basic grounding in the nature of resource development impacts, impact assessments, and the policy considerations related to the assessment of resource developments also require such a reference. That such an effort can be only partially successful, given the complexity and rapidly changing nature of this field, is evident. However, it is our hope that such an effort, by summarizing the state-of-the-art in the assessment of impacts of resource developments, will serve to improve that art as well.

F. Larry Leistritz
Steven H. Murdock

Acknowledgments

In the completion of this work, the support, encouragement, and assistance of numerous persons and institutions have been invaluable. The Department of Agricultural Economics and the North Dakota Agricultural Experiment Station at North Dakota State University and the Department of Rural Sociology, the Texas Agricultural Experiment Station, and the Center for Energy and Mineral Resources at Texas A&M University have all helped to support this effort and receive our sincere appreciation.

Numerous persons have provided assistance in manuscript preparation. In this regard, the assistance of Pat Walker, Theresa Dreher, Cheryl Peterson, Jani Richter, Cindy Weise, Nancy Lohmeyer, Pamela Hopkins, John de Montel, John Womack, Carol VavRosky, Banno Parpia, and Sean Hwang is gratefully acknowledged. In particular, the able assistance and dedication of Cindy Danielson and Becky Dethlefsen in typing the final copy as well as many of the earlier drafts; of Rana Shames in proofreading and editing references in many chapters; and of Rita Hamm in reviewing, editing, and indexing large portions of the manuscript and suggesting substantive changes which greatly improved the quality of the manuscript deserve special recognition. We also extend our sincere appreciation to our series editor, Charles Wolf, and to our managing editor, Miriam Gilbert, for their encouragement and for their suggestions, which clearly improved the quality of the manuscript. We extend special appreciation to Karen Clauson, our technical editor, whose countless hours of assistance made completion of the manuscript possible.

We also extend our appreciation to numerous colleagues and associates who provided invaluable advice in reviewing and commenting on the manuscript. Don Scott, Arlen Leholm, Ron Luke, Ken Nygard, Laurent Low, and David Rice all reviewed and commented on parts of the manuscript. To each of these we extend our appreciation. We particularly wish to thank James Copp, Donald Senechal, Thor Hertsgaard, John Thomas, Eldon Schriner,

Norm Toman, Glenn Pederson, Robert Chase, and Rita Hamm, who each reviewed the entire manuscript and provided numerous helpful suggestions.

Finally, we wish to thank our wives and families for patiently enduring the long hours and pressures that accompany such an effort and for their general encouragement and understanding.

F.L.L.

S.H.M.

1
Introduction: Dimensions of Impact Assessment

Any attempt to assess the impacts of resource developments will involve an examination of an extremely broad range of theoretical and methodological considerations. It is necessary then to begin the discussion by specifying: (1) the rationale behind the focus of the work; (2) the specific focus and limitations placed on the effort; (3) the range of conditions and factors likely to significantly affect key impact categories; and (4) the basic organization of the text.

RATIONALE FOR AN ASSESSMENT OF SOCIOECONOMIC IMPACT ASSESSMENT TECHNIQUES

Recent trends toward industrial decentralization have led an increasing number of firms to locate new facilities in rural areas (Summers et al., 1976). Similarly, changes in the nation's energy supply patterns point toward the increasing development of large-scale energy resource extraction and conversion projects in sparsely populated rural areas, particularly in the western United States. These developments present both benefits and problems to the communities nearby. While new industrial and resource development projects offer the benefits of new jobs and provide a stimulus to the local economy, they also pose the problem of rapid population growth -- a problem which few rural communities are prepared to handle.

The socioeconomic changes occurring during the construction and subsequent operation of large energy conversion plants exemplify the paradoxical effects of many types of industrial facilities on rural areas. Such projects often lead to long desired increases in local employment and to general economic growth in the area. However, the total magnitude of economic growth associated with such projects, the rapidity of the fluctuations of such patterns during the lifetime of the project, the public service demands created by growth, and the uncertainty of the timing and specific location of many of the impacts create severe planning problems for local areas.

For example, in sparsely populated rural areas, the construction of energy facilities has sometimes led to a doubling
or trebling of population in nearby communities in only a few
years with rapid growth beginning as early as the first year
of construction. This growth often fluctuates widely during
the development period with rapid growth occurring during the
construction phase followed by relative stability during the
facility's operation and by rapid population decline during
the post-operation phase. Similar patterns of growth are
often associated with the construction of large military installations and reservoirs.

Because public service needs fluctuate with population,
local areas are often faced with the difficult decision of
whether to build facilities to meet the anticipated requirements during a project's construction phase and then face the
possibility of substantial excess capacity during the operational phase or simply to attempt to make do during the construction phase and to build to meet the long-term needs resulting from the project. Added to such difficulties is the
fact that local officials often must plan with the realization
that the demands for new services resulting from a new project
are likely to precede the revenues from it (Gilmore et al.,
1976a) and with the realization that changes in the project's
construction schedule or in the settlement patterns of new
workers can often change the expected impacts (Murdock et al.,
1978). Given such a decision making environment, the need for
timely projections of the magnitude and location of economic,
demographic, fiscal, and other likely impacts of new development projects and thus the importance of the impact assessment
process that produces such information is apparent.

Socioeconomic impact assessments are also being conducted
to meet expanding regulatory demands. Federal agencies involved in major development projects are required, by the provisions of the National Environmental Policy Act of 1969
(NEPA), to prepare environmental impact statements in order to
ensure that their actions are planned with a full understanding
of the consequences (Council on Environmental Quality, 1973).
When the impacts of a project are potentially large, a number
of other federal agencies with service or resource management
responsibilites in the area also may require data from the impact assessments in order to plan their programs.

States have also shown increased interest in the impact
assessment process, and a number have enacted environmental
and/or facility siting legislation which imposes impact assessment requirements similar to those of NEPA (Auger and Zeller,
1979). Some states have imposed impact assessment, monitoring,
and mitigation requirements which go beyond those of NEPA.[1]
In addition, many states utilize information from impact assessments not only to assure the continued viability of affected communities but also to plan their own public service
programs.

Private resource development firms also have an increasing number of reasons to be vitally concerned with the impact assessment process. First, impact assessments are required as a prerequisite to obtaining necessary permits, and inadequacies of impact assessments have led to substantial delays of major projects. Second, unmanaged boom growth can lead to socioeconomic problems which adversely affect worker productivity and project costs (Gilmore and Duff, 1975). Finally, in some cases developers may be required to plan for and accept financial responsibility for the mitigation of adverse impacts as a condition for development (Watson, 1977).

Thus, federal and state officials, local leaders in affected communities, and private entrepreneurs all require information about the economic and social changes that may accompany development in order to formulate appropriate responses and to meet legal requirements. Such information must be obtained in a readily useable and interpretable form.

The assessment of the impacts of resource developments, however, often places heavy demands on the social science analysts who must perform such assessments, on policy and decision makers whose agencies are responsible for the completion of such assessments, and on decision makers who must plan facilities on the basis of these assessments. For each, the common task is to obtain the expertise necessary to carry out and evaluate such assessments.

In addition, the rapidity of the development of the science of impact assessment further accentuates the learning problems involved. Demands for timely impact information have led increasingly to the development of computerized socioeconomic impact assessment models. These models provide a relatively wide range of outputs and do so in a flexible and timely manner. The models, however, differ widely in data input requirements, computational procedures, outputs, and in many other respects. Given the diversity of such models and their clear utility in producing timely and flexible information bases, a careful and systematic comparison of the conceptual and methodological basis of such models is essential. The information and knowledge bases necessary to make such evaluations, however, are even more extensive than for noncomputerized models.

Unless a sufficient knowledge base can be obtained, research analysts and decision makers cannot address many of the questions that should be answered before the assessment process begins. These questions include:

1. What economic, demographic, public service, fiscal, or social analysis techniques are available for impact projections and which are likely to be of greatest utility under a given set of circumstances?

4

2. What are the factors likely to affect the magnitude,
   form, and distribution of economic, demographic,
   public service, fiscal, and social impacts?
3. What are the most frequent informational needs of
   decision makers in impacted areas?
4. Which of the computerized impact projection systems
   best meets the decision makers' needs, and what are
   the costs and problems involved with the use of such
   models?

To summarize, the knowledge base necessary to perform
socioeconomic impact assessments and to monitor and utilize
them is extensive and increasing rapidly. There is a clear
need for a consolidated single source reference on the assessment process which brings together:

1. A discussion of the alternative methods for assessing major types of impacts and the conceptual bases,
   relative strengths and weaknesses, and data base and
   resource requirements of each alternative;
2. A consideration of the salient features of the process of rapid economic and population growth which
   are likely to influence the nature and magnitude of
   each type of socioeconomic impact and thus to affect
   the information needs of planners, policy makers, and
   the public;
3. A description of the present state-of-the-art of impact assessment and the most frequently used methods;
   and
4. A consideration of the characteristics and features
   of the various computerized impact projection models.

This book is an attempt to provide such an information
source addressing the needs of decision makers and research
analysts.

SPECIFIC FOCUS AND SCOPE

The focus of this book is the assessment of the socioeconomic impacts of resource developments in rural areas and some
of the conceptual, methodological, and policy considerations
associated with impact assessment methods.

Resource Development in Rural Areas

The term resource development is used very broadly in the
analyses and discussion to include the development of any previously undeveloped resource of an area. Although emphasis
is given to natural resource developments, such as water and
energy resource developments, industrial developments in-

volving new uses of human resources, such as labor supplies of rural areas, are also considered. Resources refer, then, to both physical and human resources.

Emphasis is also placed on development occurring in rural areas. In part, this reflects the fact that an increasing number of resource developments are being located in rural areas. It also reflects the authors' experience and training. Although assessment principles are similar for urban and rural areas, some differences in technique are evident. References will be made to differences for various types of areas, but emphasis will be placed on assessment techniques for rural areas.

Conceptual, Methodological, and Policy Considerations

Conceptual, methodological, and policy considerations include a broad range of materials. The conceptual considerations of interest here are limited to the conceptual approaches that are the bases of methods presently used in impact assessments.

The methodological considerations are restricted to a general discussion of the computational procedures involved in various assessment methods, the relative strengths and weaknesses of each method, and the data needs and resource costs associated with the use of each method. This part of the discussion is the focal point of the work and is presented in greatest detail.

The policy considerations emphasized in the work are the information needs of policy and decision makers rather than the political considerations related to such factors as the need for impact assessments and modes of public participation. The policy focus is directed toward making impact assessments more directly serve the information needs of different types of policy and decision makers.

Projection of Socioeconomic Impacts

Although a large number of types of impacts are likely to result from resource development, the focus of this work is on those related to socioeconomic dimensions, and, within the socioeconomic realm, to indicators of change in economic, demographic, public service, fiscal, and social dimensions. The discussion deals specifically with the projection of impacts -- events that would not occur were it not for resource development being undertaken in the area. Such projections inevitably involve projections of two sets of conditions -- baseline conditions without the project and impact conditions with the project. Both baseline and impact projection techniques for assessing socioeconomic impacts are discussed for each type of impact.

FACTORS AFFECTING SOCIOECONOMIC IMPACTS AND IMPACT ASSESSMENTS

Although six specific chapters of this work each discuss some of the factors affecting a particular type of impact, it is essential to obtain a broad overview of the total range and interrelationships of socioeconomic dimensions that are likely to affect an impacted area. The intent of this section is to provide the reader with a better understanding of the total context of resource development impacts and the factors that must be considered in the impact assessment process.

The factors likely to affect impacted areas are extremely complex, and a comprehensive discussion of these is beyond the scope of this work. (However, see Murdock and Leistritz, 1979.) Among the most significant of these impact dimensions, however, are the factors shown in Table 1.1. Two categories of causal factors are included in Table 1.1: (1) characteristics of resource development projects; and (2) characteristics of areas where development projects are sited. These categories include factors which are instrumental in determining the nature and extent of a project's socioeconomic effects. Six categories of project effects also are included:

1. Characteristics of project work forces;
2. Effects on the local trade and service sectors and on other basic industries;
3. Effects on population growth and the location and characteristics of new populations;
4. Effects on public services and community infrastructures;
5. Effects on public sector costs and revenues; and
6. Effects on social organization, values, attitudes, and perceptions.

Although a realistic assessment of the economic, demographic, and social changes likely to occur in impact situations requires a detailed understanding of the interrelationships among the various dimensions, the intent here is only to provide the reader with an initial understanding of the importance of these dimensions and particularly of the importance of their many possible forms of interaction.

Causal Forces

The first two dimensions listed in Table 1.1, project characteristics and site area characteristics, have a pervasive influence on all other impact dimensions. The characteristics of the resource development project and the characteristics of the site area interact to influence virtually all impact dimensions and all phases of the impact process.

Project Characteristics. Project characteristics are particularly important in influencing work force characteristics. Resource development projects differ in their total work force requirements, in the timing of those requirements (particularly the relative magnitude of construction and operation work forces), and in the mix of skill levels required. Skill requirements in turn influence the extent to which a project utilizes local labor and the wage and salary levels of project workers. The nature of the technology, coupled with the project's construction schedule, will determine the size of the peak work force which in turn is a key factor in determining the nature and magnitude of population, public service, and fiscal effects.

The project's resource requirements and linkages with other economic sectors are key determinants of secondary economic effects. Development projects differ substantially in their economic linkages. The resource requirements of a given technology, such as use of water and land, are primary determinants of effects on other basic sectors, such as agriculture. The level of investment in project facilities may be a major factor in determining the local public sector revenues generated by the project. In addition, project characteristics may have other, more subtle, effects. For instance, the aesthetic aspects of the facility together with its impacts on the physical environment may affect local residents' perceptions of the project and may alter their basic orientation toward land use.

Site Area Characteristics. Characteristics of the site area likewise have an influence that is pervasive across all impact dimensions (see Table 1.1). An area's natural resource base is a major determinant of the feasibility of locating various types of facilities there. Present patterns of resource utilization and ownership in the site area may affect the potential for use of these resources by development firms.

The size of the local population, residents' skill levels, and the extent of underemployment and unemployment may determine the proportion of a project's employment needs which can be met by local recruitment. Site area characteristics, including amenities and climate, may also influence worker productivity. For example, certain types of construction activities are severely constrained during the winter months in many northern areas, while in areas with milder climates construction activities can proceed virtually year round, and peak work force requirements may be smaller.

Site area characteristics may influence the population effects of a new project in several ways. First, as noted above, they may have a substantial influence on the number of project workers hired locally and, conversely, on the number who will be inmigrants. Second, site area characteristics will have a substantial influence on the settlement patterns

TABLE 1.1. KEY ECONOMIC AND SOCIAL IMPACT DIMENSIONS

ITEM	KEY COMPONENTS	RELATIONSHIPS TO OTHER IMPACT DIMENSIONS
Causal Forces:		
Project Characteristics	Work force -- magnitude, skill level requirements Linkages to other sectors Investment Resource requirements	Strong relationship to all impact dimensions Relationships to work force characteristics, secondary economic effects, and fiscal effects are especially important
Site Area Characteristics	Population -- size, composition, skill levels Economic structure Resource ownership Public service infrastructure Tax System Unemployment and underemployment Social organization and structure	Strong relationships to all impact dimensions
Project Effects:		
Work Force Characteristics	Local hire rate Worker demographic characteristics Origins of immigrants Worker productivity	The major determinant of characteristics of new population Also influences secondary economic effects and public service requirements

Category	Components	Relationships
Characteristics of New Populations	Total population change Population composition Location of population growth	The major determinant of effects on public services and infrastructure Closely related to secondary economic effects, fiscal effects, and social effects
Secondary Economic Effects	Indirect and induced employment and income effects Effect of linked industries Effects on local trade and service firms Effects on wage rates and unemployment	Closely related to population effects Also related to public service, fiscal, and social effects
Effects on Public Services and Community Infrastructure	Housing Public utilities Quasi-public services (e.g., medical care) Effects on service structures	A major determinant of fiscal effects Also related to social effects and work force characteristics
Fiscal Effects	Public sector revenues Public sector costs Timing and jurisdictional distribution of costs and revenues	Related to public service and social effects Project and site area characteristics strongly influence fiscal effects
Effects on Social Organization, Values, Attitudes, and Perceptions	Social organization Attitudes Perceptions Values	Related to some degree to all impact dimensions

of inmigrating workers and their families. The number of communities within commuting distance of the project site, the quality of the local transportation networks, and the availability of housing and public and private services in the impact area communities all may influence worker settlement patterns. Finally, the availability of housing and services, together with the degree of isolation of the site area, may influence the proportion of the inmigrating construction workers who bring their families to the site area.

The secondary economic effects of a project are influenced substantially by site area characteristics. The area's economic structure will affect the developing firm's ability to purchase supplies and materials locally and may influence the propensity of project workers to purchase goods and services locally. In addition, present residents' skill levels will affect the availability of workers for certain types of enterprises and thus may enhance or reduce the likelihood that various types of linked industry may develop in the area (Gilmore et al., 1975).

Public service and infrastructure effects of new projects are influenced by site area characteristics. Any excess capacity present in an area's public infrastructure will affect its ability to absorb new populations and the cost of meeting growing demands for services. The cost of expanding services such as water and sewer may be substantially influenced by the site area's topography and geology. Existing land ownership patterns and topography may influence the availability of land for new housing development.

Fiscal impacts of new resource development projects are influenced substantially by site area characteristics. Differences in state and local tax structures can greatly affect the magnitude and timing of revenues derived from a new project and the accompanying population growth and secondary economic activity (Stinson and Voelker, 1978). In addition, the arrangement of jurisdictional boundaries in relation to the project site and location of worker's residences can, in some cases, lead to substantial mismatches of project-related revenues and costs.

Finally, areas may differ considerably in their residents' values, attitudes, and preferences toward development, social change, and conservation. The basic characteristics of indigenous social groups, of social organizations, and of social structures will determine many of the social effects of a new project. For example, if an area has a substantial number of elderly persons or other persons on fixed incomes, it can be expected to receive lower levels of benefits from development than if other population characteristics are evident (Albrecht, 1978).

Project Effects

The six categories of project effects also include a number of key dimensions and relationships.

Work Force Characteristics. Project work force characteristics form some of the key dimensions of economic and social impacts and have a substantial influence on other impact dimensions. Some of the major characteristics of interest are the proportion of the workers who are inmigrants to the area, the number and demographic characteristics of their dependents, their wage and salary levels, and their geographical origins.

The population effects of a new development project are strongly influenced by project work force characteristics. The proportion of the project work force who are inmigrants, together with the demographic characteristics of these migrants, is a major determinant of the population increase associated with a new project (Murdock et al., 1980a). In addition, increased employment opportunities resulting from a new project may lead to increased labor force participation by women and to other indirect population changes such as lower fertility levels. Increased employment opportunities likewise may lead to substantially reduced levels of out-migration from the site area.

Work force characteristics also may be an important determinant of the secondary economic effects of a new project. The propensity of project workers to purchase goods and services locally rather than in distant trade and service centers, together with the wage and salary levels of the project workers, is a major determinant of the indirect and induced employment and income effects of a new project (Tweeten and Brinkman, 1976). In addition, the extent of local hiring by the project may have a major effect on the supply of labor available to local trade and service firms. In some cases, local firms have had difficulty in competing with higher wage levels offered by a new industry.

Public service effects also depend in large measure on work force characteristics. Local hiring by the firm will affect the labor supply available to local public entities and to firms engaged in construction of housing and public facilities (Gilmore, 1976). In addition, the demographic characteristics of inmigrating project workers will affect the type of housing they desire (Leholm et al., 1976b; Wieland et al., 1977), and workers' salary levels will influence their ability to pay for different forms of housing.

The employment opportunities resulting from a new project may have several effects on local youth. The new employment opportunities associated with development may lead to the retention of more young adults in impact areas and also may discourage local youths from acquiring higher levels of education.

Further, the higher incidence of wage labor associated with
development may increase the formalization of work roles and
work-related status differences.

Characteristics of New Populations. Population characteristics of special importance are the magnitude of population change resulting from the project, the rate of that
change, the age-sex composition of the new population, and the
location of population change within the study area. These
characteristics of project-related populations have substantial implications for public service requirements and can be
expected to be a major determinant of the social and fiscal
effects of a project.

Population growth associated with a new project, together with the location of that growth, is the key determinant of additional public service and infrastructure
requirements. Substantial population growth in a rural community is likely to result not only in increased demands on
public services but also to increasing formalization of service structures. The composition of new populations can be
expected to affect the mix of service needs experienced. The
composition of these populations (particularly the number of
secondary workers in inmigrating households) will also affect
the labor supply available to local trade and service firms
and public service entities. Likewise, the composition of new
populations may affect the propensity to spend locally, with
single workers and those with permanent homes outside the area
expected to have smaller local expenditures. The residential
location of inmigrating populations will in large measure determine the location of secondary economic impacts.

Socioeconomic characteristics of new populations will affect their perceptions of site area communities and the long-
term residents' perceptions of them. Origins of inmigrating
workers may affect the social acceptance and levels of integration of workers' families into the community. Thus, social
acceptance and integration may be less difficult to the extent
that inmigrants have a regional cultural background similar to
that of present area residents.

The socioeconomic characteristics of new residents may
affect their levels of participation in community activities
and organizations. Problems of integration of new residents
into the community are likely to increase with the magnitude
and rate of population growth. Further, rapid population
growth is often associated with substantial increase in rates
of crime, juvenile delinquency, and other manifestations of
deviant behavior (Cortese and Jones, 1977).

Secondary Economic Effects. Another important category
of project impacts is its secondary economic effects. The
projects' purchases of supplies and materials from local firms

together with expenditures by project workers typically result
in increased business activity and employment in the local
trade and service sectors. A major project may also lead to
the development of linked industries in the area. These industries may be either backward-linked (i.e., supplying inputs
to the project) or forward-linked (i.e., processing products
or by-products).

Secondary economic effects of a new project may have substantial interactions with several other impact dimensions.
Growing indirect and induced employment associated with the
project is likely to lead to some inmigration of indirect
workers and their dependents. The growing demand for labor
may alter local patterns of underemployment, unemployment, and
income distribution but may also lead to substantial increases
in local wage rates and interindustry competition for labor.

Secondary economic effects also have a number of social
implications. Increased incomes may have at least three effects. First, area residents' exposure to information on
outside areas may increase. Second, area resident's interaction with others from outside the local community may also
increase. Third, area residents' awareness of social class
differences may increase as income differentials increase.

Effects on Public Services and Community Infrastructure.
A new development project may lead to substantial changes in
local public services and facilities (infrastructure). Important dimensions of public service impacts include changes
in requirements for housing (both number and types of units);
for public utilities, such as sewer and water; for public services, such as education and fire and police protection; and
for quasi-public services, such as medical care. In addition,
the changes in levels and types of public service needs which
accompany development often lead to changes in the organization of service delivery systems.

Public service and infrastructure effects can be expected
to have significant interactions with a number of other impact
dimensions. Lack of satisfactory housing and services may
influence worker productivity and turnover rates (Gilmore,
1976). If an area lacks the necessary services that workers
and their families desire, firms may be forced to pay higher
wages to compensate for these deficiencies (Mehr and Cummings,
1977). If public services are inadequate to meet basic needs
and residents feel the local quality of life has been de-
graded, business may regard the area as unfavorable for new
investment (Gilmore, 1976). Furthermore, initial strains on
particular types of services may cause shifts to alternative
service forms leading to extensive strains on those services.

Costs of public services may affect the cost of new housing units if local governments impose hookup fees or other
forms of user charges to recover the cost of service expansion. Conversely, the pattern of new housing development can

have substantial effects on the costs of providing services.
For example, dispersed patterns of housing development may
lead to higher costs for school busing, fire protection, and
sewer and water service.

If rapid community growth leads to a decrease in the
quality and range of services available to the residents,
their perceptions of the local quality of life are likely to
be lowered (Murdock and Schriner, 1979). Conflicts may arise
between new and longtime residents regarding adequacy of
present service structures. Poor quality housing and services
may lead to increased strains in family relationships (Murdock
et al., 1980b).

Fiscal Effects. The changes in public service and facility requirements associated with development of a new project typically are reflected in changes in costs incurred by
local governments. These changes in public sector costs together with the changes in revenues of local jurisdictions
resulting from the new project and associated economic growth
constitute the fiscal effects of the project. Key dimensions
of these fiscal effects include not only the magnitude of
changes in costs and revenues but also their distribution
through time and among jurisdictions.

Fiscal effects of a new project have substantial interactions with other impact dimensions. The tax structure of an
area may influence its attractiveness as a site for a new
project. Once a project is under construction, however, local
governments may find it necessary to raise tax rates in order
to meet growing needs for services. Higher taxes coupled with
rising costs of living in the impacted area may influence some
longtime residents to leave the area. Because impacted communities often are constrained in their ability to borrow --
by bonding capacity limitations and because additional revenues
from a new project often lag behind additional costs -- local
governments often experience severe cash flow problems during
the early years of project construction. These revenue short-
falls may seriously hinder local officials in their efforts to
meet growing service needs.

Fiscal problems of impacted communities may become a substantial source of local conflicts. Decisions regarding bond
issues and increases in tax rates may lead to conflicts between inmigrants and longtime residents.

Effects on Social Organization, Values, Attitudes, and
Perceptions. A major development project may lead to a variety of changes in the social structures of the site area. In
particular, such developments are likely to change the way in
which persons in rural areas interact with and relate to one
another, to change existing organizations and institutions, to
change leadership and other status arrangements in rural communities, to decrease the levels of social control and quality

of life, and to create possible conflicts between new residents and longtime residents in impact areas. Each of these impacts is likely to alter the way of life of the affected communities.

The social effects of a project have pervasive interactions with other impact dimensions. Before a project is even initiated, pressure from local groups with negative perceptions of development may lead developers to institute modifications to reduce the potential environmental damage of a project. Residents of potential site areas may differ in their receptiveness to a new project, and these attitudes may influence site selection (Albrecht, 1978).

Residents' attitudes may also influence the employment and population effects of a new project. Aspirations and career patterns of indigenous populations may affect their desire to seek employment. Residents' perceptions of the desirability of growth may affect their receptiveness to new populations, while the preference patterns of nonlocal workers and factors such as the presence of family in the impact area may affect the settlement choices of inmigrants (Wieland et al., 1979). Public views toward growth may influence local attempts to capitalize on new business opportunities associated with development. Family structure and values of local residents may affect the propensity for women and other residents to seek the new employment opportunities associated with development (Albrecht, 1978).

Attitudes and preferences of local residents and inmigrants may have substantial effects on public services (Murdock and Schriner, 1979). If inmigrants are characterized by preferences for higher levels of public services than are longtime residents, substantial increases in the overall level of service demands may be experienced. Further, organized action by groups of area residents have sometimes led the developing companies to assist in financing housing and services. Attitudes of fiscal conservatism on the part of longtime residents may hinder the passage of new bond issues, and their perceptions of acceptable tax levels may limit the ability of local governments to raise tax rates.

Finally, the site area's original social structure may have a substantial influence on subsequent social effects (Murdock and Schriner, 1978; Murdock, 1979). Thus the initial patterns of dominance and power concentrated in specific groups may affect levels of receptiveness to new groups, and the levels of conflict between new and longtime residents may be affected by interrelationships in baseline social structures. In addition, initial hostile relationships are likely to lead to further increases in conflict.

In summary, these are some of the major factors and their interrelationships that are of obvious importance in impact situations. Whether implicitly or explicitly, these factors and their interactions must be considered in the impact assessment process.

ORGANIZATION OF THE TEXT

The text consists of nine chapters in addition to this introductory chapter. Each of the first five chapters is devoted to a particular impact category (i.e., economic, demographic, public service, fiscal, and social), and the chapters are organized in the order that the issues they address are likely to be considered in developing or evaluating an impact assessment. Within each of these chapters, we briefly examine the following topics: (1) the conceptual basis of the alternative methods used in the given area of impact assessment as well as the relative strengths and weaknesses of each alternative and the data and resource requirements for implementing each alternative; (2) the key impact and policy decisions that are likely to affect the magnitude and distribution of the given type of impact in a given geographical area and that must be considered in modeling the specific type of impact; and (3) the actual projection techniques employed in current impact assessments (the state-of-the-art) and in the integration of impact dimensions.

The next three chapters examine specialized issues. Because of the importance of systematically interrelating the various impact dimensions, Chapter 7 examines techniques for integrating or interfacing economic, demographic, and other assessment methods.

Because of the increasing importance of the computerized forms of impact assessment models, Chapter 8 presents a comparison of the basic characteristics and relative strengths and weaknesses of the most widely used computerized models.

Chapter 9 deals with the utilization of impact assessments in the policy process. Factors affecting the utilization of assessments by decision makers are examined, major model validation techniques are discussed, and conditions for a successful impact assessment effort are presented.

The final chapter presents a brief conclusion which attempts to both summarize some of the major findings and to point out those areas where additional conceptual and analytical refinement appears necessary.

The topics addressed in the text are broad in scope and inclusive of only some of the many aspects of social and economic impact assessment. They represent, however, very important aspects of the impact assessment process.

NOTES

1. Impact assessment refers to efforts to anticipate the economic and social changes resulting from a new project.

<u>Monitoring</u> usually refers to efforts to discern changes in economic and social indicators soon after they occur. Monitoring efforts sometimes provide the basis for updating impact projections (Auger and Zeller, 1979). <u>Impact</u> <u>mitigation</u> refers to efforts to minimize those economic and social changes which are viewed as undesirable and to enhance those changes which are considered benefical.

2
Economic Impact Assessment

The general purpose of economic impact assessment is to measure changes in the level of economic activity which result from a specific action such as the introduction of a new plant into an area. Indicators of economic activity which are frequently used in impact assessments include industrial output (gross receipts or value added), employment, and personal income. Economic impact analysis thus measures changes in activity levels for the entire economy of the area affected by a new project, including both the private sector and the public (government) sector.[1] Effects on the public sector are frequently subjected to additional, more detailed study often referred to as public service analysis (see Chapter 4) and fiscal impact analysis (see Chapter 5).

A realistic assessment of the impact of a large-scale project typically requires projection of the level of economic activity which would be expected to prevail with and without the presence of the project. The results of this latter projection, often termed a baseline projection, can then be compared with the former projection which assumes development of the project. The difference between the two projections measures the impact of the project. Assessing the impact of a major project thus frequently involves a combination of the techniques often used in regional economic forecasting and those used in more traditional impact analyses (Richardson, 1972).

The purpose of this chapter is threefold. First, the conceptual bases and methodological alternatives for economic impact assessment are reviewed. Conceptual bases examined include economic base theory, location theory, and central place theory. The review of methodological alternatives places heavy emphasis on export base (economic base) and input-output techniques and includes an evaluation of the strengths and weaknesses, data requirements, and types of outputs associated with each method. Other techniques,

19

including intersectoral flows and econometric models, also are examined. Secondly, the characteristics of the impact process which are especially important in determining the economic effects of major projects are discussed, and the information needs of decision makers with respect to economic impacts are described. Finally, the techniques which are typically being employed in economic impact assessments and the ways in which they are applied are examined.

CONCEPTUAL BASES AND METHODOLOGICAL ALTERNATIVES IN ECONOMIC IMPACT ASSESSMENT

Over the past three decades, the factors leading to differing rates of economic growth among regions have received increasing attention. Regional scientists, principally economists and geographers, have developed a number of theoretical concepts which provide the conceptual foundations of economic impact analysis. A number of specific impact assessment techniques or models also have been developed based on these concepts. The purpose of this section is to describe first the conceptual foundations and then the major methodological alternatives for economic impact analysis.

Conceptual Bases

Three concepts of particular relevance to economic impact analysis are reviewed here. These are the export base (economic base) theory, location theory, and central place theory. Export base concepts underlie all the techniques commonly employed in economic impact assessment. Location theory is important in explaining why firms locate where they do, and it forms the underpinnings for most new firm feasibility studies. In the context of economic impact assessment for major development projects, location theory provides the basis for estimating the potential for development of linked industry in the impact area and for evaluating the potential of an area's export sectors. Central place theory deals with the hierarchy of interdependence among trade centers. It provides a means to assess the prospective geographic distribution of impacts. Through identification of the threshold or minimum market size necessary to support various types of trade and service activities, it also provides a framework for assessing the likelihood of change in the composition of the local trade and service sector in response to project development. These, then, are the principal conceptual bases underlying most impact assessment efforts.

Export Base Theory. Export base theory provides the conceptual foundation for all operational impact assessment models. This theory, which has origins in Keynesian national income and growth model analysis, was originally outlined by Haig (1926) and Hoyt (1933). More recently, the concept has been thoroughly discussed by Isard (1960), and its applications at the community level are described by Tiebout (1962), among others.

A fundamental concept of the export base theory is that an area's economy can be divided into two general types of economic units. The basic sector is defined as those firms which sell goods and services to markets outside the area. The revenue received by basic sector firms for their exports of goods and services is termed basic income. The remainder of the area's economy consists of those firms which supply goods and services to customers within the area. These firms are referred to as the nonbasic sector or sometimes as residentiary or local trade and service activities.

A second key concept in export base theory is that the level of nonbasic activity in an area is uniquely determined by the level of basic activity, and a given change in the level of basic activity will bring about a predictable change in the level of nonbasic activity. This relationship is known as the multiplier effect. Thus, export base theory emphasizes external demand for the products of the basic sector as the principal force determining change in an area's level of economic activity.

The basis for the multiplier effect is the interdependence (or linkages) of the basic and nonbasic sectors of an area's economy. As the basic sector expands, it requires more inputs (for example, labor and supplies). Some of these inputs are purchased from local firms and households. As the firms in the nonbasic sector expand their sales to the basic sector, they too must purchase more inputs. Again, a portion of these inputs comes from other local firms which in turn must purchase more inputs and so on.

Increased wages and salaries paid to labor and management by the basic sector, together with similar payments by the nonbasic sector, lead to increases in the incomes of area households. Some of this additional income is spent locally for goods and services, some is saved, and some leaves the area as payments for imported goods and services (or as additional tax payments to government). To the extent that additional income is spent locally for goods and services, the output of local firms is increased and additional cycles of input purchases and expenditure result. This cycle of spending and respending within the local economy is the basis for the multiplier effect.

Export base theory is a subset of the general subject of regional income theory (Richardson, 1969). The regional income equation which forms the basis for export base theory is:

$$Y = (E-M) + X' \qquad (2.1)$$

Where:

Y = net area product or income
X' = area exports (assumed to be exogenously deter-mined)
E = expenditures
M = imports.

Equation 2.1 simply states that area income is equal to domestic spending plus exports. Exports are thus treated as the only source of autonomous demand for the area's products.

The relationship presented in Equation 2.1 can be restated as follows:

$$Y = \frac{a - b + X'}{1 - (e-m)} \qquad (2.2)$$

Where:

e = marginal propensity to spend
m = marginal propensity to import
b = value of imports when Y = 0
a = value of expenditures when Y = 0
Y and X' are as previously defined.

The values of e, m, a, and b are assumed to be constant in a given area in the short run, although their values may vary substantially among areas. Thus the level of exports (or basic income) determines the area's total income and output.

The effect of an additional dollar of exports on area income is shown by taking the derivitive of equation 2.2 with respect to X':

$$\frac{dY}{dX'} = \frac{1}{1 - (e-m)} = K \qquad (2.3)$$

Because the value of (e-m) is expected to lie between 0 and 1, the value of K in equation 2.3 is expected to exceed 1. K is frequently termed the export multiplier.

The magnitude of the multiplier effect is determined by the proportion of a given dollar of additional area income which is spent locally. This relationship is often expressed as the marginal propensity to spend locally (Tweeten and Brinkman, 1976). Referring to equation 2.3, the marginal propensity to spend locally is simply the quantity (e-m). High multiplier values are associated with high values of e and low values of m. The value of e can be expected to vary slightly among areas, but the major deter-

minant of the variation in multiplier values is the value
of m. The more diversified and self-sufficient the area's
economy, the lower will be the value of m and the higher
the multiplier. Larger regions, then, tend to have higher
multiplier values (Harvey, 1973).

The model presented in Equation 2.1 can be broadened
to include other sources of autonomous demand, as in equation 2.4:

$$Y = C + I + G + X' - M - T \qquad (2.4)$$
Where: C = consumption expenditures
        I = investment expenditures
        G = government expenditures
        T = tax payments
        Y, X', and M are as previously defined.

The expanded model includes investment and government
expenditures as additional sources of autonomous (that is,
determined outside the area) demand for an area's goods and
services. Consumption expenditures and imports are generally considered to be determined by the level of local
income. Tax payments, except to local governments, represent a flow (or leakage) of purchasing power from the local
economy, and the amount of taxes paid is also treated as a
function of area income. In the expanded model, area income
depends on the level of exogenous expenditures $(X + I + G)$
and on the values of the marginal propensities to consume
(c), to import (m), and to tax (t). If the values of c, m,
and t are taken as predetermined, at least in the short
run, a constant multiplier relationship and area income can
again be derived.

The model outlined in equation 2.4 can be further
generalized to an interregional trade model with n interde-
pendent regions. In this case, exports of a given region
are no longer exogenous to the model; rather, they are
determined by the import demands of other regions. While
models of this form are conceptually superior to the
single-region model, such models have never been implemented empirically because of severe data limitations. Economic impact analysts thus typically utilize single-region
models. The implementation of such models, however, generally follows the expanded definition of exogenous expenditures or basic income (see equation 2.4). Federal government expenditures, expenditures by tourists and
recreationists, and other exogenous consumption and investment expenditures as well as exports are thus considered to
be components of the area's basic income.

Numerous authors have examined the strengths and limitations of the export base model. (In particular, see
Levan, 1956; Tiebout, 1962; Garnick, 1970; and Shaffer,
1979.) A major conceptual limitation of the model is that

it emphasizes changes in external demand for an area's products and completely ignores the factors affecting the area's ability to supply those products (Richardson, 1978). Some authors are concerned with the model's apparent lack of policy content and particularly with the inability of the single-region model to explain why exports change or what conditions internal or external to the region will be conducive to growth (Tweeten and Brinkman, 1976).

Other limitations of the export base model include the potential for changes in the ratio of basic to nonbasic activity over time and the possibility of lags in the adjustment process. The basic to nonbasic employment ratio may change over time because of differential rates of change in productivity of the two sectors. For example, rapid productivity increases in the basic sector may allow more nonbasic sector employment to be supported with a given level of employment in the basic sector. In growing regions, furthermore, the basic to nonbasic ratio may change over time because of the import substitution which often accompanies regional growth.[2] Lags in adjustment of nonbasic activity to changes in the level of basic activity also present a problem (Stinson, 1978a). The export base multiplier provides an estimate of the increase in nonbasic activity which would be expected as a result of a given change in basic activity. It does not, however, provide any insight regarding the time period required for full adjustment to occur. Lags also may present a problem in initially measuring the relationship between basic and nonbasic activity that prevails in a given economy (Gillies and Grigsby, 1956). Despite these limitations, however, the export base model is widely used as the basis for impact analyses.

Location Theory. Location theory is closely related to the concept of comparative advantage and emphasizes the tendency for firms to locate where they can earn the greatest profit on their investment. The conceptual location model based on profit maximization implicitly incorporates both cost and market demand factors. Development of location theory began with the work of Von Thunen in the early 19th century. Major contributors include Weber (1929), Hotelling (1929), Losch (1940), Greenhut (1956), Moses (1958), and Smith (1971).

Location theory indicates that industry location decisions are guided by the comparative costs of producing, transporting, and marketing a product from plants at various alternative locations. Location theory concepts also are useful in explaining the reasons for the development or growth of an export sector in a given area (e.g., unique resources, production cost advantages, transportation advantages). Thus, it provides a conceptual framework for assessing likely future trends in an area's export sectors.

Industries can be classified according to their general pattern of response to location factors. Those industries which require large quantities of resources whose transportation costs are quite high tend to locate close to the source of these resources and are termed resource-oriented industries. Industries which require large marketing outlays per dollar of output or whose product is bulky and expensive to transport tend to locate close to major market centers and are termed market-oriented industries. A third group of industries is the footloose industries whose profits do not vary greatly whether they are located close to raw material sources or to market centers.[3]

A final factor to be considered in assessing probable locations for industry is agglomeration economies. Agglomeration economies refer to cost savings which are realized when firms locate in proximity to one another. Agglomeration economies fall into two major categories: (1) economies external to the firm but internal to the industry; and (2) economies external to the industry. Economies external to the firm but internal to the industry might include such factors as: (1) the ability to support and have access to research and development facilities; (2) the development of a skilled labor pool; (3) the growth of auxiliary industries; and (4) the development of markets for raw materials. The other form of agglomeration economies is economies external to the individual industry. The cost savings which occur when firms from different industries congregate in the same local area are often referred to as urbanization economies (Isard, 1960) or economies of urban concentration (Hoover, 1948). These might include such factors as: (1) access to a larger market; (2) the development of pools of managerial talent; (3) the presence of specialized commercial, banking, and financial facilities; (4) development of improved transportation and communication facilities; and (5) the existence of social, cultural, and leisure facilities. Some observers believe that these agglomeration advantages are even stronger than those internal to an individual industry (Richardson, 1969).[4]

In the context of economic impact assessment for large development projects, location theory is useful as a conceptual basis for assessing the potential for development of linked industry as well as for evaluating the potential of an area's basic sectors. Export base theory provides the basis for a generalized assessment of the increase in local trade and service activity that would normally be expected to occur in response to a given level of additional basic activity. When a major new industry locates in an area, however, the possibility exists that a series of specialized firms will establish themselves in the area either to supply inputs to the industry or to utilize its products.

Firms which supply specialized inputs to the industry are
often termed <u>backward-linked</u> while those that utilize its
products are often termed <u>forward-linked</u>. Location theory
provides a general framework for evaluating the likelihood
that new backward- and forward-linked industries will
develop as the result of the location of a major facility
in a given area.[5]

   <u>Central Place Theory</u>. Central place theory attempts to
explain the location and development of "central places"
(cities, towns, and villages) in terms of functions performed and services provided, not only for the residents in
each center but also for the tributary populations surrounding each center.[6] According to this theory, an urban
center's primary function is to act as a service center for
its hinterland or trade area. The services provided by
central places can be ranked into higher and lower orders
depending on the minimum market size (sometimes called the
demand threshold) required to support the service. Some
goods and services can be efficiently supplied only from
very large centers while others are more efficiently supplied from smaller centers. Thus, trade and service centers
can be classified into a functional hierarchy according to
the types of services they provide. (For examples of empirical efforts to classify trade and service centers, see
Borchert and Adams, 1963; Berry, 1967; and Voelker <u>et al.</u>,
1978.)

   The trade areas of higher order trade centers overlap
those of the lower order centers. Residents of a small
rural town are likely to purchase some types of goods and
services locally but will obtain other, more specialized
services from higher order centers. If a new development
project should bring increased employment and income to the
community, the result will be increased levels of trade and
service activity not only locally but also in the higher
order centers.

   Central place theory provides a conceptual basis for
assessing the potential geographic distribution of the impacts of a new project. If the functional hierarchy of
central places in a region can be identified and the rank
and market area of each center can be established, the
effects of the project on each center can be estimated. The
approach that is typically taken is to integrate central
place concepts into an export base framework. Thus, the
level of nonbasic activity in any central place is assumed
to be a function of the level of basic activity in its
trade area.

   These, then, are the major conceptual bases for economic impact assessment. The next section of this chapter
examines the principal forms of empirical models which have
been developed to estimate economic impacts.

Methodological Alternatives

During the last two decades, interest in regional and urban planning and in small-area policy analysis has increased. The last decade has also been a period in which increasingly rigorous requirements for socioeconomic impact assessments and impact mitigation planning in connection with large-scale development projects have been established (Watson, 1977). These two developments have led to growing interest in techniques for regional economic forecasting and for estimating the localized impacts of new projects. In this section, the major methodological alternatives for economic impact assessment are briefly reviewed. The two principal methods used in economic impact assessment are the export base and input-output techniques. Both of these techniques are reviewed in some detail, including a discussion of each model's basic concepts, its data requirements, the nature of its outputs, and its conceptual and pragmatic strengths and limitations.

Several other types of models also have some potential for application in economic impact assessment. These include the intersectoral flows or from-to model, econometric models, and multiregional models. These models are described more briefly, with emphasis on their general strengths and limitations as tools for localized impact analysis.

Export Base Models. The export base (or economic base) model is one of the earliest empirical models to be employed in economic impact studies. Despite the subsequent development of more complex and detailed techniques, export base models are still used in most impact studies. A number of variations of the export base model have been developed.

Export base models can be broadly classified according to the indicator used to measure economic activity (i.e., employment or income). Employment is more frequently used because employment data are more readily available for small areas than are measures of income, value added, or other potential indicators. In addition, employment is a major target variable for planners and decision makers.[7] Problems arise, however, because employment may not be a very sensitive indicator of economic activity in sectors which are experiencing technological change. Thus, a sector's output and income may rise relative to employment, especially if the innovations are labor saving. When rates of productivity change are much different for the basic and service sectors, the base-service employment ratio may shift substantially. Another problem arises from the fact that basic employment is aggregated for multiplier estimation, and the same multiplier is assumed to be applicable to all basic jobs, no matter in what industry they occur.

This practice can lead to misleading results if different basic industries have substantially different wage rates and/or local input purchasing patterns. A unit change in employment in a high-wage industry will generate more total employment and income in the local economy than an equal increment in a low-wage industry, but the aggregate employment multiplier masks this effect.

The problems associated with the use of employment as a measure of economic activity can be largely overcome by substituting income for employment in the export base model. The use of income has the distinct advantage of accounting for wage-rate differentials among industries. Businesses are sometimes reluctant to release wage and salary information, however, and it is frequently difficult to obtain reliable estimates of nonwage income. The task of dividing nonwage income into basic and nonbasic components is even more difficult. Finally, income may be quite variable from year to year, and this may complicate the task of multiplier estimation, particularly if time series regression techniques are employed.

The simplest form of the export base model is based on dividing the total economic activity of the study area into two components:

$$E_t = E_b + E_s \qquad\qquad (2.5)$$

Where: E_t = total employment (or income)
E_b = basic employment (or income)
E_s = nonbasic or service employment (or income)

Given the assumption that the proportion of basic to total employment is constant, an employment multiplier, K_1, can be derived:

$$K_1 = \frac{E_t}{E_b} = 1 + \frac{E_s}{E_b}$$

To estimate the value of the employment multiplier for a given area, the analyst requires employment data for at least one recent year and a basis for dividing employment into basic and nonbasic categories. Because employment data at the county level are readily available from the U.S. Department of Commerce, the estimation process can be inexpensive and rapid.

The employment multiplier of the form, K_1, has been widely criticized because it reflects only the average relationship of basic to total employment in the local economy and because this average relationship may not be a good estimator of the change in total employment which will result from a change in basic employment (Weiss and Gooding, 1968; Lewis, 1976). An alternative formulation of the model, which is sometimes employed to overcome this problem, uses changes in basic and nonbasic employment over a period of time to estimate the multiplier.[8] This model can be expressed as:

$$\Delta E_t = \Delta E_b + \Delta E_s$$

Where: Δ indicates the change in each variable over the specified time period and E_t, E_b, and E_s are as previously defined.

In this model the multiplier, K_2, is:

$$K_2 = \frac{\Delta E_t}{\Delta E_b} = 1 + \frac{\Delta E_s}{\Delta E_b} .$$

A number of methodological alternatives must be addressed prior to the implementation of export base models. The principal alternatives involve the following factors: (1) method of identifying basic and nonbasic employment (or income); and (2) estimation of disaggregated or industry-specific multipliers. The implications of these alternatives are examined in the following paragraphs.

Identifying Basic and Nonbasic Employment. The first major decision confronting the analyst is determining the most appropriate procedure for identifying basic and non-basic employment. Four general approaches have been used to classify employment into basic and nonbasic categories: (1) the assumption approach; (2) the location quotient method; (3) the minimum requirements approach; and (4) the primary data technique.[9] The assumption approach is apparently the most widely used method. Using this method, the analyst identifies certain industries which are assumed to be basic. Agriculture, mining, and manufacturing are frequently assumed to be basic. The remainder of the area's employment is thus assumed to be nonbasic. These assumptions, however, may prove to be inaccurate. Some manufacturing, such as printing and publishing, and some food processing may be locally-oriented while many financial services, for example insurance and banking, often serve a market larger than the immediate area in which the establishment is located. In regions where tourism and recreation activities are prominent, a number of sectors which are traditionally regarded as nonbasic may be supported in substantial measure by the expenditures of tourists. The proportion of their employment which results from tourist expenditures should properly be classified as basic. If the assumption method results in an underestimate of basic employment, the employment multiplier will be over-estimated and subsequent estimates of the impact of a new facility are likely to be too high. Conversely, if basic employment is

over-estimated, the multiplier value and subsequent impact
estimates will be too low.

Attempts to improve the accuracy of employment classification over that resulting from the simple assumption
method have resulted in three alternative approaches. The
first two, the location quotient and minimum requirements
approaches, are statistical methods which compare the
area's employment patterns with those of the nation. The
third involves using knowledge of the local economic structure, gained either through a survey or by less formal
means, to assign each industry's employment between the
basic and nonbasic categories.

The location quotient method assigns employment to
basic and nonbasic categories by comparing the proportion
of the region's employment in a given industry with that
observed in some benchmark region, usually the nation. The
location quotient is defined as:

$$LQ_i = \frac{E_{ir}}{E_{in}} \Big/ \frac{E_r}{E_n}$$

Where: LQ_i = location quotient for industry i
E_{ir} = employment in industry i in the region
under study
E_{in} = employment in industry i in the nation
E_r = total employment in the region
E_n = total employment in the nation

The location quotients indicate the relative specialization
of the region in each industry. A location quotient greater
than unity indicates that the region has more than its
proportionate share of national employment in that industry. In such cases, the excess employment over propor-
tionality is assumed to be export related.[10] The economic
base employment multiplier is then computed by estimating
basic employment for all industries with location quotients
greater than one, summing the export employment of all
those industries, and dividing this sum into total employment (Isserman, 1977b).

The location quotient approach is useful as it takes
account of "indirect" exports (that is, firms who sell to
other local firms which in turn sell to customers outside
the region) as well as direct exports (Tiebout, 1962). This
method does, however, have several deficiencies. First, it
involves an implicit assumption that consumption patterns
and productivity rates are uniform across the nation.
Secondly, international exports and imports are ignored.
Finally, by assuming that the production of each industry
goes first to satisfy local needs and that only the excess

31

is exported, the location quotient approach ignores cross-hauling of goods. This leads to underestimation of the export base and an over-estimate of the multiplier. However, this systematic bias in the multiplier estimates may become less serious as the level of employment disaggregation increases (Levan, 1956; Isserman, 1977b).

A second statistical approach to employment classification is the minimum requirements approach (Ullman and Dacey, 1960). This technique involves identifying a number of representative areas and calculating each industry's percentage of employment in each area. The smallest percentage of employment found in each industry across the various sample areas is then interpreted as the minimum required to satisfy internal needs. These minimum requirements are then compared to the employment structure of the study area, and employment in any industry which exceeds the minimum requirement is classified as basic.

The minimum requirements technique has many of the same deficiencies associated with the location quotient method. Again, national uniformity in consumption patterns and productivity is implicitly assumed. This technique is likely to systematically over-estimate basic employment as the areas with the lower percentages of employment in a given industry may in fact be importing a substantial proportion of their requirements for output from this industry.[11] Finally, the reliability of this technique is reduced as employment is disaggregated into smaller sectors because disaggregation leads to estimates of minimum requirements which approach zero for most sectors.

An evaluation of the estimation error associated with both the location quotient and minimum requirements techniques was undertaken by Greytak (1969). He finds that both techniques result in export estimates which deviate substantially and systematically from those actually observed. While subsequent work by Isserman (1977b, 1980) demonstrates that the performance of the location quotient technique is improved substantially by disaggregation of industrial sectors, the desirability of specific knowledge about the area under study appears obvious.

The final approach for determining basic employment, the primary data technique, involves obtaining additional information regarding the composition of the local economy. In some cases, a number of firms in each industry may be interviewed to determine the percentage of their sales which are to customers outside the area. This technique can be expected to yield more accurate results than the methods discussed earlier, but the data collection process may become expensive if a large number of firms are involved. The quality of the results is also dependent on the ability of producers to accurately estimate the areal distribution of their customers (Pfister, 1976). Finally, the analyst must attempt to detect indirect exports. The interview technique sometimes can be supplemented with information from secondary sources, such as a state directory of manufacturers, and can be used in conjunction with the location quotient or minimum requirements techniques.

Estimating Disaggregated Multipliers. Another approach which can be used to overcome the problems posed by differentials in wage rates and input purchase patterns among basic industries is to estimate separate multipliers for each basic industry (Weiss and Gooding, 1968; Braschler, 1972; McNulty, 1977). An excellent example of this approach is provided by Bender (1975). In this analysis, all employment in four specified industries was assumed to be basic, and all employment in the remaining industries was assumed to be nonbasic. Cross-sectional data from a large number of counties were used in a regression analysis to estimate separate multipliers for each of the four basic industries.[12] The disaggregated model can be summarized as follows:

$$E_t = a + b_1 X_1 + b_2 X_2 + b_3 X_3 + u \qquad (2.6)$$

Where:
E_t = total employment,
X_1, X_2, X_3 = employment in three different basic industries,
b_1, b_2, b_3 = industry-specific employment multipliers, each of which indicates the change in total employment associated with a one unit change in employment in the respective basic industry,
u is a stochastic disturbance term.

Strengths and Limitations of Export Base Models. Although the export base model has definite limitations as a general theory to explain regional growth, it has found widespread use in impact analysis. One reason for the popularity of this model is undoubtedly its simplicity and low cost (Pfister, 1976). The model can be, and generally is, implemented using secondary data exclusively. Further, the necessary computations can be completed in a relatively short time and do not require access to computer facilities, at least for the simpler formulations of the model. This model, however, provides very limited impact information. In essence, the export base model indicates only the aggregate effect on an area's nonbasic employment (or income). Further, in the simpler formulations of the model, all basic employment is assumed to have the same local multiplier effect. Such aggregate models ignore the differences among basic industries in input purchase patterns, wage rates, and worker spending patterns.[13] Refine-

ments of the model alleviate the problems associated with
the aggregate employment multiplier either by substituting
income for employment in the multiplier analysis or by
estimating separate multipliers for each of the area's
important basic sectors.[14] These refinements, however, come
at the cost of greater data requirements. To summarize, the
export base model usually provides highly aggregated estimates of economic impacts. Analysts who desire more detailed impact projections, including estimates of effects
on individual sectors of the local economy, have often
turned to input-output models.

Regional Input-Output Models. Regional input-output
models have been utilized extensively in regional impact
studies.[15] These models are based on analysis of the interdependence of a region's industries and households as suppliers of inputs and purchasers of products. In developing
an input-output model for a given region, the regional
economy is divided into sectors (groups of similar economic
units), and the transactions among the various sectors are
estimated. The quantitative estimates of the interdependencies among the various sectors then provide the basis for
tracing the multiplier effects of an exogenous shock to the
economy in a more detailed manner than do export base
models. In general, a regional input-output model can be
viewed as a disaggregation of the export base model which
allows for consideration of a large number of local industries with varying proportions of basic activity and for
consideration of several sources of exogenous demand for
the region's products (Richardson, 1972; Romanoff, 1974).

Input-Output Structure and Assumptions. The basic equation of the input-output model is:

$$X_i = \sum_{j=1}^{n} x_{ij} + Y_i \qquad (2.7)$$

Where: i and j = 1, 2 ... n
x_{ij} = the amount of industry i's output required for the production of industry
j's output,
Y_i = sales to final demand by industry i,
x_i = total output of industry i.

Equation 2.7 describes a system of linear equations, one
for each industry (or producing sector) of the regional
economy. The output of each industry is divided between
intermediate products (or interindustry transactions) described by x_{ij} and final products (Y_i). Final products or

sales to final demand are generally assumed to consist of
sales for consumption, investment, government, and exports.
   To facilitate empirical implementation of the model,
the following assumptions are made:

   a. Each industry produces a single, unique product.
   b. There are no economies or diseconomies of scale.
   c. Each industry has a single production process and
      no substitution among inputs is possible.[16]

Assumptions b and c imply a constant relationship between
each sector's output level and its input requirements:

$$x_{ij} = a_{ij}X_j \qquad (2.8)$$

   Where: a_{ij} is the production coefficient specifying
           the amount of output from industry i
           needed to produce one unit of the output
           of industry j, and X_j is the output level
           of industry j.

   By substituting equation 2.8 into equation 2.7, we
obtain:

$$X_i = \sum_{j=1}^{n} a_{ij}X_j + Y_i \qquad (2.9)$$

Equation 2.9 is a system of n linear equations which may be
solved for X_i if the values of the a_{ij} and Y_i are known.
   In matrix notation, equation 2.9 may be written as:

$$X = AX + Y \qquad (2.10)$$

Equation 2.10 can then be solved for the vector X as follows:

$$X = (I - A)^{-1}Y \qquad (2.11)$$

   Where: X is a vector of output for each industry, X_i
           (i = 1, ..., n)
           A is a matrix of production coefficients (also
           called direct requirements coefficients or
           technical coefficients)
           I is an identity matrix
           Y is a vector of sales to final demand for
           each industry
           $(I - A)^{-1}$ is a matrix of interdependence coef-
           ficents which show the direct and indirect
           requirements for output from each sector to
           support one unit of sales to final demand. (For
           a detailed discussion of the technical and inter-
           dependence coefficients and their interpretation,
           see Mierynk, 1965; or Doeksen and Schreiner, 1974.)

Implementation of the input-output model, equation 2.9 or
2.11, requires independent estimates of the technical coefficients (a_{ij}) and the sales to final demand (Y_i). Given
these estimates, the input-output model can be used for
both impact analysis and regional forecasting (Richardson,
1972).

   Use of Input-Output Multipliers. Impact analysis involves estimating the effect on the regional economy of a
specified change in the output of one or more economic
sectors. Input-output (I-O) provides a mechanism for estimating the effect of a new project on output, income, and
employment for the regional economy as a whole. It can also
provide estimates of changes in output and employment for
each sector. Final demand, output, income, and employment
multipliers derived from the input-output equation system
provide useful summary measures of the relationship between
expansion or contraction of a given sector and the total
change in economic activity created throughout the economy.
   The final demand multiplier for a sector measures the
change in total output from all sectors resulting from a
one dollar change in sales to final demand of products of
that sector. The output multiplier for a sector measures
the change in total output from all sectors resulting from
a one dollar change in the output of that sector (Roesler
et al., 1968). Both final demand and output multipliers can
be computed directly from the matrix of interdependence
coefficients. The choice between these two multiplier forms
in impact analysis depends primarily on the relative availability of information on sales to final demand versus
output for the sector to be analyzed. It is critical,
however, that analysts not confuse the two multiplier
forms. The income multiplier measures the total change in
income (of households) throughout the economy resulting
from a one dollar change in income in a given sector.
   The employment multiplier, as computed from the I-O
model, is defined as the total change in employment due to
a one unit change in employment in a given sector. The
basic assumption in computing employment multipliers is
that there is a linear relationship between employment and
output of a sector. Computation of employment multipliers
requires an estimate of the direct employment requirement
(that is, the person-years of employment per unit of output) for each sector. Given this information, the I-O
interdependence coefficients matrix can be used to compute
the direct and indirect employment requirements and the
employment multiplier for each sector. (For further discussion of input-output multipliers and the details of their
calculation, see Miernyk, 1965; and Doeksen and Schreiner,
1974.)
   A number of factors affect the magnitude of the multi-

pliers estimated from the input-output framework. First, multiplier values may differ substantially from sector to sector because of differences in the linkages of the individual sectors with other sectors of the regional economy. A sector which depends heavily on other local sectors for its inputs will typically have higher multiplier values than one which imports most of its input requirements. Secondly, multiplier values tend to vary directly with the size of the region being studied, for the same reasons discussed earlier in connection with export base models. Finally, input-output multiplier values are affected by the structure of the model itself. In particular, some regional I-O models include households as a producing sector; these models are said to be closed with respect to households. Such models reflect the induced effects of the expansion of a given industry (that is, the additional household consumption which results from the additional income associated with industrial expansion) as well as the indirect effects (arising from additional requirements for production inputs) and the direct effects (that is, the initial increase in the industry's output).

Input-output models used in impact assessments for major projects typically are closed with respect to households, although this is not always the case. Multipliers derived from I-O models of this type are termed Type II multipliers to distinguish them from the Type I multipliers which reflect only direct and indirect effects. The income and employment multipliers derived from the closed I-O model are closely analogous to those from export base models. In fact, it has been demonstrated that the export base income multiplier and the consolidated closed I-O multiplier are mathematically identical (Billings, 1969). Both reflect direct, indirect, and induced effects of exogenous changes in demand for a region's output, and both are average rather than marginal multipliers. Further, empirical comparisons of the two multipliers, using similar definitions of basic activity, indicate that their values tend to be similar (Garnick, 1970).

Given the conceptual and empirical similarity of the export base and input-output multipliers, the major bases for selecting between the two models are the required level of detail for the analysis, the availability of necessary data, and the time and resources available to the analyst. I-O models clearly provide more detailed impact projections (that is, they show effects on output and employment by sector), and they are more sensitive to differences in input purchasing patterns and salary levels among sectors. These models are capable of extension to allow projection of employment by occupation (Drake et al., 1973), and they can also be employed to project changes in income distribution (Sherafat et al., 1978). Another extension of the I-O

model is to incorporate coefficients reflecting the resource use and environmental emmissions per unit of output
for each sector. The model can then be utilized to estimate
changes in resource utilization and environmental quality
associated with the various economic projections and to
analyze economic-environmental trade-offs (Isard et al.,
1972). However, input-output models also impose substantial
data requirements. The data requirements of the input-output
model are discussed in the next section.

   Input-Output Data Requirements. The most difficult
and time consuming task in implementing a regional input-
output model is developing estimates of the direct requirements
coefficients (technical coefficients). These coefficients
are frequently estimated using primary data collected through
an extensive survey of firms and households in the study area.
(For a detailed discussion of the procedures involved in
developing input-output coefficients from primary data, see
Richardson, 1972.) These data provide a detailed description
of the interdependencies among the sectors of the local
economy. The time and expense required to prepare input-output
tables based entirely on primary data are considerable, however, and may exceed the resources available for many impact
studies.[17]
   In an attempt to reduce costs associated with regional
input-output analysis, a number of techniques for developing input-output coefficients totally or partially from
secondary sources have been developed. All of these techniques are based on adjusting coefficients already available
for some larger area (such as the nation or the state) to
approximate the interindustry relationships of the study
area. The principal difference among these techniques is
the extent to which they require collection of primary data
from local firms. These methods can thus be catagorized as
either limited survey (or semisurvey) or nonsurvey techniques.[18]
   The limited survey techniques require some primary
data collection but employ simplifying assumptions to reduce the number of sectors from which data must be collected, or the amount of information required from each
respondent, or both. Representative of these methods are:
(1) The Rows-Only Approach (Hansen and Tiebout, 1963); (2)
The Columns-Only Approach (Harmstrom and Lund, 1967); (3)
The Technique for Area Planning, or TAP (Bonner and Fahle,
1967); (4) The Rectangular Matrix Method, or RMM (Davis,
1976); and (5) The RAS Method (Stone, 1961). All of these
methods allow for significant reductions in data collection
requirements, accompanied by some loss of accuracy. Several
recent analyses, however, suggest that the loss in accuracy
may not be severe (Smith and Morrison, 1974; Davis, 1978).
The semisurvey techniques may offer an attractive com-

promise in many situations where the detail provided by an input-output analysis is desired but resource limitations prevent a standard survey.

Nonsurvey techniques rely entirely on secondary data sources. These methods fall into three major categories: (1) the location quotient approach; (2) the commodity balance approach; and (3) the iterative procedures approach (Morrison and Smith, 1974). Evaluations of the accuracy of these techniques have led to differing conclusions regarding their acceptability. Several studies have concluded that the level of error present in such analyses is unacceptably great (Miernyk, 1976; Schaffer and Chu, 1969). These authors conclude that, at a minimum, supplementary surveys are required to supply coefficients for primary industries and for industries in which the region is specialized. Other analysts, however, believe that nonsurvey methods can be used to develop coefficients with satisfactory levels of accuracy in a very cost-effective manner (Boster and Martin, 1972).[19]

If an input-output model is to be used as a forecasting tool, projections of sales to final demand are an essential data requirement, and estimates of future changes in the I-O technical coefficients also may be required. The problem of projecting sales to final demand has two aspects: (1) projecting sales to final demand under baseline conditions; and (2) projecting changes in sales to final demand associated with a new development project. Developing projections of sales to final demand is a challenging task. Because the issues involved in projecting sales to final demand are similar to those associated with projecting basic employment, however, this subject will be examined in the subsequent section on economic impact assessment techniques.

If projections are being made over a substantial time period, it is also necessary to consider forecasting changes in the I-O technical coefficients. There are at least five reasons why regional input-output coefficients may vary over time: (1) changes in relative prices of inputs; (2) changes in product mix; (3) technological change; (4) economies of scale; and (5) changes in regional trade patterns (Richardson, 1972). There is some evidence, however, that these coefficients may be relatively stable over time, at the regional level (Miernyk, 1968). The major exception may be in rapidly growing regions where import substitution effects can be substantial.

There are several alternative methods of forecasting changes in I-O coefficients at the regional level. Most of these are imperfect, however, and rely heavily on the analyst's judgement (Richardson, 1972). Some of these approaches are: (1) to obtain national projections of changes in coefficients and apply them proportionately to the regional coefficients; (2) if two I-O tables are available for the region, to compare the coefficients and use this as the basis for forecasting a third table of direct require- ments coefficients; and (3) using data from a regional I-O survey, to apply the "best practice" technique described by Miernyk (1968).[20] The use of these techniques may not be feasible in many impact studies, but, if long-range fore- casts are required, the analyst should at least consider the possibility of changes in the I-O coefficients (Harmstrom and Lund, 1967).

Strengths and Limitations of Input-Output Models. Like export base models, input-output models have been used extensively in assessing economic impacts at the local, state, and national levels. Criticisms of the I-O model from a theoretical standpoint focus mainly on its assump- tion of constant coefficients. This criticism is valid, but it should be recognized that the principal alternative model, the export base model, shares this shortcoming. The problems posed by constant coefficients can be overcome, as discussed earlier, but only through substantial effort and at the cost of increased data requirements. Another similar- ity between the input-output and export base models is that both are equilibrium models which indicate the estimated secondary economic effects once the local economy has fully adjusted to a change in basic economic activity. Neither model provides an estimate of the time path of adjustment, and this characteristic can pose problems when they are used to assess the impacts of large projects. (The export base model may offer greater potential for extension in this regard, however).

In summary, the input-output model provides more de- tailed impact estimates than the export base model and shares many of that model's basic assumptions. The data collection and analysis requirements associated with I-O models have been the major impediment to their more wide- spread utilization.

Other Economic Impact Models. A number of other models have occasionally been utilized in economic impact assess- ment or have potential for such application. This section briefly reviews a number of these models, including the intersectoral flows or from-to model, regional econometric models, and multiregional models.

The Intersectoral Flows or From-To Model. The intersec- toral flows model combines elements of the input-output and export base models. The concept was introduced by Levan (1961); examples of empirical applications include studies by Hansen et al. (1961) and Kalter (1969). The key element

of the model is a table showing the distribution of the
sales of each local sector to other local sectors, exports,
and other forms of final demand. From this table can be
derived estimates of: (1) direct input requirements; and
(2) direct and indirect requirements similar to those developed in input-output models. The direct and indirect requirements coefficients can then be used to derive employment or output multipliers for each local sector (Doeksen
and Schreiner, 1974).

The from-to model is clearly a compromise between the
export base and input-output models. Unlike the input-output
model, the from-to model ignores data on imports. This
leads to at least one major advantage and one disadvantage.
The advantage is that data requirements of the from-to
model are greatly reduced, compared to the input-output
model. The disadvantage is that there is no cross-checking
mechanism such as that contained in I-O models (where the
rows and columns must balance). The from-to model, then,
offers a potential alternative to analysts who desire more
detail than is provided by export base models but want to
avoid the expense of developing an input-output model.

Econometric Models. A relatively recent development
in regional economic analysis has been a growing interest
in regional econometric models. These models are generally
based on time series data (that is, observations on the
same economic variable on a regular temporal basis).
Regression analysis is the principal statistical tool used
to estimate the relationships between economic variables.
The interest in developing econometric models at the regional level has been fostered in large measure by the
development of econometric models for forecasting wages,
prices, income, and output at the national level. (For
example, see Evans and Klein, 1968.) Regional analysts
rapidly perceived the potential for developing regional
models which could be linked to these national models and
which would use as exogenous variables the forecasts of the
latter (Klein, 1969). A number of econometric models have
been developed for multistate regions (Crow, 1973); for
states (Adams et al., 1975); and for substate areas
(Glickman, 1977).

The development of regional econometric models has
been hampered by substantial data constraints. Whereas
national models are typically based on quarterly data,
regional models must rely on annual data, and the published
data series are often quite short. Scarcity of data has led
to model structures which are usually quite simple, relatively static, and lacking in spatial disaggregation
(Glickman, 1977). Very few models have been estimated for

substate areas, and these have generally been for SMSAs.

While national and regional econometric models are a promising tool for those engaged in regional analysis, it does not appear likely that they will soon replace the more traditional economic impact assessment techniques. Data availability likely will continue to severely limit their application in nonmetropolitan substate areas. State and national econometric models may prove useful, however, in developing regional projections of sales to final demand or basic employment.

Multiregional Models. Regional analysts have long been intrigued by the concept of multiregional or inter-regional economic models which could explicitly quantify the linkages among the various regions of a nation. Such models would circumvent one of the major problems of single-region economic base or input-output models -- that being the need for exogenous projections of exports. In a multiregional model, the exports of a given region are determined by the import demands of all other regions. Two forms of multiregional models are of particular interest in the present context. These are multiregional or inter-regional input-output models and the Harris Multiregional, Multiindustry Forecasting Model.

The theoretical structure of interregional input-output models was first discussed nearly three decades ago by Isard (1951), but little progress was made in applying such models until recent years because of data limitations and computer capacity constraints. Work by Polenske (1969) and Almon et al. (1974) has recently stimulated renewed inter-est in interregional models, and some progress has been made in adapting the multiregional framework to substate areas. For example, a twelve-region model for the south-western United States has recently been implemented, based in large measure on the work of Almon. The model's twelve regions include the seven state planning districts of New Mexico; the states of Arizona, Colorado, Utah, and Texas; and the rest of the United States (Brown and Zink, 1977). Multiregional I-O models, then, show potential as a tool for regional analysts, but the data requirements of these models and the resources required to implement them are substantially greater than those associated with single-region models.

The Harris Model is of interest because it has been used extensively in impact analysis by the U.S. Bureau of Land Management (Betters, 1979) and by Resources For the Future (Krutilla et al., 1978). This recursive econometric model is capable of developing annual forecasts at the county level (for all of the 3,111 counties in the United States) for 99 industry sectors, 4 government sectors, and

28 types of construction activity. The model is based on location theory coupled with input-output analysis. The location of the various industries is allowed to shift over time in response to changes in the demand for their products and the price and availability of inputs. The model is described in considerable detail in Harris (1973), and its usefulness in the impact assessment and planning process is evaluated by Betters (1979).

Comparison of Alternative Economic Impact Assessment Methods. The purpose of this section is to provide a brief summary and comparison of the strengths and weaknesses of the alternative economic impact assessment techniques discussed above. The comparison of the major alternatives is summarized in Table 2.1. In examining Table 2.1, it should be noted that all of these models can be critized on several grounds. All are essentially "static" models which assume fixed relationships between local sectors. This characteristic can potentially be altered in most of the models, but only at the cost of greater data requirements and with willingness to assume that past trends of change in intersectoral relationships will continue. Incorporation of dynamic properties (e.g., changes in basic/service ratios, lags) generally is simplest in the export base models. None of the models directly account for the import substitution effects which may accompany regional growth. Likewise, all of these models assume no underemployment of resources (i.e., no excess capacity) in the local economy.
Other limitations shared by all the models compared in Table 2.1 include their lack of mechanisms for estimating the timing and geographic distribution of economic impacts. Problems in estimating the timing of secondary economic effects are endemic to export base and input-output models because these are equilibrium models which estimate the secondary economic effects once the local economy has fully adjusted to a change in basic economic activity. Export base and input-output models also typically do not provide estimates of the geographic distribution of secondary effects. These models are typically estimated at the county or multicounty study area level and provide estimates of the total secondary effects within the area. One recent study (Chalmers et al., 1977), however, illustrates a method of modifying the export base (income multiplier) model to provide estimates of the distribution of secondary effects among counties in an impact area.
In summary, there is probably no single ideal model for local area economic impact analysis. The choice among models must be determined through a balancing of model capabilities and resource requirements. In making this choice, however, it is important that both the nature of

the impact process and the information needs of decision
makers with respect to impact assessment and mitigation be
considered. These topics are discussed in the next section.

FACTORS AFFECTING ECONOMIC IMPACT ASSESSMENTS

In the actual projection of economic impacts, the key
factors affecting the results include the nature of the
project and characteristics of the site area. These causal
forces interact through the complex process of regional
economic adjustment to determine the nature, magnitude, and
distribution of impacts. Impact assessment techniques must
be designed to account for these interactions. Because
impact assessments are intended to be tools for decision
making, assessment methods also should be structured to
produce projections in the form which will be most useful
to policy makers and managers. The purpose of this section
is to describe those characteristics of resource development projects and site areas which are likely to affect the
nature of the impacts experienced, to examine the salient
features of the economic adjustment process, and to discuss
the information needs of decision makers relative to economic impacts.

Project Characteristics

The characteristics of the development project are
central in determining the nature and extent of all forms
of economic impacts. Project characteristics of particular
interest include work force (number, skill levels, and
timing), investment, input purchase patterns (by sector and
by location of suppliers), specific forward linkages to
other sectors, and natural resource requirements. Work force
characteristics are of obvious importance. Development
projects differ in their total work force, in the relationship between construction and permanent work forces, and in
the mix of skill levels required for each phase. Skill
requirements in turn influence the project's ability to
utilize local labor and also are instrumental in determining the wage and salary levels of project workers (which
may in turn affect wage levels in other industries).
A project's resource requirements and linkages with
other economic sectors are key determinants of secondary
economic effects. Resource and industrial development projects differ substantially in their economic linkages --
both forward to processors of their products and by-products
and backward to suppliers of inputs. The resource requirements of a given project, such as use of water and land,
are primary determinants of effects on other basic sectors,
for example, agriculture. The level of investment in

TABLE 2.1. COMPARISON OF STRENGTHS AND WEAKNESSES OF ALTERNATIVE ECONOMIC IMPACT ASSESSMENT TECHNIQUES

ALTERNATIVE MODELS

1. Export Base -- Aggregate Employment Multiplier	2. Export Base -- Disaggregated Employment Multiplier	3. Export Base -- Income Multiplier	4. I-O Location Quotient	5. I-O Primary Data
Major Strengths:				
Data are readily available	Provides for differentiation of multiplier estimates among basic industries	Provides differentiated multiplier estimates	Provides differentiated multiplier estimates and also accounts for input purchase linkages	Provides differentiated multiplier estimates and also accounts for input purchase linkages
Resource requirements are modest -- less than for any other alternative	Can provide a labor income multiplier indirectly (through the application of assumed wage rates to number of jobs in each sector)	Can provide an employment multiplier indirectly (through the application of wage rates to nonbasic income)	Provides estimates of employment, income, and output effects	Provides estimates of employment, income, and output effects
Can be modified to incorporate timing and geographic distribution of secondary effects	Data are readily available	Data are readily available	Identifies incidence of economic impact by sector	Identifies incidence of economic impact by sector
Can provide a labor income multiplier indirectly (through the application of estimated wage rates to the number of jobs in each sector)	Can incorporate timing and geographic distribution of secondary effects	Can incorporate geographic distribution and, potentially, timing of secondary effects	Amenable to expansion to examine changes in employment by occupation, resource use, etc.	Amenable to expansion to examine changes in employment by occupation, resource use, etc.
		Modest resource requirements	Estimates of activity by sector can be advantageous for subsequent tax calculations	Estimates of activity by sector can be advantageous for subsequent tax calculations

Modest resource requirements		Resource requirements are moderate, but data problems may increase costs in rural areas (because of non-disclosure in secondary sources)	Primary data allows possibility of adjusting coefficient over time via "best practice technique"
		Coefficients are acknowledged to be somewhat biased	High data collection and processing costs
		Does not directly estimate timing or geographic distribution of effects (these can be incorporated through side-calculations)	Does not directly estimate timing or geographic distribution of effects (these can be incorporated through side-calculations)

Major Weaknesses:

Does not provide for differentiation of multiplier estimates among basic industries	Employment may be a less sensitive indicator of economic activity than income	Income data poses some analytical problems -- particularly the division of nonwage income into basic and non-basic categories
Employment may be a less sensitive indicator of economic activity than income	Provides only aggregate measures of secondary effects -- no distribution by sector	Provides only aggregate measures of secondary effects
Provides only aggregate measures of secondary effects -- no distribution by sector		

project facilities may be a major factor in determining
the local public sector revenues generated by the project.
The adequacy of local revenues can be expected to influence
public sector decisions regarding investment in infrastructure which may in turn affect local business investment
decisions (Gilmore, 1976).

Site Area Characteristics

Characteristics of the site area likewise have an
influence that is pervasive across virtually all economic
impact dimensions. An area's natural resource base, labor
force, and level of economic development can have considerable influence on the economic impacts resulting from a
given project. An area's natural resource base is a major
determinant of the feasibility of locating various types of
facilities there, and resource ownership patterns may play
a key role in determining the distribution of royalty
payments to area residents.

Site area characteristics may greatly affect the composition of a project's work force. The size of the local
population, residents' skill levels, and the extent of
underemployment and unemployment could determine the proportion of employment needs that could be met by local recruitment. Site area characteristics, including amenities and
climate, also may influence worker productivity.

The secondary economic effects of a project also may
be greatly influenced by site area characteristics. The
area's economic structure will affect the development
firm's ability to purchase supplies and materials locally
and also may affect the propensity of project workers to
purchase goods and services locally. Areas with more diversified economies and better developed trade and service
sectors thus typically experience greater secondary economic effects.

Interactive Effects of Project and Area Characteristics

The economic effects of large-scale development projects also result in large part from interactions between
the scale of the project, the timing of project events, the
ability to use local resources, and the characteristics of
the site area. The direct employment effects of a large
development project typically occur in two phases: the
construction of the facility and its subsequent operation.
Construction work force requirements generally are much
greater than operational requirements. As a result, the
socioeconomic impacts of such facilities are cyclical,
being greatest during construction phases, reducing
markedly from construction to operation periods, and poten-

tially declining even more dramatically once the operational life of the project has ended.

The extent to which the project's employment requirements are met by local workers plays a key role in determining the magnitude of other economic effects and also influences other impact dimensions. When most of the workers can be recruited locally, inmigration and local population growth are minimized as are impacts on public services. Other local employers may experience difficulty in retaining skilled employees, however, and local wage rates may increase substantially. The extent to which project construction jobs are filled by inmigrating workers is almost certain to affect the percentage of project payroll which is spent locally and hence the magnitude of secondary employment and income effects. The settlement-commuting patterns of the project work force will also influence the geographic distribution of secondary economic effects.

Because of the rapid fluctuations in direct employment requirements between project construction and operation phases, the assumptions regarding the timing of increases in indirect employment are of obvious importance to the accuracy of not only the total employment projections but also subsequent projections of population changes and public service requirements. At least three hypotheses have been advanced to explain the response of secondary employment. The first is that lags in employment response are typical and occur because time is required for the local multiplier process to work itself out and for a new equilibrium to be achieved.[21] The second hypothesis is that, during construction of a large project, secondary employment growth will be further retarded because the economic stimulus is perceived as temporary and because rapidly growing boomtowns are not viewed as attractive sites for new business investments (Gilmore, 1976). Finally, some analysts (Auger et al., 1976; Denver Research Institute, 1979) have hypothesized a "construction accelerator effect" on secondary employment associated with major projects. The rationale for this effect is that a major development will lead to substantial construction of new housing, public facilities, and business structures. Thus, sizeable work forces may be required to build the new facilities and, in addition, these secondary construction activities will have their own multiplier effects on the local trade and service sectors. The result could be major increases in secondary employment during the early years of the project, followed by some reduction in secondary employment levels as the local economy achieves a new equilibrium condition. Efforts to measure the timing of secondary employment growth in impacted rural areas have produced somewhat contradictory results (Conopask, 1978; Thompson et al., 1978; Gilmore and

48

Duff, 1975), and more research is clearly needed on this topic.

Because a large project may lead to very substantial growth in the affected area, the potential exists for import substitution and for significant changes in regional trade patterns; and the existing hierarchy of trade centers may be altered. Impact analysts must take these effects into consideration in developing their projections.

Impact assessments must also take account of the possible effects on other basic sectors resulting from development of the proposed project. Such effects may be the result of direct competition for resources such as land, water, and labor or could possibly result from the effects of air pollution or aesthetic aspects of the project. The aesthetic aspects of a project, together with its impacts on the physical environment, could, for example, have negative effects on an area's present recreation and tourism industry.

While most impact assessment efforts have been directed toward evaluating potential effects in terms of estimating overall changes in employment, income, and other indicators for a given area, the distribution of these effects also must be considered. While it appears that local workers who obtain employment will experience substantial income gains and that the effect of most projects will be to increase average per capita income levels (Leistritz et al., 1980a), little is known concerning the effects of large projects on income distribution. Some segments of the local population, such as the elderly, may experience little change in their incomes as a result of development but may experience substantial increases in living costs (Thompson et al., 1978). These persons could suffer as a result of development. More detailed evaluations of the distribution of development-related benefits and costs may be required before the desirability of these developments can be adequately assessed.

Information Needs of Decision Makers

The decision-making environment which exists in a rapidly growing rural community has several specific implications with respect to the information needs of planners and policy makers. First, because many of the necessary decisions must finally be resolved at the local level, projections of changes in population, service needs, and public sector revenues must be provided for individual jurisdictions. This obviously means that economic impacts also must be projected for individual jurisdictions. Secondly, because the timing of socioeconomic changes is critical in local planning and decision making, annual

projections are extremely useful. The need for annual projections, in turn, requires impact analysts to address
questions concerning the time path of economic adjustment.
Finally, because many local decisions require evaluation of
the project's effects in the context of the entire regional
economy and its dynamic functioning, impact projections
must indicate not only the likely consequences if the
project is developed but also the expected future without
development, or baseline situation (Morse, 1980).

The nature of the decisions confronting impacted communities appears to indicate greater needs for specificity
of impact projections by time period and geographic unit
than by economic sector or occupation group. Thus, employment projections clearly must be provided annually and at
county or subcounty levels, but projections of employment
by industry and occupation often appear less essential.
Such disaggregated projections may be important, however,
in order to link the economic projections to subsequent
projections in the demographic, public service, and fiscal
areas. Projections of employment by occupational category,
for example, might be extremely useful in estimating the
extent to which employment requirements can be satisfied by
the existing population (see Chapter 7) as well as in
guiding regional employment and vocational training programs. Likewise, projections of income distribution are
very helpful in estimating the types of housing which may
be required, and projections of output or gross business
volume by sector are desirable as input to the fiscal
impact analysis (see Chapter 5). Finally, disaggregated
projections can be very useful in identifying the incidence
of project-related benefits and costs among groups in the
local population.

A final consideration which affects the information
needs of decision makers is the substantial degree of
uncertainity often associated with resource development projects. During the planning stages of such projects, uncertainty as to whether the facility will actually material-
ize, when construction will begin, and whether the project
may be developed only to later be abandoned as infeasible
increases the complexity of impact management planning
(Leistritz et al., 1980b). Uncertainty regarding the potential distribution of impacts at the community level makes
the decision making process even more difficult. Even after
project development is underway, changes in construction
schedules can lead to substantial increases or decreases in
work force levels and hence in community population, school
enrollment, and other critical variables. These uncertainties
imply that impact assessment cannot be a one-time effort and
that impact models should be capable of projecting the implications of a number of development scenarios. These models
must also be capable of readily incorporating new information

(such as a revised work force schedule) and producing revised projections in a timely manner.

ECONOMIC IMPACT ASSESSMENT TECHNIQUES

The actual preparation of an economic impact assessment involves a number of specific steps. These include: (a) description of the project's characteristics; (b) delineation of the study area; (c) developing baseline projections; and (d) projecting the impacts of development. These steps will be discussed in the sections which follow.

Description of the Project

Before the effects of a new development project can be evaluated, of course, the characteristics of the project which are important in determining its economic impacts must be quantified. These characteristics include work force requirements, level of capital investment, amount and composition of local input purchases, level and types of output, and natural resource requirements.

The nature of a project's work force is one of the most critical factors determining its socioeconomic impacts. Many assessments conducted in the mid-1970s considered only the size of the peak-year construction work force and permanent work force requirements (Berkey et al., 1977). Many analysts, however, now attempt to obtain estimates of the size of work force by year during the construction phase, and some assessments have utilized quarterly work force projections during the construction period (National Biocentric, Inc., 1977). Work force requirements are sometimes estimated by craft or occupational category in order to facilitate subsequent estimation of local hiring rates, although the more typical practice is to utilize only total work force (Berkey et al., 1977). The average earnings of the workers during construction and operational phases is frequently estimated, and the income distribution of project workers at each phase is occasionally estimated (Denver Research Institute, 1979). These estimates of income distribution are often used in subsequent analysis of housing demand.

The capital investment for the new facility as well as its expected output generally must be estimated to enable subsequent calculation of tax revenues (see Chapter 5). In addition, the analyst should attempt to estimate the extent of purchases of supplies and materials which will be made in the impact area. Some analyses have included detailed estimates of local purchases (Dalsted et al., 1976), but many have simply incorporated the assumption that these purchases will be minimal and, hence, that the only secondary impacts of the project will arise from local expenditures of project payrolls. An exception to this treatment frequently occurs, however, when purchases of a particular type of input are expected to be quite large (for example, purchases of electricity by a synthetic fuel plant). In these cases, the input supply facility may be treated as a linked industry, in which case its expected employment would be added to the basic employment created by the project.[22] The prospect of linked industry development must be considered on the output side as well. For example, synthetic fuel plants might give rise to fertilizer manufacturing facilities utilizing by-product ammonia. Specific venture analysis or feasibility studies may be required to determine the likelihood that such forward-linked industry will develop in the impact area.

The description of project characteristics also should include a compilation of major resource requirements (such as land required for the plant site or for mining and water required for cooling and other plant operations). This information can be utilized to estimate impacts on other basic industries such as agriculture.

Information concerning project characteristics can be derived from several sources. Interviews with officials of the company or agency developing the project are the most frequent source of such information, particularly for project-specific assessments. Analyses which involve a wider region and/or a longer time frame may require that information from developers be supplemented with data from secondary sources. Government and industry publications which provide compilations of development plans may be consulted (for example, U.S. Department of the Interior, 1978), but information from these sources should be cross-checked with that available from local planning officials and industry representatives. Federal and state agencies which have responsibility for permitting or licensing new projects can be a valuable source of information concerning those projects which are scheduled for development in the near future. When specific information regarding the work force requirements and other characteristics of a new project is not available from the developer, secondary sources may be consulted. For example, estimates of work force requirements for several types of energy facilities are found in Stenehjem and Metzger (1976) while work force and material requirements for similar types of facilities have been estimated by Stanford Research Institute (1975). Data from such sources also can be used as a check on information obtained from developers.

Delineation of the Study Area

An important decision in any impact assessment is the identification of the study area. Two general considerations affect this choice. First, the study area should approximate an economically self-contained region, as defined by established

trade patterns. Second, the definition of the study area
should allow detailed analyses of the jurisdictions which will
be most seriously impacted by the project. In order to achieve
both of these objectives, some analysts define two impact areas:
(1) a _regional_ impact area which approximates a functional
economic area or the trade area of a regional wholesale-retail
center (Berry, 1973); and (2) a _local_ impact area which includes
those jurisdictions where most of the direct employment and
population effects of the project will be experienced (Chalmers
and Anderson, 1977). When the study area is thus defined at
two levels, the usual approach is to provide a summary of
economic effects for the regional impact area and more detailed
analyses for individual jurisdictions within the local impact
area.

The regional impact area is typically defined on the
basis of information from secondary sources which identifies
regional economic relationships and the trade areas of various
centers. Bureau of Economic Analysis (BEA) Economic Areas
(U.S. Department of Commerce, 1977) are sometimes used as the
regional impact area. State planning districts or Council of
Governments areas provide an alternative basis for defining the
regional impact area (Leholm et al., 1976c).

The local impact area is generally defined in terms of
the anticipated residential patterns of inmigrating workers
(see Chapter 3). Data availability usually requires that
the local impact area be defined along county lines, although
it is possible to use census county division or enumeration
district boundaries.

In sparsely populated regions where the market areas
of the wholesale-retail trade centers are quite extensive, the
regional impact area will typically be much larger than the
local impact area. In more densely settled regions of the
country, less difference will exist in the geographic boundaries
of the two areas, and in some cases the two areas may coincide.

Baseline Projections

Baseline projections are estimates of the socioeconomic conditions likely to prevail in the impact area if
the proposed project is not developed. The first step in
developing baseline economic projections for an area is to
project the levels of activity for each basic industry over
the course of the projection period. These activity levels
may be measured in terms of employment, income, output,
and/or sales to final demand with the choice depending on
the economic impact assessment technique which is employed.
The length of the projection period is frequently determined by the specific planning or assessment guidelines
under which the study is being conducted or by specific
characteristics of the proposed project.

The economic impact technique which is employed most frequently is the export base employment multiplier (Berkey et al., 1977). When this technique is used, economic trends in the basic sectors are measured by employment. The basis for projecting basic employment is to assess the profitability and growth potential of each industry. Location theory concepts discussed earlier provide a framework to guide this evaluation. Key sources of information include industry experts (for example, persons within the local industry and research economists employed by public and private organizations), state and local planning organizations, and federal agencies. Projections of employment by industry at the national level can be valuable in evaluating those industries whose market is national and can provide insights regarding market forces and productivity trends.[23] Recent employment trends of the various industries in the area also provide some guidance, but the analyst should not rely on simple extrapolation of past trends to the exclusion of other procedures and information sources. After projections of basic employment for the area have been developed, the economic base multiplier is applied to the projected basic employment to estimate total employment.

The estimates of employment under baseline conditions are frequently used as the basis for projecting changes in area income and population. Income projections are usually developed by first estimating the average annual wage and salary levels for basic and nonbasic workers. This wage and salary figure may then be adjusted through time using productivity factors. Total wage and salary payments are projected by applying these adjusted wage and salary levels to the projections of basic and nonbasic employment. Other components of personal income (for example, proprietors' income and transfer payments) are then estimated as a function, usually a constant percentage, of wage and salary income. Population effects are typically estimated through the use of assumptions regarding local labor force participation rates and worker demographic characteristics. When local employment requirements exceed the locally available labor force, inmigration is assumed to occur. This topic is discussed in considerable detail in Chapters 3 and 7.

When the export base income multiplier technique is utilized, the projections of basic sector activity are developed in terms of income. The key considerations in projecting basic income are similar to those discussed with respect to basic employment. An additional problem in developing income projections is that it is frequently difficult to obtain reliable data on nonwage income and even more difficult to allocate this type of income into basic and nonbasic components. Once baseline projections of basic income have been developed, the income multiplier is applied to estimate nonbasic income. These income projections may then be used as the basis for employment estimates (by first applying a nonwage income adjustment and then using projected salary levels for basic and nonbasic workers to convert income to employment).

When input-output techniques are utilized, baseline projections of sales to final demand by the various sectors are required. Developing baseline projections of sales to final demand is a challenging task. Many of the considerations outlined earlier with respect to projecting basic employment apply, however. The number of final demand components for which projections are developed will differ depending on the specific model structure. National forecasts of rates of growth in output or final demand of various industries can be useful inputs into the regional forecasting process as can the historic performance of the region's major industries. Detailed analyses of the export prospects of the region's individual industries can be invaluable if available to the analyst. (For a detailed discussion of procedures for developing regional forecasts of sales to final demand, see Richardson, 1972, Chapter 9.)

Once the final demand projections have been completed, the input-output interdependence coefficients are applied to estimate output by sector for the target years. Projected ratios of output per worker are then frequently applied to develop estimates of future employment for each sector (industry). A further refinement which is sometimes employed is to multiply the vector of employment by industry by a matrix containing the projected occupational distribution in each industry to obtain estimates of employment by occupation for future years.

One of the conclusions that may be reached in the course of projecting the future of the basic sectors is that there are many factors which contribute to uncertainty. A variety of alternative assumptions about the future of certain sectors may appear plausible. Thus, it is often necessary to recognize that there are several possible futures for the area and that more than one baseline projection may be appropriate. In such cases, as many sets of basic sector projections as appear desirable can be constructed, and baseline economic assessments can be carried out for each. It will still be necessary, however, to ultimately choose one of these alternative baselines as the most likely future to which the impacts of the project will be compared.[24]

While some impact assessment efforts have included development of detailed baseline projections for both regional and local impact areas, many assessment reports have drawn their baseline projections exclusively from existing

studies (Berkey et al., 1977). This practice may be appropriate if state or regional planning agencies or other
groups have recently completed such forecasts and at times
may seem necessary in order to conserve project resources.
Projections from secondary sources should be carefully
evaluated, however, to ensure that their assumptions are
appropriate in light of current conditions.

Impact Projections

The purpose of economic impact projections is to estimate the effects of a project on selected economic variables in the affected area. While a number of economic
indicators may be considered, those which are most frequently used are employment, income, and output. As noted
earlier, it is important that these economic variables be
projected in temporal and geographic dimensions which are
meaningful to decision makers and that the economic projections be developed in sufficient detail to support subsequent demographic and fiscal analyses.

Secondary economic effects are most frequently estimated
using the employment multiplier technique (Berkey et al.,
1977).[25] A variety of approaches are used in estimating employment multipliers, with the most frequent being the assumption method and the location quotient technique (Denver
Research Institute, 1979). Income multipliers have been used
in a number of studies (TERA Corporation, 1976; Chalmers and
Anderson, 1977). Input-output analysis has been employed in
a few project-specific assessments (Leholm et al., 1976a, b;
Toman et al., 1976) but has been more frequently utilized in
regional assessment studies (Auger et al., 1976; Gray et al.,
1977).

The types of information reported differ considerably
between studies. Estimates of total secondary employment are
reported most frequently, often on an annual basis. Changes
in income are reported less frequently while only a few studies,
usually those utilizing input-output techniques, have reported
employment by industry or occupation.

An important issue in evaluating impacts of large projects
is how to account for the differences which may exist in
multiplier effects between construction and operational periods
and, more generally, for the time which may be required for
complete economic adjustment to occur. According to Berkey and
associates (1977), very few of the environmental assessment
reports completed during the mid-1970s for energy development
projects considered these timing questions. More recently,
however, their importance has been generally recognized.

A number of different techniques have been employed to
deal with timing effects in impact assessments. Some analysts
have examined the proportion of the project work force that is

estimated to be inmigrants and assumed that a smaller percentage of these workers' income is spent locally (Mountain West Research, Inc., 1979), thus reducing the magnitude of secondary effects during construction periods. A second approach which is sometimes used in conjunction with the first involves the concept of a "ceiling to nonbasic employment growth" (Mountain West Research, Inc., 1979). The basis of this concept is that the local trade and service sector will not expand during the construction phase beyond that level of employment which can be sustained during the post-construction period. A third approach uses a smaller employment multiplier during the construction phase but does not compare the secondary employment levels of the two phases (Briscoe, Maphis, Murray, Lamont Inc., 1978; Murphy and Williams, 1978). A fourth approach involves applying a lag factor to all changes in nonbasic employment. Alternative formulations of the lag factor include the following: (1) a three year lag with one-third of the total estimated employment change occuring each year (Denver Research Institute, 1979); (2) a four year lag with 71 percent of estimated employment occurring in the first year, 17 percent in the second, 8 percent in the third, and 4 percent in the fourth (Stenehjem and Metzger, 1976); and (3) a quarterly income lag model with respending in each quarter amounting to 59 percent of that in the preceding quarter (TERA Corporation, 1976). The accelerator effect has been incorporated into at least two impact modeling systems (Auger et al., 1976; Denver Research Institute, 1979). The coefficients utilized are acknowledged to be somewhat judgemental, however.

The geographic distribution of secondary economic effects has received less attention than their timing. Within local impact areas, secondary effects are generally assumed to occur in the same community where the direct project workers reside. While differences in the magnitude of multipliers between local and regional impact areas indicate that some secondary effects occur outside the local impact area, few analysts have attempted to estimate the distribution of these effects among jurisdictions. At least three different techniques have been employed to estimate the geographic distribution of secondary effects. Chalmers and his associates (1977) integrated central place concepts into an income multiplier framework to estimate the distribution of secondary income effects among counties in a regional impact area. Another approach employs the gravity model technique to distribute secondary effects among communities in local and regional impact areas (Leistritz et al., 1979a). The third approach, developed by Stenehjem and Metzger (1976), involves use of a linear programming model to allocate workers to places of residence on the basis of commuting distance, housing availability, and budget constraints. As is the case for the timing of secondary

effects, however, scarcity of data indicating the actual
geographic and temporal distribution of secondary effects
in rapid growth areas has severely limited attempts to test
and refine such models.

The effects of a new project on other basic sectors
have been examined by only a few studies (Whittlesey, 1978;
Dalsted et al., 1976).

In summary, economic impact analysts have employed a
variety of techniques in conducting their studies. A chrono-
logical comparison of impact assessments suggests that techniques are becoming more sophisticated and that analysts
are giving more attention to simulating the timing of
economic effects. Impact assessments have been limited,
however, in two major respects. First, many studies have
not utilized the more advanced techniques that were available. In fact, some studies have not even considered secondary effects, and many have been limited in their economic
evaluation to the estimation of aggregate secondary employment effects. Second, the effort to develop more adequate
impact assessment models has been constrained by a scarcity
of data reflecting the actual effects of rapid growth in
rural areas. Impact studies to date, then, have been more
productive in generating hypotheses than in developing verified estimates of key relationships. Future analyses should
focus both on synthesizing more comprehensive impact assessment systems and on empirical testing of existing models
and relationships.

SUMMARY AND CONCLUSIONS

The purpose of this chapter was to review the conceptual bases and methodological alternatives for economic
impact assessment, to describe the features of the impact
process which influence the information needs of decision
makers, and to examine the techniques which are typically
applied in impact assessments for large projects. The export base (or economic base) theory is the basis for all
economic impact assessments. Location theory and central
place concepts also are important in some aspects of impact
analysis. The principal methodological alternatives for economic impact assessment include various forms of export
base employment or income multiplier models and input-output
models. Multiregional models also may be applicable in some
situations.

When large projects are located in rural areas, growth
may be quite rapid. Because labor requirements may fluctuate both within and between development phases, impacts
are likely to be cyclical with employment and total regional income increasing rapidly during the project construction

period and decreasing somewhat once construction is completed. A substantial decrease in the area's economic activity may later occur when the operational life of the project has ended. The rapid rate at which economic and associated demographic and fiscal changes may occur and the possibility of substantial differences in these effects among individual jurisdictions indicates a need for economic impact assessments to include substantial emphasis on the timing and distribution of impacts. Impact projections also should be presented in a form which allows comparison of future conditions if the project is developed with those likely to prevail if the project were not developed. Finally, impact assessment techniques should allow decision makers to cope effectively with the uncertainties frequently associated with major projects.

The techniques which have been employed in many impact assessments appear rather simplistic. In some cases secondary employment and other indirect economic effects have not even been addressed. In others, impact projections developed using one set of techniques have been compared with baseline projections developed using considerably different approaches and incorporating assumptions which may be invalidated by recent events. Impact assessment practices have emphasized use of the simplest assessment techniques, particularly aggregate employment multipliers, despite their acknowledged limitations. Given the needs of decision makers in impacted areas, it appears that greater attention should be given to assessing the distribution of impacts over time, among jurisdictions, and among population groups. Models which take account of interproject differences in salary levels and input purchasing patterns and which provide disaggregated impact projections probably should be utilized more extensively. While data requirements have limited the use of some of these techniques, particularly input-output models, other modeling forms (such as disaggregated employment multipliers and intersectoral flows models) appear to offer substantially greater analytical power with only moderate increases in data requirements.

Economic impact assessment has been limited in another important respect, however. The information base concerning the effects of rapid economic and population growth in rural areas is simply insufficient to allow adequate assessment of many impact dimensions. More extensive longitudinal and comparative analyses of areas experiencing such growth are essential if the quality of impact assessments is to be improved. In summary, improving the quality of impact assessments appears to require both more extensive utilization of the more sophisticated analytical systems and greater efforts to determine the nature of actual development effects in order to more accurately calibrate these models.

NOTES

1. It should be noted that, while the techniques of economic impact analysis are most frequently applied in cases where a new project is contemplated, these methods are equally adaptable to the case of reduction or elimination of an activity.

2. Import substitution is the process by which an area develops the capability of producing internally goods and services which formerly were imported.

3. Other, more detailed, classifications of industries according to their location characteristics also have been proposed. For example, see Perloff (1961).

4. It should also be noted, however, that diseconomies may be associated with high levels of urban concentration. Congestion, air quality degradation, and higher costs for providing certain public services may result from increasing levels of urban concentration and may be reflected in increased tax rates and labor costs for firms in these locations (Tweeten and Brinkman, 1976).

5. An example of the application of location theory principles to the evaluation of linked industry prospects is provided by Gilmore et al. (1976b).

6. The original development of central place theory came primarily from the work of Christaller (1933) and Losch (1940). Subsequent contributions have come from Berry and Garrison (1958), Dacey (1966), Berry (1967), and Parr et al. (1975).

7. This tendency for planners to focus on employment effects and multipliers may not be entirely desirable. For example, some sectors may have substantial income effects but only modest employment effects (Scott and Braschler, 1975). Both effects should be considered in development planning.

8. A third estimation approach may be feasible if data are available for several time periods. This approach utilizes regression analysis to estimate the coefficients of the equation:

$$E_t = a + bE_b + u$$

Where: b is the multiplier estimate
a is a constant
u is a stochastic disturbance term
E_t and E_b are as previously defined.

This estimation technique is generally considered to be more reliable than the other two but also imposes greater data requirements (Weiss and Gooding, 1968; Pfister, 1976).

9. Another approach to identifying basic employment is the econometric approach recommended by Mathur and Rosen (1974). For a critique of this technique, see Isserman (1980).

10. The proportion of an industry's employment to be assigned to the basic sector is calculated as follows:

$$E_{irb} = E_{ir} \frac{(LQ_i - 1)}{LQ_i}$$

11. One case in which the minimum requirements approach may be appropriate is in estimating sales of certain types of goods and services to tourists. For a discussion and example of this application, see Pfister (1980).

12. A unique feature of this study is that not only are sector-specific multipliers estimated but also selected community characteristics (i.e., distance to the regional trade center and median family income) are incorporated as factors influencing the multiplier values. Other studies usually have either estimated sectoral multipliers without regard to the influence of community characteristics (Braschler, 1972; McNulty, 1977) or have estimated the influence of community characteristics on the aggregate multiplier (Lewis, 1976).

13. Such differences can have significant effects on multiplier values. For example, Garnick (1970) found differences in multiplier values within aggregated export base sectors up to a factor of three in some cases.

14. Another advantage of the export base model when multiplier values are estimated statistically is that confidence levels can be associated with the multiplier estimates.

15. This section draws heavily on the work of Richardson (1972), Miernyk (1965), and Isard (1960). Pioneering works in input-output analysis include Leontief (1936), Leontief (1941), Chenery (1953), and Isard and Kuenne (1953).

16. In using the input-output approach, it is also implicitly assumed that input supply functions are perfectly elastic and that each industry (sector) is operating at capacity.

17. For example, Pleeter (1980) estimates that such an effort for a small area "could cost $250,000 and take two years to complete."

18. Yet another approach to estimating sector-specific multipliers, while avoiding the expense of a complete I-O study, is termed the short-cut multiplier approach (Drake, 1976). This method is based on the assumption that the indirect impacts of any change within a specific economic sector is

a linear function of the direct impact. Sector-specific multipliers for 56 industrial sectors have been calculated for each of the 173 BEA economic areas through regionalizing the 1967 BEA national input-output model (U.S. Department of Commerce, 1977). These multipliers reflect sectoral differences in indirect and induced effects but do not indicate the distribution of these effects among sectors.

19. For detailed discussion of the various semisurvey and nonsurvey techniques, see Richardson (1972) and Shaffer (1979). Other recent efforts in this area include Boisvert and Bills (1976); Henry et al. (1980); and Stevens and Trainer (1980).

20. One source of projections of changes in national I-O coefficients is the INFORUM Model. For a detailed discussion of the structure of this model and the procedures used in projecting changes in technical coefficients, see Almon et al. (1974).

21. Another factor which could contribute to the apparent lag in secondary employment response in some areas is the existence of excess capacity in the local trade and service sectors. That is, existing firms may be able to accomodate substantial increases in business volume before additional hiring or facility expansion is required.

22. Linked industry can be defined as those economic activities which in some cases may be, but in all cases theoretically could be, vertically integrated into the primary resource development project (Denver Research Institute, 1979).

23. As discussed previously, a number of national and nationally-linked state econometric models have been developed in recent years. Projections developed from these models can be a useful source of insights concerning national trends and their regional implications.

24. Development of realistic baseline economic projections also requires that changes in the structure of the local economy be taken into account. As service employment apparently is becoming a larger part of the employment mix in many rural areas (Bender, 1980), this factor should be given careful consideration in developing baseline (and impact) projections.

25. It is interesting to note, however, that a survey of Environmental Assessment Reports for energy facility construction projects indicated that the majority did not address secondary employment effects (Berkey et al., 1977).

3
Demographic Impact Assessment

Assessment of the demographic impacts of resource developments represents one of the most important steps in the socio-economic assessment process. Determining the number and the characteristics of people moving to each geographical entity in the impact area is essential for assessing other population-related impacts such as public service demands, fiscal impacts, and social impacts. In fact, to many planners and decision makers the magnitude of population impacts is synonymous with the magnitude of all impacts. Assessing the size, distribution, and composition of project-related populations is thus of utmost importance and is the major topic of concern in this chapter. As in the preceding chapter, the discussion first examines conceptual and methodological alternatives in demographic impact assessment, then examines policy and impact process-related factors affecting the choice of alternative methodologies. Finally, the methodologies presently employed in impact assessments are examined.

CONCEPTUAL BASES AND METHODOLOGICAL ALTERNATIVES IN DEMOGRAPHIC IMPACT ASSESSMENT

The conceptual and methodological alternatives for projecting population change are widely known, and numerous excellent works describing specific projection alternatives are available (Shryock and Siegel, 1973; Bogue, 1974; Pittenger, 1976; Morrison, 1971; Irwin, 1977). As a result, our discussion of these techniques will be more limited than in other chapters.

Definitions, Distinctions, and Principles

Foremost among the distinctions usually made by demographers in determining population change are those made between population estimates, population projections, and population forecasts. Population estimates refer to population data obtained for periods which fall between dates for which actual population counts are available, such as estimates for 1975 obtained by using 1970 and 1980 census data, or determinations of population for dates that are only a few years past the last population count and for which data on actual counts could hypothetically have been obtained. In other words, estimates refer to data obtained on population levels for past or present periods for which population censuses are not available. Estimation procedures do not provide data on future population levels and are thus not applicable to impact assessments that must determine future levels of population. Estimation techniques are thus not examined here. (For an examination of these techniques, see Morrison, 1971.)

Projections, on the other hand, refer to determinations of future population levels. They consist of computations of the future levels of population that will exist in an area if certain sets of assumptions prove to be valid. Thus, a projection of the 1990 population for the Western United States, based on the assumption that 1970-1980 fertility, mortality, and migration levels continue from 1980 to 1990, is an example of a population projection. Such projections will be correct only if the assumptions on which they are based are correct, and thus they consist of little more than the tracing of the logical consequences of a set of assumptions.

A population forecast also refers to determinations of future population levels. Unlike a projection, however, the term "forecast" has a connotation of certainty, of total correctness, of judgement that most demographers wish to avoid. As many scholars point out, this distinction is often recognized only by demographers (Keyfitz, 1972), and the terms forecast and projection are used interchangeably in discussions of demographic assessments.

Whatever the term used, however, it is clear that any projection, estimate, or forecast is likely to vary in accuracy in accordance with the characteristics of the projection area and the projection technique. Shryock and Siegel (1973) note several general principles which bear on the accuracy of projections. Perhaps the most important of these is that any projection is only as accurate as the assumptions on which it is based, and will only be correct if its assumptions are correct. The assumptions underlying a projection must be critically examined. In addition, they note that population projections are generally more accurate if performed:

1. For an entire nation or large geographic region rather than for a small component area or subregion;
2. For total populations rather than for subpopulations or population subgroups;
3. With series using data directly related to population change (births, deaths, and migration data) rather

than using data that provide indirect or symptomatic
indicators of population change (automobile regis-
tration, housing counts, etc.);

4. For shorter rather than longer periods of time;
5. For areas in which past trends are more likely to
   continue rather than new patterns to arise; and
6. For areas undergoing slow rather than rapid change.

As will soon become evident, in areas such as those
undergoing rapid change due to resource developments, few of
the above factors operate to increase projection accuracy.
It is essential, however, to keep each of these distinctions
in mind in the evaluation of alternative procedures.

Alternative Techniques

There are numerous alternatives for classifying population projection techniques (Shryock and Siegel, 1973;
Morrison, 1971; Pittenger, 1976; Irwin, 1977; Barclay, 1958),
but one of the most useful classification schemes is that presented by Irwin (1977). He suggests that projection techniques can be divided into five types:

1. Extrapolative, Curve-Fitting, and Regression-Based
   Techniques;
2. Ratio-Based Techniques;
3. Land Use Techniques;
4. Economic-Based Techniques; and
5. Cohort Component Techniques.

Although the computational procedures utilized for each of
these methods differ, as described below, the rationales and
conceptual bases for choosing one or the other of these techniques appear to lie in the factors of data availability, the
desire for detail in demographic outputs, and the desire to
simulate demographic processes.

Of the five techniques, the cohort component requires the
largest input of data. Data are required on fertility rates,
mortality rates, and migration rates, both for present and
future periods. The other techniques tend to concentrate on
the projection of total populations; thus, detailed data on
demographic processes are not required. The data requirements
of these techniques, then, are often less demanding than for
component techniques.

As with other projection processes, however, a lack of
detail in inputs also leads to the inability to obtain detailed
outputs. Because the cohort component technique usually involves the use of data for specific age and sex groupings
(cohorts), its outputs provide a greater degree of detail on
demographic structure than is provided by other procedures.
When detailed data on demographic structure, such as age and

sex, are deemed necessary and the required input data are available, cohort component techniques are usually selected for use.

Conceptually also, the major distinctions are between cohort component techniques and all other projection procedures. Noncomponent techniques tend to use either direct projections of total population or to use symptomatic indicators of population, such as employment levels, to project population. To many demographic analysts, noncomponent approaches are seen as less acceptable than component techniques because they ignore the basic demographic processes that are known to determine population size -- fertility, mortality, and migration. Simulating these processes as a way of determining population should provide more accurate assessments in which the roles of the various processes are more clearly understood. Although there is little indication that cohort component processes are more accurate than noncomponent techniques in actual projections (Ascher, 1978; Bjornstad et al., 1975; Isserman, 1977a), their ability to provide detailed age structure data and potential for simulating demographic processes, and hence potential to provide more accurate projections once the effects of the components are correctly understood, has led to their predominant use in demographic projections, and in many impact assessments.

In fact, however, the selection of techniques for use in assessments has been too restrictive, and each of the five sets of techniques cited above is appropriate for some aspects of impact assessments and should be given careful consideration by impact researchers. Each is discussed briefly below.

Extrapolation Techniques

Extrapolation techniques include a wide range of procedures which attempt to predict the path of future population growth on the basis of past trends in total population growth. Included among such techniques are: (1) arithmetic and exponential growth rate techniques; (2) curve-fitting techniques including those utilizing polynomial, Gompertz, and logistic curves; and (3) regression-based techniques (linear as well as nonlinear). Basic to all such techniques is the tendency to project only total population size with the use of assumed levels, rates, or trends in growth over time.

The simplest techniques are clearly the arithmetic techniques. These consist of simply taking a level of numerical growth, usually based on past patterns, and assuming that it will continue for some period of time. Computationally, this can be expressed as:

$$P_2 = P_1 + (P_0 - P_1) \qquad\qquad (3.1)$$

Where:　P_2 = population for projected period

P_1 = population for baseline period

$P_0 - P_1$ = numerical change for known period from P_0 to P_1

For projections for very short periods of time, this technique may be quite useful. For longer periods, particularly for areas that may show dramatic population changes, such as re-source development areas, this technique is likely to be less acceptable.

Slightly more complicated are those procedures involved in exponential projection techniques. These involve using rates of annual or continuous growth. The most basic of these derivations is similar to the compound interest formula used in basic accounting. The formulas for annual and continuous compounding are:

Annual:　$P_2 = P_1 (1+r)^t$　(3.2)

Continuous:　$P_2 = P_1 e^{rt}$　(3.3)

Where:　P_2 and P_1 are as in equation 3.1

r = rate of growth per unit of time (t)

t = time period

e = natural log value

The effect of using this procedure is that population from each previous period of growth (defined by t) is added to the base population before the next period of growth (annually or continuously) is computed. The basic rate used in this pro-cedure is nearly as easy to obtain as the values for arithmetic estimates of change. Given population growth for two known consecutive time periods, the rate of growth can be determined by the following formula in which natural logarithms are used to reduce the tedious nature of the necessary calculations.

$$r = \frac{\text{Log } \frac{P_1}{P_0}}{t \text{ Log } e} \quad (3.4)$$

Where:　r = rate of growth for the time period from P_0 to P_1

P_1 = population of the area at the last formal population count

P_0 = Population of area at some period preceding P_1

t = number of units of time (usually single years) between P_0 and P_1

e = natural log value

Determination of the value of t is often done with the value of P_2 set at twice the value of P_1. This provides an assessment of the time necessary to double (the doubling time of) an area's population.

In general, exponential techniques are superior to arithmetic procedures but are still heavily dependent on assumptions about past rates of growth continuing in the future. For projections for short time frames and for areas with relative socioeconomic stability, exponential techniques deserve careful consideration.

Polynominal growth techniques might also be used. They form the basis for many of the curve-fitting techniques and, thus, require brief discussion. Unlike arithmetic techniques, they involve patterns or trends which form curves that, when graphed, are nonlinear in form. Whereas a linear model would be of the form:

$$Y = a + bX \qquad (3.5)$$

a polynomial would include one or more additional terms, such as:

$$Y = a + bX + cX^2 ... zX^n \qquad (3.6)$$

and would form a curve rather than a straight line.

Although one might find a given polynomial formula that accurately described the growth of a particular area's population over a given period, such a curve would be unlikely to describe future patterns. Such techniques are seldom used to project population. However, their conceptual and computational procedures form the general basis on which the more generalized curve-fitting techniques described below are based.

Among the more generalized curve-fitting techniques are the Gompertz and logistic curves which became popular in the work of Pearl and others in the 1920s and 1930s. Each of these two techniques produces a curve that is asymptotic (that is, "s" shaped) over time. Whereas the Gompertz curve is somewhat skewed, the logistic curve provides a smoother curve more closely resembling a normal curve. The formulas for these curves are:

Gompertz Curve: $\qquad P_2 = KP_1^{r^t} \qquad (3.7)$

Logistic Curve: $\qquad P_2 = \dfrac{K}{1 + e^{P_1 + rt}} \qquad (3.8)$

Where: $\qquad P_2$ = population for projected period

$\qquad P_1$ = population for baseline period

K = upper asymptote
r = growth rate per unit of time
t = time period over which growth occurs

Although these curves have provided relatively accurate predictions of population for several periods (Ascher, 1978),
they are not widely used in present day projection procedures.
    More commonly used are regression-based techniques in
which the relationship of various factors to population growth
are known and used to predict future population levels. These
techniques require establishing a set of factors or independent variables that accurately predict population levels for
some past period and assuming that the past relationships
between these predictor or independent variables and population
levels will persist in the future. Given projections of the
future values of the predictor variables, one can then predict
future population levels. The nature of the independent-
dependent variable relationships is generally assumed to be
linear in form, meaning that a straight line jointly determined by the values of the independent variables will predict
the rate of change in the dependent variable, population, with
a minimum of error. This straight line relationship is referred to as a linear relationship and can be determined computationally in simple and multiple regression forms by the
following formulas:

Simple regression: $Y = a + b_1 X_1$ (3.9)
Multiple regression: $Y = a + b_1 X_1 + b_2 X_2 + \ldots b_n X_n$
                                                (3.10)

Where: Y = dependent variable
        a = origin or intercept value
        b = slope or amount of change in Y per unit of
            change in a given X (X_1, X_2... etc.)
        X = independent variables

Projections of population using regression techniques may use
past or projected future values of such independent variables
as size of labor force, income, wage levels, vital rates
(births, deaths, and migration), population density, or similar factors as predictor variables.
    Regression-based techniques have been widely used for
population estimates for periods after the last population
count by the Bureau of the Census in methodologies termed ratio
correlation techniques (discussed below). Their use is less
desirable for projections, however, because they require data
on the predictor variables and projections of each predictor
variable for the future period. They also require assuming
that the historical relationships between the independent variables and population (the b_1 through b_n values) will persist

throughout the projection period.

Whatever the specific form of the extrapolation techniques used, their advantages lie in the fact that they use historical data, which are relatively easy to obtain, to make projections and consist of generally easy to complete computational forms. On the other hand, the dependence on past patterns can also be a major source of error in rapidly changing (impacted) areas. In addition, in some techniques, data needs, particularly the projections of predictor variables needed to determine future populations, may place considerable data collection demands on the research analyst. Finally, these techniques seldom provide sufficient detail on the demographic characteristics necessary for public service and other planning needs. For such methods, then, the data needs can vary from little more than total population figures for two past censuses (arithmetic or exponential techniques) to data on multiple variables for past and future time periods (multiple regression-based methods). These methods may provide adequate short-term projections for past periods and for populations whose compositions are unlikely to alter rapidly over time. These methods, however, should be used carefully and with full knowledge of their limitations.

Ratio-Based Techniques

Ratio techniques consist of procedures in which the population of a subarea is projected on the basis of its proportion of a larger area's projected population. In general, the ratio techniques are subarea techniques that are used in conjunction with other projection procedures. They are frequently used in allocating regional or county populations to municipalities (Murdock et al., 1979b; U.S. Bureau of the Census, 1953).

Although the proportion or ratio of the subarea's population to the larger area's population may be assumed to remain constant over time, it is more common to trend area ratios over time and adjust the sum of area projections to the projection of the total area's population (Pittenger, 1976). The trends in shares are usually determined either by an extrapolation of baseline patterns or by a regression or similar procedure. When regression techniques are used with the subarea's share serving as the dependent variable and the subarea's population attributes as the independent variables, the technique is often termed the ratio correlation technique.

Ratio techniques are most widely used in projecting population for subareas of cities and municipal populations from county or regional totals. Their utility as a major projection technique is clearly limited, but their use in subarea analysis is likely to remain extensive.

The advantages of such techniques lie in their relatively limited data requirements and simple computational procedures. Potential disadvantages stem from the need to assume a given ratio or trend in ratios of subarea to area populations over time and from the lack of demographic detail provided by the outputs of such procedures.

Land Use Techniques

Irwin (1977) delineates two separate types of land use approaches; these include what he terms: (1) the "saturation" approach, in which projected populations for an area are limited by the number of housing units that can be built in the area; and (2) density methods, in which limits are placed on the population in an area on the basis of predetermined levels of population per unit of area. Both techniques are most often used in projections of subarea populations in urban areas (Portland State University, 1975; Greenberg et al., 1978). These techniques, like the ratio techniques, are seldom used except as part of more comprehensive procedures.

The "saturation" method is usually used by assuming a standard number of housing units per unit of area and then computing population on the basis of an average number of persons per unit. Among the problems with this method are the determination of the upper limit for housing units per unit of area and the need to obtain recent average household size estimates. For many local areas, for example, the failure to take into account the relatively rapid decline in average persons per household has resulted in inflated population estimates.

The density method may be particularly useful for projecting subarea populations within urban areas undergoing rapid growth. In such areas, extrapolation of past trends may quickly lead to unreasonable population levels. Controls on subarea population levels are essential.

Land use models are often problematic for use in rural areas because land use is seldom a major limitation on population growth, but land use factors should be considered within any impact projection. The advantages of these methods are clearly their utility in limiting the rate of growth in component areas to feasible levels while their disadvantages lie in the difficulty encountered in determining the density limits for housing units for an area and in the lack of demographic detail produced by such procedures. Particularly for rural areas that are not geographically confined, growth limits may be extremely difficult to determine. On the other hand, in some rural areas, topographic features or land ownership by the federal or state government may limit the potential geographical expansion of a jurisdiction (city). In such cases, land use models may be applicable. To summarize, although past use of land use models have been restricted to large urban areas, their possible use in impact assessments for rural areas should be given serious consideration as a potential addition to more widely used techniques.

Economic-Based Techniques

Economic-based techniques, as the name implies, project population on the basis of assumed relationships between economic patterns and population change. As the name also suggests, they tend to be the techniques for population projection most widely used by economists. They have been widely used in the OBERS (U.S. Bureau of Economic Analysis, 1974) and National Planning Association (Lee and Hong, 1972) national economic models and are particularly attractive when population growth in an area is expected to result largely from economic development. As will soon become apparent, they have received widespread use in impact assessments.

The basic methodology of such projections involves using an economic model to determine employment changes and then using either a direct or an indirect method to determine either total population change or the level of change within a key demographic component (usually migration) resulting from the project employment. In the simplest procedure, projections of population are determined by applying a population to employment ratio to the projection of employment. This technique, however, relies on some very simple assumptions. In particular, the assumption of a constant number of persons per employee is often questionable because of wide variation in dependency rates for rural areas. This technique is, thus, of decreasing significance as a means of population projection.

A more widely used procedure is to match the economic projections of labor demand with projections of labor supply to determine migration levels. In this mode of use, an economic-based technique is usually used in conjunction with a cohort technique (cohort survival technique) that is used to project all but the migration component of the population dimension. Labor supply is usually determined by applying total, age, or age and sex-specific labor force participation rates to population projections (total, age, or age and sex-specific). Labor demand is then matched with labor supply to determine migrating workers. If the labor supply exceeds demand, workers are assumed to outmigrate. If demand exceeds the labor supply, then workers are assumed to inmigrate. In- or outmigrating workers are then converted to population estimates by the application of various assumed demographic profiles for migrating workers. In specific applications, however, each of the major steps of:

1. Projecting labor demands over time;
2. Projecting labor supplies over time;
3. Matching of labor supplies and labor demands;
4. Determining levels of migration; and
5. Projecting the total population changes accompanying the migration of labor

requires a detailed set of procedures and extensive sets of
assumptions. Each of these steps for standard models is briefly reviewed below.

The projection of labor demands is described in detail
in Chapter 2. As noted in that chapter, an input-output model,
an export base model, or some form of shift-share analysis is
generally used to project labor demands resulting from
economic activity.

The projection of labor supplies usually involves the
projection of at least two major dimensions: (1) a baseline
or closed population to serve as the base to which employment
levels must be applied; and (2) the expected levels of labor
force participation of persons in the closed population over
time. The baseline population is often simply the last population count of persons, adjusted for mortality and fertility
changes since that count. The levels of labor force participation assumed for the projection period are the key part of
this technique and, if they are in error, the level of migration predicted will be in error. In general, the rates assumed to prevail are allowed to vary over time. For local
areas, these trends over time are often tied to national projections of labor force participation rates published by the
U.S. Bureau of the Census and the Bureau of Labor Statistics.
This patterning of local to national rates may be done by calculating a ratio of local to national rates at a known (census)
period and then assuming this ratio will be maintained over
time or by altering the ratio in a prescribed manner over time.
The fixed or projected ratios for each period are then applied
to the projections of national participation rates to obtain
local rates for use in projecting employed population. This
technique can be used with total population labor force participation rates or can be made characteristic-specific (i.e.,
age-specific or age and sex-specific). Whatever technique is
used, the participation rate when applied to the baseline or
closed population value becomes the major determinant of labor
supply. This supply is usually further adjusted by the local
level of unemployment or underemployment before being matched
with labor demands.

The matching of labor demands and labor supply may involve
relatively simple or highly complex procedures. This is, both
labor demands and supplies may involve one type of demand and
supply or several. In a procedure developed by Hertsgaard
et al. (1978) and Murdock et al. (1979b), for example, at least
four separate types of demand and supply are used, and supplies
are examined with age and sex detail. Whatever the level of
complexity, however, the key assumption is that demands that
cannot be met by the local population will be met by inmigration while excess supplies will lead to outmigration. A large
body of research in economics points to a general relationship
between employment and migration (Sjaastad, 1962), but there
is some evidence that this relationship is weaker and less

pervasive now than at previous periods, and that employment changes are more directly related to inmigration than to out-migration (Greenwood, 1975; Ritchey, 1976).

In recognition of the fact that not all migration behavior is economically motivated, the determination of the level of migration resulting from the matching of labor supplies and demands is often altered by incorporating noneconomic procedures or by adjusting the basic matching or interfacing procedure. For example, the OBERS projections maintain three separate population groups: (1) those under 15 years of age; (2) those 15-64 years of age; and (3) those 65 years of age and over. Only the under 15 and 15-64 age groups' levels of migration are determined by the employment matching procedure. The age group 65 years of age and older is projected largely on the basis of past trends with little regard being given to area employment patterns. In other procedures, some populations, such as those at military installations, colleges, and universities, are treated in "special population" procedures and are exempted from employment matching routines. Finally, some techniques have been developed which allow the labor supply in an area to exceed labor demands or demands to exceed supplies by predetermined rates, before outmigration or inmigration occurs (Hertsgaard et al., 1978). In sum, then, the step of determining the level of migration resulting from labor market changes has come to use techniques that are increasingly complex and increasingly sensitive to differences in demographic composition.

Given that the matching procedure has been completed and the number of migrating (in- or outmigrating) workers determined, the last step is to convert projections of migrating workers into projections of population. This usually involves applying a set of assumed worker-related population characteristics to the projections of the number of inmigrating workers. Though simple computationally, the characteristics assumed for workers (such as family size, dependent characteristics, etc.) will markedly affect the levels of population projected. As with the use of data on average size of households or other similar characteristics, in projections the determination of the characteristics to be assumed for inmigrating workers must be a careful process.

Economic-based techniques are becoming increasingly popular and are evolving rapidly (American Statistical Association, 1977). Their advantages lie in the fact that, unlike many purely demographic techniques, economic-based techniques allow the economic changes expected to take place in an area to be taken into account. They thus represent important attempts to integrate factors that are clearly interrelated.

Their weaknesses must also be recognized. The number of explicit assumptions on which such projections are based is large. Accurate projections of both economic and demographic factors and their interrelationships are thus required by such techniques. Since the errors made in assumptions for basic factors at the beginning of such computational procedures may be magnified as the computations proceed (Alonso, 1968), such a large number of sequentially-linked assumptions may be problematic. In addition, the data requirements of such models are often extensive. Data on economic and demographic trends such as labor force participation rates, family size, and many other dimensions must be obtained for the projection period. Finally, because they have been developed recently, these techniques have received even less validation than other procedures (see Chapter 9), and it is unclear whether such techniques provide more or less accurate population projections than demographic techniques alone (Kendall, 1977). Economic-based techniques represent an important set of methods that are worthy of concerted attention but which also require additional analytical verification.

Cohort Component Techniques

Cohort component projection techniques are perhaps the most widely used techniques for determining future population levels. They are often seen as the most complex and sophisticated of the purely demographic techniques and are usually preferred by professional demographers because they involve the direct simulation of the demographic processes of fertility, mortality, and migration that produce changes in population size.

As the name implies, the basic characteristics of these techniques are the use of separate cohorts, persons with one or more common characteristics (usually similar ages, i.e. persons born during the same period), and the separate projection of each of the major components of population change -- fertility, mortality, and migration -- for each of these cohorts. These projections of components for each cohort are then combined in the familiar "demographic bookkeeping equation" (Barclay, 1958; Bogue, 1974) as follows:

$$P_{x + t} = P_x + B_{x + t} - D_{x + t} + M_{x + t} \qquad (3.11)$$

Where: $P_{x + t}$ is the population projected at some future date t years hence.

P_x is the population at the base year x.

$B_{x + t}$ is the number of births that occur during the interval t.

$D_{x + t}$ is the number of deaths that occur during the interval t.

$M_{x + t}$ is the amount of net migration that takes place during the interval t.

When several cohorts are used, P_{x+t} may be seen as:

$$P_{x+t} = \sum_{i=1}^{n} P_{ci, x+t} \qquad (3.12)$$

Where: P_{x+t} is as in equation 3.11

$P_{ci, x+t}$ = population of a given cohort at time $x+t$

and $P_{ci, x+t} = P_{ci, x} + B_{ci, x+t} - D_{ci, x+t} + M_{ci, x+t}$ $\qquad (3.13)$

Where: all terms are as in equation 3.11 but are specific to given cohorts ci

In general, single-year or five-year age and sex cohorts are used in conjunction with age and sex-specific survival rates, fertility rates, and migration rates. The technique is seldom used for geographic areas smaller than counties because of the difficulty of obtaining birth, death, and migration data for these areas and because of the widely known problems of applying rates (or percentages) to small population bases (Irwin, 1977). Whatever the geographical level of analysis, however, there are four key steps in the procedure:

1. The selection of a baseline set of cohorts for the area of study;
2. The determination of appropriate baseline migration, mortality, and fertility measures for each cohort for the projection period;
3. The determination of the method for projecting trends in fertility, mortality, and migration rates over the projection period; and
4. The selection of a computational procedure for applying the rates (from 3) to the cohorts over the projection period.

Each of these four steps involves consideration of numerous alternatives that are discussed briefly below.

Selection of Baseline Cohorts. The selection of baseline cohorts is usually done by selecting data from the last population census. The data so selected are age and sex cohorts in single- or five-year age groups. Of all the data requirements, the baseline cohort data required for the procedure are the most readily available. In addition, the major adjustments to such baseline data that may be necessary (in addition to those noted below) are relatively simple, such as the adjustment of cohort counts for census undercounts (Pittenger, 1976;

Irwin, 1977).

Determination of Appropriate Baseline Measures. The
selection of the appropriate migration, fertility, and mortality rates to be used in the projection is the key step in
the projection process. The accuracy of the assumptions about
these rates and their trends over time will determine the
accuracy of the projections. The selection of these rates
involves numerous considerations.

Determination of Mortality Rates. Mortality levels are
easy to discern because of the ready availability of data on
mortality and the relatively slow rate of change in mortality
levels over time (at least in developed areas of the world).
Life tables for states and other areas are published periodically (for example, see National Center for Health Statistics,
1975), and, generally, state level rates can be assumed to be
applicable to local areas without markedly affecting the
results of the analysis. Given a life table, the mortality
measure most often used is the age and sex-specific survival
rate which indicates the probability of persons of a given
age living from period (x) to the next period (x + t). So
considered, the survival rates for any age group can be computed from the number of survivors column of the life table
with the following formula:

$$S_{x,x+t} = \frac{L_{x+t}}{L_x} \qquad (3.14)$$

Where: $S_{x,x+t}$ = probability of a member of a cohort
              surviving from the time period x to
              x + t

       L_{x+t} = number of persons in the cohort alive
              at the end of the period, x + t

       L_x = number of persons in the cohort alive at the
              beginning of the period, x

These rates are computed for each cohort, including the beginning cohort which consists of persons born during the projection period from x to x + t and for persons at the end of their
life cycles (for a description of the special procedures
necessary to compute survival rates for beginning and end of
life cohorts, see Irwin, 1977). The rates so obtained are
those that are applied to age and sex cohorts to age or survive them to the next projection period. As with the choice
of cohorts, either single- or five-year survival rates can be
computed.

An alternative to life table derived survival rates are
national census survival rates, computed from census data at
the national level. National level data are used to control

78

for the confounding of mortality and migration factors. Thus, when national data are used, the effect of migration on age groups can be assumed to be negligible because inmigration is a very small percentage of total national population change. To compute these rates, age groups at two consecutive censuses are examined in the following computational form:

$$S_{x,x+t} = \frac{P_{x+t}}{P_x}$$ (3.15)

Where: $S_{x,x+t}$ is as in equation 3.14

P_{x+t} = population in a given cohort at the second census period

P_x = population in a given cohort at the first census

The problem with this method is that the national rates computed are less likely than rates derived from state life tables to reflect local conditions and hence these rates are generally used only when appropriate life tables are not available.

Determination of Fertility Rates. The methods for determining fertility levels fall into three general categories. These are: (1) period fertility measures; (2) cohort fertility measures; and (3) marriage-parity-interval progression measures (Shryock and Siegel, 1973).

Period fertility measures are among the most often used measures of fertility in projections. They involve the use of rates showing the number of births likely to occur to a group of women during the projection period. The rates used most often indicate the number of births per female in the reproductive age groups of the population (usually defined as those women 15-44 years of age) and are termed General Fertility Rates (GFR's) and computed as follows:

$$GFR = \frac{B_t}{FP_{t\ 15-44}}$$ (3.16)

Where: GFR = general fertility rate

B_t = births during projection period t

$FP_{t\ 15-44}$ = fertility of population age 15-44 years of age during projection period t

They may also be made specific to given cohorts (single- or five-year cohorts). In such cases they are termed Age-Specific Fertility Rates (ASFR's) and computed as follows:

$$ASFR_i = \frac{_iB_t}{_iFP_t} \qquad (3.17)$$

Where: $ASFR_i$ = age-specific fertility rates for females
in age group (cohort) i

$_iB_t$ = births to women in age group i during projection period t

$_iFP_t$ = female population of age group i during
projection period t

To compute these measures, data are obtained on births
(for GFR's) or births by age of mother (for ASFR's) from state
health and vital statistics departments or the National Center
for Health Statistics and on populations from a recent population census. Usually the average number of births for three
years centering on a year for which there either was a population count (such as a census year -- 1980) or for which
acceptable population figures are available is used. The use
of an average of three years of births is employed in order
to reduce the chance of obtaining a numerator that is nonrep-
resentative of the actual number of births to such age groups.
This is essential because of the relatively wide fluctuations
in the number of births that occur from year to year in some
populations. Such rates are computed for each single- or five-
year age group (15-44 years of age) given data on births by
residence and age of mother and data on the number of females
in each age group.

The distinctive characteristics of these rates are that
they are rates computed at a given point in time. They do not
take into account the fact that the time period covered by a
set of projections will involve the fertility experiences of
women as they age over the projection period. Rather, these
period measures are based on the experiences of women at different ages at one point in time.

Cohort fertility measures attempt to overcome the limitation noted above for period measures by attempting to simulate a set of rates that will characterize the actual experiences of a cohort of women as they age through the life cycle.
The most widely used form for simulating these experiences
is to choose a set of age-specific fertility rates that would
result in the average female giving birth to a given number
of children by the completion of her reproductive years. Among
the "targeted" values often chosen is the level of 2.1 births
per female. This number of births is termed the "replacement
level of fertility" and is that number of births necessary for
the women in a population to replace themselves and their
mates, taking into account (the .1) that some women will die
or not produce children during their reproductive lifetimes.
These targeted levels of cohort fertility (such as the 2.1

80

noted above) are the sum of a set of ASFR's for women in each
of the reproductive cohorts and are termed the Total Fertility
Rates (TFR's) (TFR equals the sum of ASFR's over all female
cohorts 15-44 years of age).

The advantage of using total fertility rates is that they
allow analysis in terms of family size and other similar concepts that are familiar to a wide range of persons who may use
the projections. Although they are often based on the experiences of actual cohorts of women that have completed their
childbearing years, the obvious disadvantage of using these
rates is the difficulty encountered in choosing the set of
rates that will correctly characterize the experiences of
future cohorts of women.

Marriage-parity-interval progression measures refer to the
use of sets of sequential probability measures that take into
account the probability that women with different marital statuses and completed family sizes will give birth to another
child during the projection period. Although this and similar
techniques may be more widely used in the future (Pittenger,
1976) and the technique is presently used in some of the U.S.
Bureau of the Census projections (U.S. Bureau of the Census,
1979a), it is a relatively complex procedure with extensive
data requirements (numbers of women by marital status, age
and parity, births by parity, etc.). Marriage-parity-interval
progression procedures have received relatively little use in
local area projections and will not be discussed in further
detail here. They are, however, worthy of further examination
(see Shryock and Siegel, 1973, pp. 789-790) and their use may
become more prevalent as the availability of detailed local
area data increases.

However fertility rates are determined, the goal at the
end of this step of the cohort-component procedure is to have
determined a set of fertility rates for each female cohort
that can be used to determine the number of births occurring
in the population during the projection period. These procedures, then, are ones aimed at providing the B_{x+t} function
in the bookkeeping equation.

Determination of Migration Rates. For local area projections, migration levels are clearly the most difficult
demographic processes to predict and the most difficult for
which to obtain current data when cohort-specific values
are required. The difficulty is further increased by the fact
that migration may involve two different forms with opposite
effects on population change. These are inmigration and outmigration. Any time an area changes from a predominance of
one of these patterns to the other (thus changing the M_{x+t}
part of equation 3.11 from a positive to a negative or from
a negative to a positive value), the increased potential for
error in the projections is evident. Projections of migration
are usually the major area of contention in population pro-

jections.

Methods for projecting this dimension fall into two broad categories: (1) net migration projection procedures; and (2) gross migration procedures. Whereas net migration procedures attempt only to discern the net difference between the levels of in- and outmigration in an area, gross migration procedures project in- and outmigration separately.

Net migration procedures usually involve projecting migration using what are termed residual methods. The formula for the residual method of migration is in fact the bookkeping equation solved for the $_{ci}M_{x+t}$ component or:

$$_{ci}M_{x+t} = {}_{ci}P_{x+t} - {}_{ci}P_x - {}_{ci}B_{x+t} + {}_{ci}D_{x+t}$$

$$(3.18)$$

Where: values are as in equation 3.11

In equation 3.18 a comparison is made between the number of persons who have survived to the end of the period, x + t, and those who at the end of the period are t years older than at time x. Thus, if ten year rates were being computed for 1980 for the age group 25-29, one would adjust the age group 15-19 in 1970 for deaths between 1970 and 1980. These rates can be computed given data on populations by age at two census counts, deaths by age, and births (for beginning cohorts) between the two census counts. In addition, useful compilations of such data for past periods have been made available by five-year age and sex cohorts for all counties in the United States, by Bowles et al. (1975) and Bowles and Tarver (1965).

The logic of the residual method does in fact underlie one complete form of population projection developed by Hamilton and Perry (1962). They propose that one simple way to project total populations or cohort populations from one census to another is to compute fertility levels and then to use a residual method to jointly compute the effects of migration and mortality. Their procedure for projecting a cohort from 1980-1990, for example, would involve the formula:

$$P_x^{90} = \frac{P_{x-10}^{80}\ P_x^{80}}{P_{x-10}^{70}}$$

$$(3.19)$$

Where: P_x^{90} = population in age group x in 1990

P_{x-10}^{80} = population in age group x-10 in 1980

$P_x 80$ = population in age group x in 1980

P_{x-10}^{70} = population in age group x-10 in 1970

82

In this equation (3.19), the ratio between population in 1970 and 1980 is assumed to continue for the next projection period. Although this ratio confounds changes resulting from migration with those resulting from mortality, it does provide an appropriate technique for use when the data necessary to separate migration and mortality are not available. It thus provides an alternative method that may be useful under some circumstances.

Gross migration measures are used less often but are somewhat more attractive conceptually because they simulate the behavior of actual individuals. Whereas inmigration and outmigration represent actions of actual individuals, net migration does not, in fact, occur. Rather it is a statistical creation resulting from a comparison of in- and outmigration. The difficulty with the use of gross migration measures is that the necessary data to determine them are often not available for local areas or, when made available, are likely to be extremely dated (U.S. Bureau of the Census, 1977). When appropriate data are available, the major mode of projection involves projecting outmigration for each area, usually on the basis of past patterns, and then projecting the pool of outmigrants as inmigrants to each area on the basis of past trends in the ratio of inmigrants in the local area to total inmigrants (Shryock and Siegel, 1973; Irwin, 1977). These methods are not often used below the multiregion level, but clearly require careful consideration.

Although additional procedures for projecting local area migration levels have been suggested (Pittenger, 1974), those discussed here are the main procedures presently in use. Each method places a heavy reliance on the use of assumptions based on past patterns. Unlike mortality or fertility patterns where some theoretical limits can be set, for migration the range of possible values and the reasons for changes in direction from in- to out- or out- to inmigration are not well understood.

Methods for Projecting Rates Over Time. Given that a baseline set of mortality, fertility, and migration rates has been established, the third major step involves developing procedures for projecting the trends in these rates over time. There are three widely used procedures: (1) continuation of baseline rates; (2) use of targeted rates; and (3) trending of local area rates to regional, national, or other "standard" area rates.

Continuation of rates determined for the baseline period may be preferable in many instances, particularly if the area is large and is not changing rapidly, and the projection is for only a short period in the future. For long-term projections, however, and particularly for areas undergoing rapid development, such assumptions are seldom warranted. Increasingly, then, projections using continuations of past trends, particularly when used for relatively small rural areas, are

being questioned and used only when projections based on
alternative assumptions are also used.

The use of targeted rates for specific periods or targeted levels of change in rates over specific periods are more
frequently employed. In using these procedures, baseline
rates are assumed to reach predetermined rates by certain
points in the projection period. Thus, the U.S. Bureau of the
Census has historically used rates of fertility that are
trended over time to reach a given level (2.1, 2.5 etc. levels
of TFR's) by a specific year (U.S. Bureau of the Census,
1979a) and have also often used targeted rates for migration
-- such as assuming immigration will be negligible by a certain point in time (U.S. Bureau of the Census, 1977).

The choice of rates using this procedure is usually tied
to a conceptual perspective on population, such as stable
population theory (a stable population being one with a fixed
level of births and deaths per year), or to assumptions that
local area rates will converge toward those of a larger area,
such as the state or nation. The rates chosen, then, are the
targeted levels that will result in a given stable population
or that characterize a large area to which local area rates
will converge.

As should be evident, this procedure is also dependent on
a number of assumptions and requires the analyst to make projections of long-term trends in each of the vital rates and
about the time period necessary for an area to reach a given
level of fertility, migration, and mortality. The task involved is clearly a difficult one.

The third approach is really a form of the other two in
that it involves choosing a standard area after which local
rates can be patterned. However, its widespread use requires
that it be given special emphasis in this discussion.

In this third approach, the trending of local rates on
the basis of larger area rates, the analyst: (1) selects a
standard population to which to relate the local area; (2)
determines the ratio or relationship of the local area rate to
the standard population rate; and (3) assumes that the local
rate will either maintain a constant ratio or relationship to
the standard population rate or change in a fixed manner over
the projection period. Using this procedure, the analyst can
make widespread use of projections made by various agencies
and groups. Thus, the work of the U.S. Census Bureau on projecting long-term national trends in fertility, mortality, and
migration have been used as the "standard" in many local area
projections (Tarver and Black, 1966; Murdock and Ostenson,
1976; Hertsgaard et al., 1978). As with the first two procedures discussed, the utility of this technique is heavily
dependent on the correctness of the analyst's assumptions about
long-term trends in vital rates and about the comparability of
local rates to those for other areas. It shares the disadvantages and limitations of the other techniques but provides the

researcher with the possibility of using the work of analysts from agencies whose long-term projections and data bases may be superior to his or her own.

Each of these three techniques for projecting trends in rates over time requires the use of assumptions that are often quite "heroic" in nature, given demographers' present ability to predict mortality, fertility, and migration phenomena. However these trends are projected over time, the population expert should be the first to view his or her assumptions with skepticism.

Selection of Computational Procedures. Although all cohort component procedures compute their final population values on the basis of the general summation procedure shown in equation 3.11, several aspects of these procedures require brief consideration. It should be made evident, for example, that few analysts using the cohort component technique feel confident enough of their assumptions about vital rates to suggest that a single set of assumptions will be correct for all areas and periods. As a result, cohort component projections will generally involve making several sets of alternative computations with different assumed rates resulting in several alternative projection series.

A number of other considerations must also be addressed. These considerations relate to adjustments required during the computations and may be most efficiently examined by presenting a standard set of steps used for deriving the values denoted in equation 3.11. Although a number of analysts provide step-by-step instructions for doing cohort component procedures (Irwin, 1977; Morrison, 1971; Pittenger, 1976; Barclay, 1958; Tarver and Black, 1966; Shryock and Siegel, 1973; Bogue, 1974), the steps delineated below appear to be the most useful for purposes of our discussion:

1. Adjust the baseline population cohorts for the correct time periods and spatial referents;
2. Adjust rates of migration, fertility, and mortality making sure that all rates are:
   (a) based on consistent population bases,
   (b) adjusted to consistent time, place, and cohort factors, and
   (c) specific to the characteristic detail desired in the projections;
3. Survive baseline population to the end of the projection period;
4. Add or subtract migrants from the baseline population;
5. Compute births and add births to initial cohorts of the baseline population in accordance with sex ratios at birth;

6. Sum cohorts as desired to obtain total population; and
7. Adjust sum of populations for subareas to population totals for the larger area.

Each of these steps entails adjustments that must be briefly mentioned.

In step one, it is essential to ensure that all data are made consistent in terms of time and place referents. That is, all population values should be adjusted for similar time frames. Population censuses, for example, are for populations as of April 1 of the census years. These figures should either be adjusted to be consistent with the periods for which other data are available, such as calendar years, or other data should be adjusted to be applicable to April 1 of the year. Whatever geographical unit has been chosen for analysis, all data must be adjusted to that unit by appropriate allocations or other procedures. It is particularly important to make sure that constant boundaries are assumed across time and have been taken into account in any historic data used. Special attention should be given to such factors in urban areas where boundary changes are frequent.

It is essential also in this initial step to consider what provisions, if any, should be made for "special populations." These are populations that are unlikely to be exposed to the same set of demographic processes as the remainder of the population and include such groups as college and university populations, military base populations, Native American populations, and institutional populations. In general, such populations are treated in one of two ways.

One commonly used procedure is simply to exclude them from the cohort component procedure and project their total levels for each projection period. For special populations in which the population totals vary little from period to period, in which the age distributions are concentrated, and for which integration with the rest of the population is limited (such as military bases and college populations), this may be an adequate way to project the influence of such groups. For other groups, their distinct demographic rates may be such and their distributions across age groups extensive enough to merit a second procedure -- the development of separate fertility, mortality, and migration rates and the use of separate cohort procedures. For example, Native American populations often have higher mortality and fertility rates than other populations and may merit such attention. In any case, it is in this initial step of determining baseline cohorts that special populations must be designated.

Step two notes that the rates for each component must also be adjusted. These adjustments include not only the same time and place adjustments as for total population bases but also those for cohorts. Whatever the level of detail for which projections are desired -- age, sex, ethnicity, etc. -- appropriate rates must be developed for each detailed characteristic. Rates must also be made consistent with the period of the projection and the size of cohorts. That is, if the projection period is one year and single-year cohorts are to be used, rates must be single-year, not five- or ten-year rates, and must be for single years of age. Pittenger (1976), among others, provides readily useable formulas for preparing adjustments of rates to appropriate periods, and Irwin (1977) provides excellent examples of adjusting cohorts to be temporally and areally specific.

Two similar concerns also relate to steps three, four, and five. One of these is the need to adjust the baseline populations to which projected rates are to be applied. For example, if a five-year projection cycle is being used, with five-year age and sex cohorts, parts of at least two different cohorts will be involved in each projection cycle. For example, if the age group of males 15-19 in 1980 is to be projected to 1985, the five-year rates should be applied to an average number of persons that are 15-19 during the 1980-1985 period. This will, in fact, include different parts of different cohorts being exposed to rates for 15-19 year olds for different lengths of time. Fifteen year olds in 1980 will be exposed to the rates for all five years (1980-1984), but 16 year olds will experience such rates for only four years, 17 year olds for only three years, etc. On the other hand, those 14 years old in 1980 will experience the 15-19 year old rates for four years, those 13 will experience these rates for three years, etc. To adjust these cohorts, an "adjacent cohort" technique (Irwin, 1977) is necessary in which an average of the two cohorts is used as the base for projections. These adjustments should be made for all cohorts before component rates are applied. Secondly, it should be noted in step five that the births produced by adjusted sets of female cohorts must be allocated to each initial sex distribution. This is usually done by taking data on sex ratios at birth, available from most state vital statistics departments, and applying them to the total number of births.

Finally, step seven points out the need to insure that, if relatively large areas with multiple subareas are to be projected, some attempt to control the sum of local area totals to the total of the larger area must be made. If this is not done, the summation of subarea migrants or births may exceed those that are reasonable for the larger area (see Irwin, 1977 and Pittenger, 1976 for further discussion of this problem).

Although the adjustments noted in the seven computational steps are all relatively minor, their omission can lead to serious errors in computations. The computations as well as the assumptions underlying the cohort component procedure may, therefore, be quite complex. Fortunately, however, a number of readily available computer programs for performing such projections are available (Bogue, 1974; U.S. Bureau of the Census, 1976).

Cohort component procedures are among the most developed techniques available for population projections. Their advantages lie in their ability to simulate demographic processes and in the age, sex, and other detail they provide in outputs. Their disadvantages are equally evident. They have extensive data requirements and rely on a relatively large number of assumptions about each of the major components. Their utility for making projections is dependent on their judicious use and the long-term development of an understanding of basic demographic processes.

Conclusions Concerning Projection Alternatives. Each of the major methods discussed, from the extrapolative to the cohort component techniques, provides procedures that are useful under particular sets of circumstances. As such, each represents a set of procedures that may be applicable for making projections of the demographic impacts resulting from resource developments, particularly for making projections of baseline conditions. The choice of the best method under any given set of circumstances will depend on a number of factors that are relatively unique to a given time and place. Data availability, the length of the projection period, and the form of outputs desired are among the key factors. As shall soon be made evident, however, many factors related to impact events and policy needs must also be considered. Overall, a wide range of potential tools for projecting population are available, but the ones that can be employed under any given set of circumstances are often much more severely restricted.

FACTORS AFFECTING DEMOGRAPHIC IMPACT ASSESSMENTS

The choice of which of the methodologies described above should be used in performing a given impact assessment is affected by a number of factors related to the nature of impact events and the needs of policy makers in impact situations. The purpose of this section is to describe some of those factors that must be considered in the choice of a projection methodology, that affect the use of impact projections, and that must be taken into account in the simulation of impact events.

Among the factors that affect demographic impacts and the choice of impact assessment methods are several of those noted earlier -- the characteristics of the project, of the project site area, and of inmigrating workers. Thus, the magnitude and distribution of project impacts will be affected by several key project characteristics:

1. Plant location,

2. Direct project employment,
3. Indirect/direct worker ratios,
4. Length of project phases (construction and operation),
5. Levels of local hiring, and
6. The developer's employment practices.

Projects located close to relatively populous areas with large employment bases are likely to draw more of their work- ers from the local area and are less likely to require the inmigration of new workers. The direct employment require- ments of the project obviously play a major role in determin- ing population impacts, with projects with larger employment demands leading to higher levels of inmigration and population growth. In addition, projects that lead to higher levels of associated or service employment (indirect or induced employ- ment) will have greater impacts on population growth. At the same time, the timing of project phases, specifically the length of the construction and operational phases, will affect the patterns of population change. Thus, in most cases popu- lation trends in resource developments follow the trends in employment patterns with project-related population peaking during construction periods and then declining and eventually reaching a relatively stable level during the operational period. Finally, the extent to which local residents are hired for project-related employment and the developer's poli- cies toward such hiring will affect population growth. That is, if more local residents are hired, fewer inmigrants will be required to fill project-related employment. Company policies toward training locals may thus have marked effects on the number of locals employed by the facility.

The characteristics of the project site may also affect population growth and its distribution within impacted areas. Among these characteristics (Murdock et al., 1980b) are: (1) local population's labor force skills and availability; (2) the number and characteristics of possible settlement sites; and (3) local communities' growth preferences. The level of local hiring will, in large part, be a function of the avail- ability of local residents for project employment and the skill levels of the population of the local area. The more persons available for project employment and the more compati- ble their skill levels with those skills required -- directly or indirectly -- as a result of the project, the fewer inmi- grants will be required. At the same time, the number of alternative settlement sites and the characteristics of these sites, particularly their ability to absorb population growth, will affect both relative population impacts for given sites and the distribution of new population between sites. Impact regions with a relatively large number of communities with well developed service bases will experience less dramatic concentrations of population growth and impacts than those regions with relatively few impact sites and with sites poorly

equipped to absorb new growth. Finally, population growth in
impact areas may be affected by more subtle factors, such as
community growth preferences. Although growth in large urban
centers is less likely to be affected by such factors, residents' desires for growth in rural communities are often
directly communicated to potential migrants and are thus more
effective in inhibiting or promoting growth.

The characteristics of inmigrating workers represent another dimension that must be considered in impact assessments
(Chalmers and Anderson, 1977). Since resource development-
related population growth is clearly economically created
growth, the characteristics of inmigrating workers and their
families are key determinants of population growth. Such
characteristics as the marital status, average family size,
and age and sex distribution of workers, spouses, and dependents as well as their community service and settlement preferences will affect the total level of population growth in an
impacted area, the characteristics of that new population, and
its distribution.

Finally, in addition to these dimensions, the legislative
mandates of impact assessments and the pragmatic considerations of decision makers also affect the demographic assessment process and the choice of an assessment methodology. Increasingly, the guidelines that govern the application of the
National Environmental Policy Act (Council on Environmental
Quality, 1973; 1978) have established the need to provide assessments that are readily understandable to, and that directly service the information needs of, decision makers. These
guidelines mandate that two separate projection procedures be
completed, one for the impact area under baseline conditions,
without the project, and one for the impact area with the project in place. Projections that take into account the standard
considerations noted in the previous section of this chapter
and ones taking the impacts of resource developments into
account must be made. In addition, attempts to plan for, manage, and mitigate the impacts of the population growth resulting from a resource development require decision makers such
as mayors, city managers, police and fire chiefs, and school
superintendents to develop policies applicable to their jurisdictions on the basis of the differences between baseline and
impact conditions.

In practice, these conditions have meant that increasing
emphasis has been placed on making projections locality and
characteristic-specific under both baseline and impact
conditions. Projections at the individual community level
and for such standard demographic characteristics as age, sex,
and race have received increasing emphasis.

When taken as a whole, the factors described above clearly
make the task of completing a demographic impact assessment a
formidable one. The population analyst must:

1. Project both baseline and impact population levels in
    which standard projection assumptions are required;
2. Project not only the total magnitude and characteris-
    tics of that growth but also its distribution and
    characteristics at the community level;
3. Make projections that take into account:
    a. the characteristics of project labor demands and
        local areas' settlement configurations,
    b. the workforce as well as the demographic charac-
        teristics of the indigenous area's population
        (i.e., availability, skill levels, etc.),
    c. the fluctuations likely to appear in various
        phases of the development project,
    d. the potential effect of nondemographic factors,
        such as development policies, community growth
        perceptions, and service infrastructures, and
    e. the extent of congruence between local skill
        levels and the skills required for the develop-
        ment;
4. Not only assess the demographic characteristics of
    residents in the area, but also the likely character-
    istics and settlement patterns of workers and the
    dependents of workers who will inmigrate into the
    area.

To summarize, the population analyst doing impact projections
must combine the standard, and often unsubstantiated, assumptions about demographic processes that must be made in standard population projections, with the additional assumptions required concerning each of the impact dimensions and the legitimate demands of decision makers for increasing specificity in
data outputs.

Clearly, an accurate assessment of demographic impacts can
only be approximated by existing techniques and knowledge
bases. It is a process that, because of its complex nature,
requires numerous compromises and simplifying assumptions. It
is one, however, that is being completed with increasing frequency, and a description of the state-of-the-art as it is now
being practiced is essential.

DEMOGRAPHIC IMPACT ASSESSMENT TECHNIQUES

The purpose of this section is to describe the state-of-
the-art of demographic impact assessment. In general, the
projection of baseline and impact-related populations has involved a number of key steps. A description of these steps
will delineate the nature of the demographic impact assessment
process and point out differences in alternative assessment
techniques. These steps include:

1. Delineation of the impact area;
2. Projection of baseline population for the impacted region and subregional areas;
3. Determination of project-related direct and indirect inmigrating workers including consideration of:
   a. characteristics of required employment,
   b. characteristics of available labor (unemployment, underemployment, skill levels and commuting patterns),
   c. indirect/direct worker ratios, and
   d. local/nonlocal worker ratios;
4. Projections of the geographical distribution (settlement patterns) of inmigrating workers; and
5. Determination of the demographic characteristics of inmigrating workers and their dependents to establish project-related population impacts by site.

Impact Area Delineation

Although the first step, the determination of the impact area, involves considerations in addition to the demographic, it is discussed here because demographic considerations often play a key role in the delineation of the impact area (Murdock and Leistritz, 1979). The impact area for socioeconomic purposes is often considered to be that area in which new project-related populations will locate, and the communities placed within the socioeconomic impact area are usually areas within commuting distance of the project site and, hence, likely settlement locations for new workers. The demographic dimension, then, plays a key role in focusing the entire socio-economic impact assessment effort.

Baseline Projections

The projection of baseline populations in impact assessments normally involves two procedures, a projection of total population at the regional or county level and an allocation or distribution of that population to subareas in the region or county. Surveys of prevailing methods (Chalmers and Anderson, 1977; Denver Research Institute, 1979) indicate that several techniques are commonly used to perform these procedures.

Projections of populations at the regional level have tended to use either a single or several separate (one for each of several types of employment) population to employment ratios, a cohort-survival, or a cohort-component method. Although use of population to employment ratios is decreasing as the need for the detail provided by cohort procedures increases, the use of population to employment ratios is still far more prevalent in baseline demographic assessments than in standard population projections. In part, this prevalence

reflects two factors -- the tendency for demographic projections in impact assessments to be made as part of the economic
portion of such an effort and secondly the need to use procedures similar to those used in the impact projections which
depend on economic assumptions. Unfortunately, however, since
population to employment ratios do not sufficiently account
for differences in population structures (particularly those
in age) or changes in those structures, they are likely to
lead to substantial errors over long projection periods. Thus,
the prevalence of such procedures in impact assessments may
not enhance the accuracy of impact projections, and the use of
cohort procedures, as described above, is becoming dominant.

The second major procedure in the projection of baseline
population involves the allocation or distribution of populations to subarea units. This is necessary because population
projections, whether done by economic-based population to employment ratios or by cohort procedures, are seldom performed
at the community level. If population projections are made
at the regional level (as is usually done when population to
employment ratios are used), this procedure involves allocations to counties and subsequent allocations to communities
within counties or a direct allocation of persons to communities and nonmunicipal areas with a subsequent summing of populations to get county totals. If projections are developed
at the county level (as in most component procedures), then
county populations are allocated to project community populations and aggregated to get regional totals. These allocations are usually done on the basis of ratioing techniques.
That is, ratios or historical trends in ratios of subarea
populations to area populations (county-region, city-region,
or city-county) are used for these allocations.

Baseline population projections in impact assessments,
then, utilize standard techniques, particularly economic-based,
ratioing, and cohort techniques. As in the use of these techniques in standard projections, the limitations and assumptions
on which they are based must be recognized and taken into
account in impact projections.

Impact Projections

Steps three through five are related to the projection of
impact populations. Although impact populations might be
determined by projecting a total population figure that includes baseline and impact populations and then subtracting
baseline projections from the total population figures, the
general pattern is to project impact-related populations
separately and to obtain total (project plus baseline) population by adding baseline and impact projections.

In addition, the impact assessment process, as usually
practiced, makes the assumption that the demographic impacts
of a resource development are a function of the number of new

persons brought to the area. Assessments of the extent to which such developments lead to the retention of existing persons are seldom made and the effects of such retention are seldom entered into other steps of the assessment process. That is, projections do not contain data on the number of locals retained in the area that would leave if the development did not take place, and the service and other needs of retained persons are usually assumed to be absorbed by existing service bases. Though the failure to develop techniques for projecting levels of population retention largely reflects the difficulty of discerning "those that would leave the area if the project did not take place," such procedures should receive attention by impact analysts.

Projection of Migrating Workers

The most difficult part of the impact projection process is step three. It involves the completion of several procedures and the use of numerous assumptions. This step, the projection of inmigrating workers, is almost the universally accepted starting point for projecting project-related populations. The reasons for the widespread acceptance of this starting point, rather than a more purely demographic one, are several. First, data on the direct labor requirements of projects are perhaps the most readily accessible of all socioeconomic data on resource developments. Secondly, although migration patterns as a whole are increasingly motivated by noneconomic factors (Long and Hansen, 1979), the migration related to resource developments is largely employment-related. Both of these factors suggest the use of employment-related migration as the key to projecting impact-related population. Finally, there simply are few alternatives to the use of employment. No clear linkages between project characteristics, other than employment, such as type of project, project production capacity, or other characteristics have been established. However desirable the development of alternative means for projecting impact populations might appear to be, few viable alternatives have been developed.

The projection of inmigrating workers may involve a relatively simple procedure or a highly complex one and may involve procedures that are based on economic factors or ones that combine basic economic and demographic procedures. In the simplest and most straightforward procedure, the steps involved are as follows (Murphy and Williams, 1978):

1. Estimates of direct employment obtained from the developer are multiplied by an employment multiplier (number of indirect workers per direct worker) to obtain estimates of indirect employment;
2. Given estimates of direct and indirect project employment requirements, estimates of the proportions of

these requirements that can be met by the local existing population are made; and

3. Local employment (step 2) at the project is subtrac-
ted from total employment requirements with the resulting difference indicating the number of workers
that must migrate into the area as a result of the
project.

In this procedure, the key values are the employment multipliers and the local worker ratios. The first of these values
can be readily obtained from state or other local economic
data (such as an input-output table), and the second has been
the focus of a number of studies (Mountain West Research,
Inc., 1975, 1977; Leholm et al., 1976b; Wieland et al., 1977,
1979) and is readily summarized in several publications
(Murphy and Williams, 1978; Bender, 1975; Murdock and
Leistritz, 1979).

The advantages of this technique are that it is computationally simple and its data needs are limited to those that
are widely available. Its major disadvantage is its neglect
of the implications of the site area's demographic structure.
It entails implicit assumptions that the site area population
is one with an average age structure, skill levels, and average levels of labor participation (i.e., a population that can
obtain a given proportion of the project jobs) which may not
be true in many rural areas with a relatively old age structure. It tends to ignore, or at least to confound, multiple
factors affecting the nature of employment requirements and
the nature of available local workers, in determining migrating workers. Even when the procedure is refined by using
separate employment multipliers for different industries and
separate local employment levels for various kinds of employment (i.e., direct, indirect, etc.) for each major project
phase (construction and operation) (Murdock et al., 1980b;
Murphy and Williams, 1978), such problems still persist. Its
use under some circumstances may still be justified, however,
if sufficient resources or data are not available to complete
projections using more complex procedures.

A somewhat more complex procedure which utilizes more
demographic input is also often used (Stenehjem, 1978; Mountain West Research, Inc., 1978). In this procedure, direct
employment and indirect employment estimates are derived as
noted above, but the application of labor force participation
rates to population projections is used as the basis for determining local labor availability.

The advantage of this technique over the one described
above, particularly if age and sex-specific labor force participation rates are used, is that the population structure of
the local area does have an effect, through participation
rates, in determining local labor availability. Thus, if a
disproportionate part of the population is in age groups with

low labor force participation rates (such as very young or
very old age groups), a smaller number of available workers
will be estimated. The disadvantage of this technique is that
appropriate baseline and projected participation rates must be
obtained. Although baseline rates are easily obtained from
census and other secondary data sources, determining those
rates that will prevail during a resource development is more
difficult. Even if some general area's (state or regional
average) rates are used as targeted values (see Hertsgaard
et al., 1978), the assumptions made concerning labor force
participation may still be problematic and require careful
preliminary analysis. In general, however, this procedure is
considered to be a more demographically desirable technique
than the one outlined earlier.

Even more elaborate techniques have been applied on some,
though infrequent, occasions. Among the more elaborate of
these are those of Hertsgaard et al. (1978) and Cluett et al.
(1977). These procedures use separate techniques to project
different types of employment and to project labor availability and a separate procedure to match employment demands to
labor availability. Hertsgaard et al. (1978) for example, use
an input-output model in conjunction with project employment
data to project four types of employment -- baseline, project
operational, project construction, and indirect. They also
use four sets of age and sex-specific employment availability
rates (one for each type of employment), that are similar to
labor force participation rates but indicate potential rather
than actual employment, to project the number of persons that
could take each of the four types of required employment. The
application of these rates to age and sex cohort data, derived
from cohort-component projections, provides four separate
labor pools composed of the number of workers by age and sex
in the local population available to take each of the four
types of project employment.

Given employment needs by type and available labor by
type, Hertsgaard et al. (1978) then apply a priority schedule
which is a set of algorithms for filling each type of required
project employment from the four labor pools given certain
assumptions about the order with which types of required employment will be filled by available workers. The result of
this procedure is the projection of migrating workers with an
excess of available employees, after all required employment
has been filled, indicating the need for worker outmigration
and a deficit indicating the need for inmigration. The final
step in this process is the adjustment of the available worker
excess or deficit by what is termed an "unallocated" labor
pool rate. This rate is a proxy for unemployment and underemployment. The procedures utilized by Cluett et al. (1977)
are similar but in addition use an algorithm that estimates
labor turnover effects on migration levels.

The advantages of these complex procedures are that they

simulate most of the major factors known to affect employment-
related migration. The Hertsgaard et al. (1978) procedure dif-
ferentiates: (1) types of employment demands that are likely
to affect levels of local employment and inmigration; (2) types
of labor availability -- the different levels of potential
(skills) in the local population for taking different types of
employment; (3) the effects of age and sex population characteristics on that availability; and (4) the effects of under-
and unemployment. These procedures are conceptually attractive. Their major disadvantages are that such procedures have
extensive data requirements, and many of these data requirements cannot be met by available data. Only extensive primary
data collection efforts can address many of these issues (see
Wieland et al., 1977), and such efforts may be too expensive
for use in many assessments.

In sum, then, in the third major step the choice of techniques can range from the relatively simple to the highly
complex. The exact choice of technique must depend on the
delicate balancing of data availability, and the time and costs
involved in altering that availability, with the need to more
effectively simulate the conditions actually affecting employment-related migration and the need to consider the effects of
population structure on local labor availability. Hopefully,
levels of data availability will increase over time and serve
to lessen the need for such compromises.

Projections of Settlement Patterns

The fourth step is the projection of the geographical
settlement patterns of inmigrating workers. This step may,
in fact, be performed with workers or be delayed until after
step five and be performed with total population. It is a
procedure that parallels the allocation of populations to
communities in baseline projections. Unlike that process,
however, the focus in impact projections is the distribution
of workers in relation to the project site rather than within
a geographically delineated county or region. This distribution involves allocating workers to places that may be located
in several separate geographical jurisdictions.

It is a vitally important step particularly in its implications for local community planning for it is in this step
that workers are allocated to local areas. Variations in the
techniques and assumptions used in this step will largely
determine the impacts that are projected for local areas.
These distributions can be affected by numerous factors. Workers' housing preferences, service preferences, willingness to
commute, and other factors may affect settlement patterns. At
best, prevailing methodologies utilize only very broad indicators of these numerous factors in their allocation procedures. Although several techniques are delineated below, the
geographical allocation of employment or population is an area

of impact assessment requiring concerted empirical attention.

At least three approaches are used with some frequency in the projections of worker distributions in impact assessments (Denver Research Institute, 1979; Chalmers and Anderson, 1977). These are: (1) judgemental weighting models; (2) delphi derived models; and (3) gravity models.

Judgemental weighting models are those models that rely on researchers' or local knowledgeables' qualitative assessments of such factors as available housing and service structures in various communities to differentially weight communities as potential settlement sites (Stenehjem and Metzger, 1976). Weights are assigned to all communities that are expected to receive workers and then the weight of each community in relation to the sum of weights for all communities is used to proportion workers to each community. These techniques have the advantage of providing input of local knowledge into the allocation process but the disadvantages of requiring the collection of such data and of having their accuracy determined by the accuracy of local perceptions.

Delphi techniques refer simply to more concerted and definitive efforts using judgemental techniques. In the delphi technique the sample of persons used to determine community weights is systematically selected to be representative of community groups with different types of knowledge on settlement choices (local leaders, merchants, real estate agents, general residents, etc.). The results of these groups' initial evaluations are summarized, and these summaries are used for additional rounds of questioning of these groups. The goal of this process is to obtain high levels of consensus on communities' relative levels of attractiveness. Although this technique is still dependent on local judgements, it has the advantage of requiring knowledgeable individuals to make concerted examinations and reexaminations of the factors that affect community attractiveness.

Gravity techniques have a long tradition of use in demography (Carrothers, 1956, Karp and Kelly, 1971) and regional economics (Isard et al., 1972) and are widely used in impact projections (Murdock et al., 1978). The premise underlying their use is that larger communities and those closer to the project site like particles affected by the physical laws of gravity will gain more population from the project (will interact more frequently) than smaller and more distant places. This relationship can be specified as follows:

$$W_{ij} = \frac{P_i}{D_{ij}} \qquad (3.20)$$

Where: W_{ij} = workers from project j going to community i

P_i = population of community i

$$D_{ij} = \text{distance from project site } j \text{ to community } i$$

For all communities in a project area, this equation is applied in the following form:

$$W_{ij} = \frac{\dfrac{P_i}{D_{ij}}}{\displaystyle\sum_{i=1}^{n} \dfrac{P_i}{D_{ij}}} \tag{3.21}$$

Where: All values are as in equation 3.20

In the gravity equation (3.21), powers are often attached to distance and/or population to indicate varying levels of influence for these factors. The major limitations of gravity models are that they are predictive rather than explanatory with an inadequate level of conceptual justification supporting their use. As a result, their use is often mechanical. On the other hand, their validity has been systematically assessed in general (Anderson, 1955) and for impacted areas (Murdock et al., 1978) and, though they had been less successful in predicting rural than in predicting urban settlement patterns, they appear to be of general utility in many instances (Wieland et al., 1979).

In addition to these three techniques, increasing use is being made of techniques that utilize either alternatives to population in the gravity formulation or that combine judgemental factors with the gravity formulation (see Hertsgaard et al., 1978; Murdock et al., 1979b; Wieland et al., 1979). Thus, Wieland et al. (1979) found that substantial improvements could be made in the predictive ability of the gravity model if sales tax receipts, which presumably reflect business infrastructure, are substituted for population in the gravity formulation, and Hertsgaard et al. (1978) and Murdock et al. (1979b) have suggested techniques that combine community attractiveness indexes, determined by local knowledgeables, with gravity formulations. It appears, then, that combinations of these methods may be more effective than any single method in determining the distribution of workers. The step of determining the distribution of workers is a critical one for projecting impacts and for use in planning for such impacts. In general, alternative series of allocation projections are desirable and useful.

Whatever the technique used, impact projection users should give critical attention to this aspect of the assessment process.

Projecting Workforce-Related Populations

The determination of the demographic characteristics of

workers is the last major step in the demographic impact
assessment process. In nearly all cases, it involves assuming
a standard demographic profile for workers and their families
and then applying this profile to the projections of in- or
outmigrating workers. The availability of these profiles is
increasing rapidly, and useful profiles are now available from
a number of sources (Mountain West, Inc., 1975, 1977; Leholm
et al., 1976b; Wieland et al., 1977). The techniques for
applying these profiles can vary from the use of relatively few
variables to the use of an elaborate array of variables describing the worker, spouse, children, and their characteristics. The simplest techniques project population by multiplying the average family size per worker by the number of inmigrating workers. More complex techniques use multiple worker-
related characteristics including the: (1) percent of workers
by age, sex, and marital status; (2) percent of workers with
dependents in the area; (3) number of dependents by age and
sex; (4) employment status of dependents; and (5) occupational
and industrial status of dependents.

The most frequently used computational procedures are as
follows:

1. The age, sex, and other characteristics of all migrating workers (direct and indirect) are determined
   by the application of rates derived from appropriate
   profiles.
2. The number of single and married workers is determined
   by the application of percentages in various marital
   statuses. Single workers are then entered as a part
   of the population total.
3. The number of married workers is multiplied by the
   percent with families in the impact area. Those without families in the area are then entered as part of
   the population total. Those with families in the
   area are entered as part of the total population and
   carried forward for all calculations involving dependents.
4. The number of spouses accompanying workers is determined by simply adding one spouse per inmigrating
   worker with a spouse in the region. Spouses are then
   added to population totals.
5. The number of children are determined by multiplying
   the average number of children per married worker with
   a family in the area by the number of these workers.
   Children are then added into the total population.
6. Age and sex distributions for spouses and children
   are obtained by multiplying their numbers by an
   appropriate age and sex distribution (usually percentages of each sex are determined and then the percentages in each group are applied to those persons

of each sex).
7. The number of employed dependents is obtained by
   multiplying an average number of additional workers
   per worker by the number of workers with dependents
   in the area.
8. Other characteristics are determined by applications
   of appropriate rates to the distributions derived
   from 1-6.
9. The total number of in- or outmigrating persons by age
   and sex is obtained by summing: the number of single
   workers, married workers without families in the area,
   married workers with families in the area, spouses,
   and children across age groups.

These calculations may become quite tedious when age, sex,
and other detailed characteristics are involved but are not
difficult to complete. Although the degree of detail noted
above may appear to be more extensive than necessary, because
the use of only total family size per worker would provide the
basic data on total population, the detail provided by the
more complex procedures is important for a number of purposes.
Data showing age and sex detail for workers and dependents
is important for health and educational planning, for development-related concerns (such as contractors and real estate
firms), and for determining the likely client or customer populations for businesses. Data on marital status and percent of
workers bringing dependents to the area can have marked effects
on population estimates and service planning. Thus, in
many early impact assessments, inflated projections of inmigrating populations resulted in large part from assuming that
the percent of married workers would be equal to the baseline
population in the area and that all married workers would bring
their families to the area. As the surveys noted above (Mountain West, Inc., 1975; 1977; Wieland et al., 1977) indicate,
however, workers inmigrating as a result of resource developments are younger, and hence less likely to be married, than
the baseline population in the area and a substantial proportion of workers will not bring their families to the impact
area, particularly during the construction of the project.
Accurate assessments of such characteristics are essential.
Projections of the workforce characteristics of dependents are equally important. Since secondary or additional
employees in the worker household will be available to take
indirect and other employment generated by the project, the
number of new secondary workers and households will be reduced
by the number of secondary workers in primary workers' households. The accurate estimation of such secondary workers is
essential to avoid inaccurately projecting the number of inmigrating secondary workers.
In brief, these and other characteristics of the migrating worker population must be projected both to provide neces-

sary planning information and to increase the overall accuracy of projections.

Conclusions Concerning the State-of-the-Art

The steps delineated above, with some variation, are the major steps generally completed in projecting demographic impacts. It is obvious that these steps involve numerous assumptions about such factors as impact events, baseline conditions, baseline populations, workforce characteristics, and inmigrating population's settlement patterns, preferences, and characteristics. As such, it is obvious that the end product of this assessment is likely to be projections that are approximations of the impacts that will actually occur.

It is essential that two final admonitions be made in relation to demographic projections. The first of these is that series of projections should be made in nearly all cases rather than a single set of projections. These series should bracket the likely range of impacts and include a middle series that is the "best guess" projection, a high series that projects the highest likely population, and a low series that presents the lowest likely projection. It makes little sense to produce such a large number of series that the range of values from the highest to the lowest projections is so inclusive as to bracket all statistical possibilities. Series produced should all be projections that are feasible under alternative sets of possible circumstances.

Secondly, it may be beneficial to use demographic projections largely as sensitizing mechanisms to assist one in understanding the implications of alternative development scenarios. As such, these projections can be useful for both the planner and the decision maker in demonstrating the implications of alternative policies and in examining potential mitigation measures and the effects of such measures. This use of projections may reflect a more pragmatic evaluation of their potential accuracy and be of as much utility as their use for more exact service planning.

SUMMARY AND CONCLUSIONS

The projection of the demographic impacts of a resource development marks an essential step in the assessment process. It provides data that are essential for public service, economic, and other planning needs and, in many ways, its magnitude delineates the magnitude of all socioeconomic impacts. Five basic methods are available for general projections of population, including: (1) extrapolative; (2) ratio-based; (3) land use; (4) economic-based; and (5) cohort component-based techniques. The major differences in these techniques lie in their data requirements, detail of outputs, and their ability to simulate demographic processes. Whereas extrapolative, ratio-based, and land use techniques have relatively limited data requirements, they also provide less detailed outputs than the more data-intensive economic and cohort component techniques. Due to their ability to simulate the actual demographic processes that determine population change, cohort component techniques tend to be the most widely used in general projections and the most preferred by demographers, but economic-based techniques are becoming increasingly popular and are the most widely used in demographic impact assessment.

In selecting a technique for impact assessments, consideration must be given to numerous factors about the project, the project area, and the potential characteristics of inmigrating workers that will affect the magnitude and distribution of demographic impacts. In particular, the labor force requirements of the project and the labor force characteristics of the local population are critical determinants, with a greater compatability between local labor availability and project labor requirements leading to fewer nonlocal employees and fewer inmigrating workers. The characteristics of these workers and their dependents are, in turn, critical in determining the total population-related impacts of the development.

In the present state-of-the-art in demographic impact assessment, almost all analyses utilize either an economic or a cohort procedure for performing baseline projections. Impact projections are made by estimating project-related employment demands and either directly projecting population via the use of population to employment ratios or by matching such demands with estimates of available labor obtained by applying labor force participation rates to the results of cohort procedures. Workers are then distributed to settlement sites on the basis of judgemental or gravity model techniques, and projections of population are developed by applying demographic profiles to estimates of migrating workers. In all cases, these techniques require the use of a large number of assumptions, and hence, several series of projections rather than a single series should be used. This use should consist largely of attempts to sensitize the public to the likely range and implications of population impacts.

The assessment of the demographic impacts of resource developments is a highly complex task requiring: (1) knowledge of demographic projection techniques, impact assessment processes, and impact events and dimensions; (2) data on the characteristics of the resource development project, the characteristics of the impact area population base, the characteristics of migrating workers and their dependents; and (3) assumptions about the future trends in each of these factors and in the baseline population of the area. It is unlikely that the trends in all of these factors will be correctly predicted in any given assessment and, thus, it is unlikely that any projection will be exactly correct. Unfortunately, the present state-of-the-art does not provide adequate information to indicate the relative effects of errors made in the assumptions for these various factors. The potential errors in demographic impact assessments must be readily acknowledged, and the implications of such errors further evaluated.

At the same time, it is evident that demographic impact projections are essential if the planning needs of impacted areas are to be met. Knowledgeable use of existing techniques and attempts to develop increasingly better simulation techniques and data bases must be the goal of those professional demographers involved in demographic impact projections. The need for the rapid development of better methods and data is critical.

For the decision maker using such assessments, the best course appears to be one of caution and skepticism. In evaluating demographic assessments, the decision maker should be careful to discern whether each of the dimensions discussed in this chapter is clearly acknowledged and the assumptions for each clearly stated in the assessment. Although assessments providing such information are not inherently superior in their ability to predict actual impact events to those with less clearly stated assumptions, they are capable of being evaluated -- a key factor for the user of an assessment. Assessments that fail to acknowledge or clearly state their assumptions should be given a particularly careful examination. Finally, it is essential that the user of such assessments remain cognizant not only of the limitations, but also of the utility of such assessments. If cautiously and knowledgeably used, demographic assessments are, with all their potential sources of error, among the best data sources available for use in judging the potential magnitude of the impacts of resource developments and, thus, among the best sources for guiding decision makers in planning for and in evaluating the meaning of resource developments for rural communities.

4
Public Service Impact Assessment

The projection of the public service impacts of resource developments is a major area of concern in socioeconomic impact assessments (Denver Research Institute, 1979; Murphy and Williams, 1978; Chalmers and Anderson, 1977). Changes in availability and quality of public services are among the most visible and widely noted impacts during any major rural development (Summers et al., 1976; Lonsdale and Seyler, 1979) and have been a topic of much discussion in the impact literature (Gilmore and Duff, 1975; Gilmore et al., 1976a; Murdock and Leistritz, 1979). The accurate projection of the magnitude and distribution of public service impacts is of vital concern to governmental decision makers, and perhaps no other single set of projections, with the possible exception of fiscal projections, is in greater demand among public decision makers. Accurate projections of service demands during a development are essential because of the lead time necessary to develop and finance public service facilities and in order to prevent the development of excess service capacity. The projection of public service demands is thus a priority area for socioeconomic impact researchers and their clientele.[1]

The projection of such services, however, though clearly essential and often not computationally difficult, requires careful consideration of numerous conceptual and analytical dimensions. A discussion of these factors provides the focus for the remainder of this chapter.

THE CONCEPTUAL BASES AND DIMENSIONS OF PUBLIC SERVICE IMPACT ASSESSMENTS

As with other areas in impact assessment, the projection of public services utilizes conceptual bases that are relatively poorly developed and is an area for which prevailing practices rather than alternative theoretical perspectives

have determined accepted techniques. In addition, it is an
area in which the dimensions analyzed are both extensive and
complex.

Conceptual Approaches

Although the techniques employed vary substantially from
one assessment to another, most reflect one of several basic
approaches. These approaches are similar to those described
by Burchell and Listokin (1978) and for fiscal analysis, and
their basic delineation is one that can be usefully employed
in the discussion in this chapter. The approaches, as outlined by Burchell and Listokin (1978), include: (1) approaches
that project service demands for new population only, utilizing averages per unit of new population and either national,
statewide, or local service standards; and (2) approaches that
attempt to take existing services into account and project new
service requirements on the basis of marginal demands (that is,
demands above those that can be met by existing service bases).

Average Unit Approaches. Perhaps the most widely used
approach is that which projects service needs on the basis of
new population only. The assumptions underlying this approach
are that existing service bases should reflect existing demands
and that no excess capacity is present in existing service
bases. These premises significantly simplify the projection
process. They reduce the information required on existing
services, which may be difficult to collect particularly in
rural areas, and require only a simple application of a set of
standard rates to projections of new population to project
service demands.

The utility of this approach is limited by the fact that
public services seldom reflect a true market system (Jones
and Murdock, 1978). That is, supply and demand considerations
seldom operate in the absence of social and political considerations. In addition, in rural areas certain services are
required (medical care units, for example) because of the
severity of a problem for those experiencing it rather than
because of the magnitude of the demand. As a result, some
services in rural areas may have significant excess capacity.
The utility of this approach thus varies with the extent to
which market factors operate within a service area. For
services such as housing and private recreational facilities,
the use of this approach is less problematic than for services
such as medical and educational services, where the significance of the need may be such as to make market processes less
applicable.

The approach is one that is relatively easy to apply but
which may be inappropriate to use in many instances where
service bases are not determined by market activities. The

use of the approach, however, is likely to remain dominant until the necessary data to assess the levels of services in rural areas improve substantially.

Marginal Approaches. The second major approach is one which attempts to take baseline conditions into account by projecting service requirements beyond those that can be provided by existing service structures. The marginal new services required are thus projected taking full account of existing service bases.

The potential sources of error underlying the premises in this approach stem from the fact that the adequacy of existing services may be nearly impossible to measure. Secondary data on rural services are often extremely limited, and the costs involved in the collection of primary data are often prohibitive. Thus, the adequacy of many services may be largely a function of citizen perception and extremely difficult to quantify, service demands may partially reflect the degree of formalization of existing structures, and the acquisition of primary data may require interviews with service personnel in each community. In sum, whereas the average unit approach is often problematic because it fails to take existing service bases into account, the marginal approach often fails because of insufficient data on service adequacy and availability in rural areas.

Standard Selection

Whichever of the two approaches described above is chosen, however, another conceptual dilemma must be addressed before service projections can be completed. This is the need to select a set of standards for projecting the service demands that will accompany new population. Again, two major conceptual approaches appear to underlie existing practices. These are: (1) the use of local or comparative area service standards; or (2) the use of generalized standards.

Local Standards. The use of local (or comparable area's) service standards, as the name implies, assumes that new persons moving to an area will demand and use services at the same level as existing residents. The validity of this premise determines the validity of using local standards and is highly variable depending on existing service bases in an area and the type of service under consideration. If existing service bases are deficient, new residents are unlikely to be satisfied with existing services. The extent to which such dissatisfaction is expressed will vary by type of service, however. Water, sewer, and similar services may be technically inadequate; but these deficiencies are often not directly evident and requirements for new services beyond existing service levels may not be recognized. On the other hand, for

services such as education and law enforcement, existing deficiencies are more likely to be directly experienced, dissatisfaction openly expressed, and new standards demanded. The use
of local standards requires careful preliminary analysis including a comparison of such standards to the minimum standards required.

General Standards. The use of general standards, such as
those for the nation, a region, or a state, is based on the
premise that new residents are likely to bring demands typical of populations in other areas, rather than of the population of the local area. New populations may have few of the
same characteristics as local populations, may have shared
few experiences similar to those of local residents, and thus
may be unlikely to perceive or demand similar levels of service. For example, whereas general medical care may seem adequate to existing residents, new residents may demand more
specialized services. In large part, then, the utility of
employing general standards versus local standards depends on
the disparity between local residents' and new residents'
service demands and on the likely influence of new residents
in changing local service demands. When substantial disparities
exist and new residents exert a significant level of influence,
the premises underlying the use of general standards are clearly
supported. However, at the present state of knowledge, the
validity of the premises underlying the use of alternative
standards has not been adequately examined. As a result, the
use of both local and general standards seems likely to
continue.

Dimensions of Public Service Projections

The range of dimensions included within public service
projections is often broad, including projections of service
demands related to:

1. housing,
2. education,
3. medical and mental health,
4. law enforcement,
5. fire protection,
6. water supplies,
7. water treatment,
8. solid waste disposal,
9. transportation,
10. social welfare,
11. libraries, and
12. recreation.

Although the methods for projecting these services will
be discussed in detail in the following sections, it is

essential to briefly delineate the dimensions usually considered
under each of these service areas. For all services, it is
essential to note that significant impact dimensions, such as
differences in construction and operational phases of projects,
site area, project, and other characteristics, must be carefully considered in projections of service impacts.

The projection of housing services usually includes an
examination of both the number and type of units required.
Because different types of housing have different effects on
local revenues and on long-term community growth, projections
of housing without consideration of housing types are generally inadequate. Thus, most projections of housing demands include projections of single-family, multifamily, and mobile
home units (Hertsgaard et al., 1978), and some include projections of temporary forms of housing as well (Ford, 1976).

Projections of educational services usually include projections of the number of students and their resultant demands
on educational personnel and facilities (Murphy and Williams,
1978; Chalmers and Anderson, 1977). Such projections will
usually include estimates of the number of primary and secondary students, the number of teachers, support, and administrative personnel, and the amount of classroom space (square feet)
required.

The projection of medical and other health services is
especially difficult because medical services are often cen-
tralized in regional clinics and hospitals. In general, in
the projection of medical services, more attention is given
to the location of such services than in other service areas.
Projections in this area may include a wide range of factors,
such as patient days and occupancy rates (Murdock et al.,
1979c), but tend to concentrate on such personnel and facility
items as the number of doctors, nurses, psychiatrists, and
hospital beds required to serve the inmigrating population.

Law enforcement and fire protection service projections
also concentrate on personnel, equipment, and facility requirements although attempts to project the number of offenses and
similar occurrences to which such services must respond are
sometimes made (Murdock et al., 1979c). In most cases, however, these projections predict the number of law enforcement
or fire department personnel required, equipment requirements
(number of police cars and fire trucks, etc.), and facility
requirements (square feet of floor space per officer, number
of jail cells, etc.).

Water supply and treatment service projections usually
concentrate on required capacity measured in gallons per
capita or per population unit (such as 1000 persons). Such
projections seldom consider the size of the functional unit
necessary for the efficient operation of such facilities.
That is, increments in such services are usually made by
adding functional units (for example, a new water treatment

facility with a specified gallons per day capacity) rather than as per capita increments. In nearly all cases, however, such projections consider only incremental service demands.

Solid waste disposal is usually considered in terms of landfill area required, and the unit of projection is usually acres. Again, such projections seldom consider the actual functional units required for the effective management of landfill operations. In addition, these projections usually include projections of service personnel and equipment (i.e., garbage trucks and bulldozers) required.

Projections of transportation needs are often absent from projections for rural areas because such services are frequently not being used at capacity levels and because the actual level of new demand resulting from new populations is difficult to predict. When such projections are made, miles of new highway construction are usually the unit of output.

Projections of social services include a wider range of phenomena than any other service area, and there is little agreement on those social services that should be projected in impact assessments. Levels of delinquency, social worker case loads, number of families receiving aid to dependent children, and the number of social workers may be included in such projections. Unlike other public service projection areas, the focus tends to be on service needs rather than on the personnel and facilities required to meet such needs. Thus, projections of rates of occurrence are performed more often than projections of personnel or facilities. These projections seldom deal with a sufficient number of social services and are generally less complete and less adequately performed than projections in other public service dimensions.

Library services are projected less often than other services and are often perceived as being less critical than many of the other services noted above. When such projections are completed, the factors normally projected are the number of volumes and floor space required per unit of population.

Projections of recreational services tend to concentrate on outdoor recreation because of the tendency for indoor recreation to be provided under private auspices. In addition, although extensive analyses have been done to determine outdoor recreational demands for various population units, the levels of demand for indoor recreation services are less well known. When projections of recreational services are made, the items most often projected are acres of open, park, playground, and campground space required per unit of population.

The alternative approaches and dimensions of service projections noted above reveal the extensive range of expertise and data required to properly describe and project public service demands resulting from a resource development. Whether local services are taken into account and local service standards applied or projections based only on new populations and general standards are employed, the projection of service demands requires the impact researcher to carefully examine the premises underlying the approach used and the level of detail and range of services to be projected. Conceptually and pragmatically, then, public services projections, though often seen as relatively straightforward (because of the ready availability of population-based standards), clearly require careful prior analyses of and extensive information on present and new populations' service requirements, if they are to be done adequately and accurately.

FACTORS AFFECTING PUBLIC SERVICE PROJECTIONS

The projection of public services requires a careful consideration not only of total service demands but also of other dimensions of service delivery and service usage in impacted rural areas. Foremost among the factors affecting the utility and accuracy of public service projections are an area's:

1. Predevelopment service levels,
2. Distribution of services,
3. Quality of services,
4. Service delivery system,
5. Perceptions of and satisfaction with local service bases, and
6. Service variability.

Each of these factors is described below.

Level of Services

One of the most obvious factors affecting the level of new services required to meet the demands of new populations is the predevelopment service level in the site area. Although an exhaustive listing of local services in rural areas in the nation is not readily available (Murdock and Leistritz, 1979), it is evident that many services in rural areas are inadequate. Rural populations have lower levels of nearly all forms of health services (U.S. Department of Health, Education, and Welfare, 1979), and rural educational services are clearly less comprehensive than those in urban areas (U.S. Bureau of the Census, 1979b). In fact, in terms of nearly all nonenvironmental dimensions, the quality of life in rural areas lags behind that of urban areas (Ross et al., 1979). The level of local services must thus be carefully considered in public service projections in rural areas. Although some services may have excess capacity (such as medical or

educational facilities), most will not, and assessments must
carefully determine the adequacy of existing services prior to
either using local standards as a means for projecting new
service needs or accepting the sufficiency of existing services.
It is essential that service projections be able to project
existing service inadequacy or excess capacity and that the
potential significance of new demands for existing service
bases be adequately examined.

Distribution of Services

It is also essential to recognize that public services
are often not appropriately located geographically to meet
the increased demands resulting from a resource development,
even when total service levels in the site area are sufficient to meet the increased demands. Thus, impact assessments
must describe the location of service bases in relation to
the location of the expected growth. In many rural areas, for
example, social services, mental health, and similar services
are provided only in regional trade centers and may be
inaccessible to rural populations that are several hours
driving distance from such centers. In addition, because
service areas are often formally defined, persons whose normal trade patterns involve one trade center may find that
their area of residence falls in the service area of another
trade center (e.g., council of government, health system agency). Inaccessibility may effectively negate the availability
of services. Before an assessment can be interpreted as indicating service adequacy or inadequacy, the question of access-
ibility must be addressed.

Quality of Services

Equally significant is the question of service quality.
The existence of the appropriate number of service units does
not insure that the quality of services is adequate to meet
either existent or projected demands. Assessing service quality is extremely difficult and requires careful consideration
because of the potential problems that may be encountered if
only quantitative assessments are made. Assessments of the
age, education, and training of service personnel and the
conditions of plant and equipment should be completed. If
medical personnel are nearing retirement, police officers
lack training in firearm useage, or fire department personnel
have received little formal training, then the use of numbers
of existing personnel as indicators of service adequacy may
lead to underestimates of service needs, while the existence
of extensive expertise may partially offset numerically lower
service levels.

Service Delivery System

Another factor affecting service projections is the need to take the characteristics of the existing service delivery system into account. The form and management of service delivery in rural areas differ substantially from that in urban areas. Delivery systems are often less formalized, and fixed management structures and routines (such as daily routes for garbage collection) may not be included in existing systems. In rapidly growing areas, such as areas being impacted by resource developments, more formalization may be necessary to meet increased demands. Although it is extremely difficult to assess such dimensions, it is essential to assess not only whether the level of existing services is sufficient but also to determine whether the delivery system and the management structure for that system are properly organized to deliver the services necessary to meet increased demands.

Service Perceptions and Satisfaction

The adequacy of a given level of services is seldom simply a function of the level of services. It is, in large part, a function of residents' perceptions. Levels of services may be differently perceived such that a relatively large number of persons in one area will perceive such service levels as sufficient to meet their needs while in another area, or for other groups in the same area, the same level of services is deemed to be inadequate (Christenson, 1976; Murdock and Schriner, 1978). Perceived levels of dissatisfaction often increase with increased levels of growth (Summers et al., 1976), and expectations rise dramatically. Although the prediction of trends in service perceptions is extremely difficult, such changes should be considered.

Service Variability

Finally, it should be recognized that the projection of service demands, though usually reported in a single part of an impact assessment and performed by only a few members of an assessment team, is, in fact, a multifaceted area of analysis. It is an area in which a broad range of dimensions unique to each service area should be examined and in which specialized knowledge of each type of service should be obtained. Service projections involve not one but several substantive areas and should involve specialists from numerous substantive fields. Thus, the delivery of medical services is clearly different than the delivery of water and sewer services, and law enforcement, fire protection, and other public services differ from housing and recreational services which are largely privately financed and managed. It

is unlikely that any assessment effort can obtain the resources necessary to involve specialists from each service
area, and recognition of the limited knowledge base upon
which most service projections are made and of the relatively
simplistic nature of this base in relation to the complexity
of each service area is essential.

The need to consider the factors noted above coupled
with the breadth of service dimensions and complexity of
premises underlying service projections clearly point to the
need for care in performing service projections. If service
projections are to be useful for infrastructure planning and
development, they must be completed with full recognition of
the complexity of the task being attempted and of the limitations inherent in the use of prevailing methods and conceptual bases.

METHODS FOR PUBLIC SERVICE IMPACT ASSESSMENT

The actual process used in assessing public service
impacts, like those used in other assessment procedures described in earlier chapters, fails to attain many of the
characteristics desired for such projections. Few adequately
assess service distributions and service delivery systems or
provide other detail required to fully characterize the complexity of each service area. Despite such weaknesses, the
techniques used have received relatively widespread acceptance. The techniques actually employed are described briefly
below.

The techniques employed in making public service projections involve the completion of three major assessment
processes. The description of these processes (the description of baseline services; the selection of a standard for
use in projecting service demands; and the projections of
service demands) provides an organizing mechanism around
which alternative methods can be described. Thus the steps
in each of these processes, data sources used in each process,
alternative methods that can be employed, and the relative
advantages and disadvantages of each method are described
below for each of the assessment processes.

Description of Baseline Services

As with all assessment processes, the first major step
involves a description of baseline service levels. To complete such descriptions, secondary, primary, or a combination
of secondary and primary data collection methods can be
employed.

Secondary data methods are almost always employed, even
when primary data collection methods are also used. The

utility of this approach varies by service area. Data on
housing are readily available from the census of housing for
each decade. For years between census periods, data from
periodic national surveys (such as the Annual Housing Survey), can be obtained and local surveys have often been
performed by local planning agencies and similar groups.

For educational services, data can be obtained on average daily attendance and number of personnel from state
departments of education and nationwide educational data are
also available from the U.S. Department of Education. Data on
law enforcement and fire services are more difficult to
obtain, but some data are usually available from the state
fire marshal and state police or other state law enforcement
agencies. In most cases, however, definitive local data on
police and fire services in rural areas are only available by
collecting primary data in local areas.

Data on medical services, though available at the national, regional, or state level (U.S. Department of Health,
Education, and Welfare, 1979) are seldom available on a
regular basis for communities in rural areas and must be
obtained from primary data collection efforts. Data on water
supplies, water treatment, and solid waste disposal are often
available from the state health department, but these services may require extensive primary data collection and updating of secondary data.

Data on transportation services are usually available
from the state highway department, data on social services
from social service agencies, and data on library services
from the state library or library association. Finally, data
on outdoor recreation services are usually available from state
recreation associations, but data on indoor recreation facilities
are seldom available except through primary data collection.

Overall, secondary data can be most readily used for
baseline descriptions of housing, education, and social services, with less certainty for law enforcement, fire, water
and waste water, transportation, and library services, and
are seldom, if ever, sufficient for characterizing medical
and indoor recreational services. In addition, secondary data
seldom allow one to adequately assess service needs. Data on
service personnel and facilities and on service usage and
occurrences (i.e., crime data) may be available, but these
data seldom indicate areal levels of need for medical, educational, social, or other services. Needs assessment data thus
form a logical, but seldom available, counterpart to secondary data in assessment efforts.

The advantages of secondary data are evident. They are
relatively easy to obtain, though often difficult to physical-
ly locate. They are less costly to collect and more likely to
have been collected for multiple areas using a common set of

procedures and guidelines than is possible with primary data. The disadvantages lie in the variable quality of such data from one service area to another, and in the tendency for secondary data to be dated and to have low levels of reliability for small areas.

Primary data collection methods are usually used to expand, update, and validate secondary data. When primary data collection methods are used, they require contact with officials in each service area. Although mail, telephone, or other forms of noncontact surveys are often used, personal surveys are the most reliable form for such data collection efforts.

Primary data methods have the clear advantages of providing comprehensive and current data that are generally well validated, though in some rural areas the part-time nature of service personnel may limit their knowledge bases concerning many services. These methods are also quite costly to complete and require extensive time and personnel resources. Because of the cost considerations, primary data cannot be used in many assessment efforts.

Finally, it should be noted that the optimum and the most widely used method for collecting data on baseline service conditions involves collecting as much data as possible through secondary means and then updating, validating, and expanding these data through primary methods. Such combined methods are usually the most desirable and efficient methods for obtaining the data necessary to describe baseline services.

Whatever method is used to describe baseline conditions, the accurate description of such conditions is essential to the assessment process. If such descriptions are incomplete or inaccurate, projected service impacts will be inadequate for effective facility and service planning.

Selection of a Standard

Although the selection of a standard to be used for projecting service demands is largely a decision making step rather than a procedural step, it is perhaps the most vital step in projecting service demands. It involves the selection of rates of service usage per unit of population and thus, as with other projection methods, the accuracy of these rates (and the assumptions underlying them) will determine the accuracy of the projections. In general, the rates used are derived from one of several alternatives. These alternatives involve the use of: (1) predevelopment local service levels; (2) comparable area service levels; and (3) general usage and engineering standards and estimates. Each of these alternatives is briefly described below.

The use of local service levels is widely accepted in

service projections. The use of these standards represents
the most conservative projection approach. Such standards are
clearly applicable to the impact area and their use has the
advantage of ready availability and relatively high credibility with many decision makers. The disadvantages of the use
of local standards are that, for a variety of reasons described
above, they may reflect already insufficient service bases and
may not accurately reflect the impacts of new service demands.

Another method for selecting service standards is to
analyze the service demands that have occurred in similar
areas during developments. Such case study or comparable area
methods have several advantages (see Burchell and Listokin,
1978). They avoid both the assumption that predevelopment
service levels will prevail during resource developments and
the use of general rates that may be derived from areas that
are significantly different than the impact area. The difficulties entailed in the selection of such standards are
twofold. First, finding an area with predevelopment service
levels similar to the impact area may be difficult. Secondly,
because of the lack of adequate data on actual service
changes that have resulted from development events, establishing standards that accurately reflect actual service changes
may be nearly impossible. The method is used relatively
sparingly, but its use is likely to increase as data on
larger numbers of impacted areas accumulate.

The third type of standards, general usage and engineering standards, are those that are most often selected.
Several sets of such standards have received widespread use.
Table 4.1 presents data on three widely used sets of rates.
The data in the table indicate the nature of such standards
and their variability. Thus, it is evident that such population-based ratios are likely to vary widely from one source
to another and should be used with caution. The advantages of
such standards lie in their widespread usage and acceptance,
their ease of application, and their grounding in analytical
analyses. The disadvantages of such standards are equally
evident. They are unlikely to be applicable to many areas,
particularly rural areas, that are dissimilar to the areas
for which they were developed. They do not reflect existing
service bases in the impact area and only occasionally reflect the functional unit thresholds for various services
(Real Estate Research, 1976).

In assessing the advantages and disadvantages of each
type of standard, it is essential to note that there has been
relatively little systematic assessment of the relative reliability and validity of any set of standards used in impact
assessments. Thus, which sets of standards (local, general,
etc.) provide the most accurate assessments under any given
set of circumstances is not clear. Such assessments are
critical, and, until they have been completed, the selection

TABLE 4.1. PUBLIC FACILITY STANDARDS FROM SELECTED SOURCES, BY SERVICE AREA

Services	THK Associates	Source — Powder River Basin Capital Facilities Study	Real Estate Research Corporation[a]
Education:			
Personnel		18.2 students/teacher	Elementary-30-32/class Secondary-30-35/class
Plant	Elementary-74 square feet/student Junior High-90 square feet/student Senior High-108 square feet/student	Number of acres/1,000 population: Elementary-3.25 (urban), 2.20 (rural) Junior High-2.08 (urban), 1.40 (rural) Senior High-3.28 (urban), 2.20 (rural)	Elementary-90 square feet/student High School-150 square feet/student
	1 elementary school-800 students 1 Junior High school-1,200 students 1 High School-1,800 students	Number of schools/1,000 population Elementary-.2558 Junior High-.0825 Senior High-.0810	.48 elementary students/household .22 high students/household
Recreation:			
Playground	1.5 AC*/1,000 population	1.5 AC/1,000 population	3.9 AC/1,000 dwellings
Neighborhood parks	2.0 AC/1,000 population	8.5 AC/1,000 population	3.3 AC/1,000 dwellings
Play field	1.5 AC/1,000 population	1.5 AC/1,000 population	-
Community park	3.5 AC/1,000 population		-
District park	2.0 AC/1,000 population	2.0 AC/1,000 population	-
Baseball field	1/1,800 population	1/6,000 population	-
Swimming pool	1/25,000 population	-	-
Tennis court	1/2,000 population	1/2,000 population	-
Golf course	1/50,000 population	1/25,000 population	-
Ice skating rink	1/25,000 population		-
Community building	1/30,000 population	1/25,000 population	-
Regional park	-	15.0 AC/1,000 population	-
Basketball court	-	2 AC/1,000 population	-
Sports field picnic areas	-	1.5 AC/1,000 population	-
Softball field	-	1/3,000 population	-

Wading pool	-	-	1/5,000 population
25-yard outside pool	-	-	1/10,000 population
50-yard outside pool	-	-	1/20,000 population
Indoor pool	-	-	1/25,000 population
Football field	-	-	1/25,000 population
Community open space	-	-	-
Library: Plant	.7 square feet/capita	Minimum: 2,000 square feet	1.0 square feet/capita
Library: Equipment	2.5 volumes/capita	10,000 volumes	minimum 15,000-20,000 volumes
Medical: Personnel	-	.75-1.25 doctors/1,000 population	-
Medical: Plant	4 beds/1,000 population	-	4.0-4.5 beds/1,000 population
Social Welfare services	-	-	.5 social workers/1,000 population
Fire: Plant	1 station/10,000 population	-	5,120 square feet
Fire: Personnel	-	-	2/1,000 dwelling unit or equivalent volunteers
Fire: Equipment	1 truck/10,000 population; 1 pumper/10,000 population	pumping capacity of 2,000-2,500 gallons/minute; 1 fire truck	2 pumpers; 1 staff car; 1 ambulance; 1,000 gallons/minute for 4 hours duration/1,000 population
Police: Plant	1 station/12,500 population	100 square feet per officer	22.5 square feet/officer
Police: Personnel	-	2 officers/1,000 population; 1/2-2/3 car/1,000 population	1.5 officers/1,000 population
Police: Equipment	1 vehicle/2,500 population	-	1 vehicle/1,000 dwelling units
Water: Supply	2.5 average gallons/day	180 gpd[b]	-
Water: Treatment	-	168 gpd[b]	150 gpd[b]/persons to operate sewer plant

*AC signifies acre.

[a] Standards shown are those for dependent outlying communities with less than 10,000 rural population.

[b] Gallons per day per capita.

Sources: THK Associates -- Gilmore et al. (1975); Powder River Basin -- Intermountain Planners and Wirth-Berger Associates (1974); and Real Estate Research -- Stenehjem and Metzger (1976).

of standards will remain less exact than desired. The selection of standards for use in the projection process must be done with full realization of the limitations entailed in the selection process.

Projections of Service Impacts

Given an adequate description of baseline conditions and a set of standards for projecting service demands, the projection of service impacts is a relatively simple process. It consists of procedures for applying the selected standards to projections of new project-related population. The population-based standards employed in such projections may be either per capita or per population unit rates (i.e., rates per 1000 population). The standards shown in Table 4.1 are typical of these rates.

Given these rates, the projection of service needs consists of the straightforward process of applying the selected rates to projections of new population. For example, given a projected new population of 10,000 persons and using the THK Associates' estimates in Table 4.1, the projections of new service needs would include projected requirements for 15 acres of playground (1.5 acres per 1000 population multiplied by 10,000 new population), 7000 square feet of library space (.7 square feet per capita multiplied by 10,000 persons), 40 new hospital beds (4 beds per 1000 population multiplied by 10,000 persons), 1 new fire station (1 station per 10,000 population), and 4 new police vehicles (1 vehicle per 2,500 population multiplied by 10,000 population).

The only variation in the application of these rates results from the use of average versus marginal approaches. When an average usage approach is employed, the projected values are reported in an unadjusted form (i.e., as noted above). If a marginal approach is used, the values projected are adjusted (upward or downward) to reflect existing service deficiencies or excess capacity. Occasional variations may be made in these procedures to adjust for unique areal characteristics or to more adequately reflect service thresholds; that is, to reflect the minimum facilities required to provide a given level of services. In nearly all cases, however, the general procedure outlined above is that employed for service projections.

The procedures utilized are easy to compute and are easy to use in a variety of geographic settings. Their disadvantages lie in the fact that they are based on standards that have not been adequately verified; fail to provide adequate assessments of needs (other than personnel and facility requirements); and seldom adequately account for distributional and quality differentials. These projection techniques clearly require additional refinement and further anlayses of their validity and reliability.

SUMMARY AND CONCLUSIONS

The projection of public services requires consideration of alternative conceptual approaches and numerous service dimensions. These projections may include or exclude consideration of predevelopment service bases and may include a wide range of widely diverse services. Service projections require adequate assessment not only of quantitative service dimensions, but also consideration of the distribution of services, the quality of services, the nature of the delivery system, service perceptions and satisfaction, and the variability that exists between various types of services. Finally, the process of projecting public services requires the completion of an adequate description of baseline service levels, the selection of a set of standards for use in the projection process, and the application of these standards to projections of new populations. Secondary or primary data approaches are usually used to describe baseline conditions. Standards are derived from local, comparative, or general sources, and the projection process usually is straightforward, involving the application of selected standards to projections of new population. Whatever the form of projection technique employed, it is evident that the projection of public services, when properly performed, is a highly complex process requiring broad-based expertise and extensive analyses of numerous areally specific socioeconomic and service delivery dimensions.

The assessment of the public service requirements resulting from resource developments requires extensive additional analysis of key premises and methodologies. Until these premises and methodologies have been adequately analyzed, the validity and reliability of service projections cannot be established. Research needs related to several dimensions of public services are thus evident.

One such area is the need for a comparable data base on service levels for all rural areas in the nation. Although quantitative needs can be assessed on a local area basis, there is no single national source of comparable data on service availability, quality, and distribution in rural areas. A data source showing quantitative service levels for small areas is essential if truly comparative analyses of the service changes resulting from developments are to be completed.

Equally important is the requirement for additional needs assessments in impact areas. These assessments are commonly completed for service planning, but seldom appear as part of impact assessments. They usually include assessments of both quantitative and qualitative service dimensions and thus provide a more holistic basis for public service analyses than is usually provided by impact assessments. The inclusion of needs assessments in the impact assessment process should receive careful consideration as a means of increasing the utility of the public service assessment process.

Related to the needs noted above is the development of methodologies that insure the systematic inclusion of service distribution, service quality, and service delivery system dimensions in the assessment process. At present, these factors enter largely as qualifiers in the descriptive phase of public service projections but are seldom used to adjust or otherwise modify the projection process. Both qualitative and quantitative methods for including such dimensions in the assessment process should be pursued.

There is also a clear need for critical analyses of the utility of various service standards. The simple availability of existing standards has, in fact, been the major reason for their use. Most standards in use have not been thoroughly analyzed in terms of either their validity or reliability. A critical examination of the sources for these standards reveals that they are derived from relatively few areas of the nation, and these areas are unlike many of the areas to which they have been applied. Analyses of service changes in impacted areas must be made to determine what levels of demand have actually been experienced as a result of resource developments. Only when such analyses have been completed can one assess when the use of local, general, or some other service standard is appropriate.

It is also necessary to more fully integrate service management and engineering considerations and research issues into the service assessment process. Most present projection techniques assume a linear relationship between population increase and service requirements. As with public costs, however, the validity of such assumptions requires extensive analysis (Lansford, 1980). In addition, it is essential that thresholds related to the management efficiency and engineering feasibility of alternative service units and thresholds be more fully included in service assessments. Increases in management personnel requirements and the minimum levels of demand necessary to merit the construction of certain facilities must be integrated into the formal projection process. Such considerations have been integrated into fiscal assessment processes, but they must be more effectively integrated into the service projection process .

Although the time and cost considerations involved in the impact assessment process will clearly lead to the continued use of averaging approaches, it appears necessary to argue for the use of marginal rather than averaging approaches.

Existing service levels in impact areas simply cannot be
ignored if an assessment is to be complete and useful to
planners and decision makers. Research to develop techniques
that more adequately use marginal approaches is thus
essential.

Finally, perhaps the most evident need related to the
assessment of public services, as well as for other impact
dimensions, is simply the need for more comprehensive data on
the actual public service impacts that have occurred in rural
areas as a result of resource developments. Such data must be
collected and subjected to careful comparative and longitudinal
analyses to discern the actual changes in service demands
that occur as an area develops. Until such data and the
results of their analysis are available, there will be little
agreement on which alternative techniques should be used in
assessment efforts. As with the assessment process as a
whole, then, the assessment of service impacts requires increased long-term research and analysis efforts.

The assessment of service impacts is often seen as one
of the least complicated steps in the socioeconomic assessment process, but this assumption is true only in relation to
the numerical computation of service demands. To effectively
understand and project the service demands of a major resource development requires an extensive base of research and
analytical information. As with other parts of the assessment
process, the assessment of public services must be refined so
that its accuracy, reliability, and validity can be assured
and its use for critical planning and decision making processes fully justified.

NOTES

1. Public service impact assessment obviously is closely related to fiscal impact assessment. The distinction between these two assessment areas is that public service
assessments focus on the magnitude, distribution, and quality
of facilities. Fiscal impact assessment examines the costs
incurred by local governments in providing additional services and compares these costs with additional governmental
revenues.

5
Fiscal Impact Assessment

The purpose of fiscal impact analysis is to project the changes in costs and revenues of governmental units which are likely to occur in response to a development project. The governmental units of primary interest are those local jurisdictions which may experience substantial changes in population and/or service demands as a result of the project (Muller, 1975). In some cases, the effect of major projects on state tax revenues and expenditures may also be evaluated (Leholm et al., 1976a; Stinson and Voelker, 1978), but such analyses are often for the purpose of identifying resources which could be used for local impact assistance programs. Some early analyses considered only the direct effects of the project, that is, the additional tax revenue produced by the plant and the added public service costs directly attributable to the plant and its workers. This approach ignores tax revenues from workers' residences and other property and also neglects both the revenues and costs which may result from the secondary (indirect and induced) effects of the project. Because the secondary effects of a project can be quite important in determining its total fiscal implications (Hirsch, 1964), most recent analyses attempt to account for both direct and secondary effects.[1] Thus, the primary objective of fiscal impact studies is to determine whether new development projects will directly and indirectly generate enough new local revenues to pay for the added public services they will require.

Fiscal impact analysis is sometimes confused with other evaluative techniques, particularly cost-benefit and cost-effectiveness analysis. The basic difference in these approaches is the scope of the analysis. Fiscal impact analysis, also often called cost-revenue analysis (Burchell and Listokin, 1978), focuses exclusively on the public sector costs and revenues associated with a particular development project or form of growth. As such, it is a practical financial planning tool, using traditional forms of cash flow analysis. The result of such an analysis is typically a statement of net surplus or

126

deficit (usually measured in dollars but sometimes in service
units or employment). The key feature of fiscal impact analysis, then, is that it focuses exclusively on the revenues received and costs incurred by governmental units. Another important feature is that the distribution of revenues and costs
through time is frequently included in the analysis. Cost
effectiveness analysis focuses on the cost of providing selected services, or more broadly, of achieving selected objectives.
This technique emphasizes determining the least cost approach
to achieving a given objective and typically considers a range
of alternative actions within the constraint of a fixed level
of resources (Burchell and Listokin, 1978). Cost-benefit analysis is the broadest of the three techniques and involves comparison of both tangible and intangible costs and benefits of a
project. The costs and benefits considered include not only
the expenditures and revenues of public sector entities but
also benefits and costs experienced by private businesses and
individuals, including both tangible and intangible benefits
and costs.

CONCEPTUAL BASES AND METHODOLOGICAL ALTERNATIVES IN FISCAL
IMPACT ASSESSMENT

Fiscal impact analysis had its origins in the 1950s, and a
number of studies were undertaken to statistically predict municipal expenditures. (For a summary of this early work, see
Mace, 1961). The cost functions or multipliers so derived
were employed in studies to determine whether certain types of
housing development "pay their own way" in terms of costs and
revenues to local governments. (For example, see Mace and
Wicker, 1968). While early fiscal impact studies tended to
focus on the implications of alternative types of housing development or alternative residential growth patterns, a few
studies examined the impacts of industrial development on local
government finances (Hirsch, 1964; Kee, 1968). During the
1970s there was a substantial increase in fiscal impact analyses in both urban and rural settings. In the urban context,
the growing interest in fiscal impact analyses arose in large
part from concern that some types of land use may have adverse
fiscal effects (Muller, 1975). In rural areas, fiscal impact
studies became more frequent as a result of industrial decentralization (Shaffer and Tweeten, 1974; Morse and Hushak,
1979). Many communities have offered tax concessions or other
inducements to encourage industries to locate in their area,
but there is growing awareness that careful analysis of the
fiscal implications of rural industrialization is needed if
these programs are to bring the desired results.

Analysis of the fiscal impacts of large-scale development
projects has received increasing attention since the enactment
of the National Environmental Policy Act of 1969 (NEPA).

During the first few years following its enactment, environmental impact statements often gave only limited attention to economic and social impacts. Court decisions coupled with pressure from local and state officials, however, have led to more thorough treatment of economic and social impact considerations (Watson, 1977). The fiscal impacts of new developments have received special attention because these effects are readily perceived by local officials and are believed to be amenable to mitigation efforts. Recent decisions by the Nuclear Regulatory Commission and the Federal Power Commission have established the precedent that firms developing new power plants may be required to compensate local governments for additional expenditures resulting from the project (Watson, 1977). A number of states have enacted legislation governing the siting of major industrial facilities (Rapp, 1976; Auger and Zeller, 1979). The state siting authorities thus created often have been authorized to include requirements for fiscal impact mitigation as conditions in the siting permits they grant. Finally, local officials may use their zoning power as the basis for negotiation with development firms.

The growing interest in fiscal impact assessment in both rural and urban contexts has led to an increasing number of such studies.[2] These have resulted in a more intensive examination of the conceptual basis for fiscal studies and also in the development of a number of specific methods of fiscal impact analysis.

Conceptual Bases for Fiscal Impact Assessment

Key concepts in the estimation of public sector costs and revenues include the basic economic principles of demand and supply.[3] These concepts were developed primarily with reference to private sector goods and services, however, and their application to public sector services is limited by a number of conceptual and practical obstacles.

Services provided by local governments have a number of unique characteristics which pose difficulties in applying the traditional supply and demand concepts. These characteristics relate to both the nature of the services produced by local governments and the environment in which governmental decisions are made. Public services are typically characterized by one or a combination of the following characteristics: (1) public or collective goods; (2) natural monopolies; (3) externalities; and (4) merit goods. It is generally the presence of these features which has led certain services to be provided by the public sector rather than by the private sector. These characteristics, in turn, complicate the task of projecting the service requirements and costs associated with growth. (For additional discussion, see Hirsch, 1973.)

The environment in which public service decisions are made also differs from that found in markets for private sector goods. Government agencies establish levels of services to be provided and taxes to be levied subject to both external and local constraints. For some services, such as education and welfare, minimum standards are established by outside authority, and the community supposedly meets these standards, generally with outside financial support. Similarly, state statutory or constitutional provisions typically establish minimum and maximum levels for tax rates and assessment ratios and limit debt issues to a specified fraction of the local tax base. Within the framework established by these external restrictions, local officials are further constrained in their decisions by voters' perceptions of "acceptable" levels of taxation and "desirable" levels of services. (For additional discussion, see Maxwell, 1969; and Groves and Bisch, 1973.)

Individuals in a community can be expected to differ in the level of services they desire and in the level of costs they are willing to incur. Further, the distribution of benefits and costs associated with a particular service is generally not uniform over all members of the community. A combination of the desire of individuals to maximize benefits from public services relative to costs and their inability individually to have a significant effect on the outcome of collective decisions provides an incentive for the formation of groups with mutual interest. The central goal of such special interest groups is to influence officials to provide a set of services from which the members of the group receive benefits in excess of their costs (Jones and Murdock, 1978). Local officials, then, can be viewed as balancing the desires of their constituents for adequate services against their need to limit expenditures to a level deemed acceptable by those constituents. (For further discussion, see Inman, 1979; Deacon, 1978; and Niskanen, 1971.)

Demand For Public Services. Demand analysis requires a thorough understanding of the characteristics of the various public services. If demand schedules are to be estimated for specific public services, meaningful output measures are essential (Hirsch, 1973). Output should be measured in terms of the number of basic output units of specified quality characteristics provided per unit of time. Very few of the public services provided by local governments, however, have basic output units with well-defined physical characteristics (water delivery and solid waste disposal are obvious exceptions). Measuring the output of many public services is quite difficult, and defining and measuring the quality of that output is even more difficult (Hirsch, 1973). In the abstract, one can view a basic service unit for many public services as having numerous quality dimensions which should be incorporated into a demand analysis. Because of the great difficulty in developing empirical measures of public service output quantity and quality, however, demand functions for many public services are difficult to estimate.[4]

In the context of assessing the impacts of a large-scale
project, the lack of empirical estimates of the factors affecting the demand for public services poses a serious problem.
There is reason to believe that the economic and demographic
changes which accompany a large-scale development will lead
to substantial shifts in the demand for various services
(Auger et al., 1978; Gilmore and Duff, 1975). There is little
basis, however, for estimating the extent of these changes in
service demands in a given impact situation.

Supply and Cost of Services. The nature of the supply
schedule for a public service depends on the characteristics
of the production function for the service and on the prices
(or supply schedules) of the major inputs (that is, labor, capital, and management). The production function describes the
relationship between various combinations of physical inputs
and levels of output. From this production function, cost
functions can be derived which describe the relationship between output level and cost per unit of output. (For a detailed discussion of production and cost functions as they relate to public services, see Hirsch, 1973.) Such cost functions provide the basis for the supply function for the service.

The costs associated with providing public services can
be categorized into capital and operating costs. Capital
costs refer to those costs associated with resources which
have a useful life of several years (for example, a building)
while operating costs refer to payments for resources which
are completely used within the current year (for example, labor
and fuel). In order to provide a realistic estimate of the
cost of providing a service, capital costs should be prorated
over the useful life of the capital good.[5]

Public service costs can also be expressed in terms of
average and marginal costs. The average cost of providing a
given service is computed by simply dividing the total cost
(operating costs plus the prorated share of capital costs) of
providing the service by the number of units of output. The
marginal cost of providing a service is the cost of providing
one additional unit of the service. Marginal costs may differ
greatly from average costs for certain services and under some
conditions. Some factors which can lead to divergence of marginal and average costs are the presence of excess capacity in
existing capital facilities, the existence of threshold effects
for certain services, and the presence of economies or diseco-
omies of scale.

If excess capacity is present in a community's capital
facilities, the marginal cost of providing additional services
may be substantially less than the average cost. This effect
is particularly important for those services for which capital
costs make up a substantial percentage of total costs (for

example, water and wastewater services).

Threshold effects refer to the fact that basic changes in the type of service facilities required tend to occur when certain population levels are reached. For example, a growing community may need to begin mechanical treatment of sewage and/or may find a change from a volunteer to a full-time fire department to be desirable. When such threshold levels of population or service load are reached, the marginal costs of providing additional services may be substantial.

Economies of scale are said to exist when larger quantities of a service can be provided at a lower cost per unit. Recent analyses suggest that economies of scale are present for most services in small communities (with populations less than approximately 20,000). The most substantial economies are typically associated with services which are capital-intensive (for example, water and sewer). Conversely, diseconomies of scale are frequently observed in very large cities. (For extensive discussions of economies of size in public services, see Gabler, 1971; and Shapiro, 1963.)

Given the conceptual model discussed above, it would appear that the most appropriate approach to fiscal impact analysis would include developing empirical estimates of the demand and supply functions for each type of service. These functions would then provide a basis for estimating changes in service output and cost associated with a new development. Unfortunately, the problems inherent in measuring public service outputs have caused most analysts to seek a simpler approach which avoids output measures and deals directly with the cost of services (Denver Research Institute, 1979). This approach requires some simplification of behavioral assumptions and tends to eliminate the distinction between forces affecting supply and those affecting demand (Margolis, 1968).

Fiscal impact analysts also typically utilize simplified assumptions in dealing with the public budgeting process. In general, it is recognized that tax rates and governmental expenditures are jointly determined by a number of factors including community preferences and local tax base. Further, in the short run, fiscal capacity rather than need is the most significant determinant of expenditure levels. (See, for example, Pidot, 1969; and Scott, 1972.) Analysts then must choose between approaches which include predicted revenues as a major determinant of costs or those which base cost estimates on a constant level of services. The former approach leads to projections of changes in the level of services which can be supported while the latter provides estimates of fiscal deficits or surpluses resulting from a project. Since fiscal surpluses and deficits provide a more concise measure and one which is more amenable to discounting, most analysts assume a constant level of services, often in conjunction with an assumption of constant tax rates. (For recent attempts to deal more explicitly with the local fiscal decision making process, see Kirlin and Brown, 1979; and Weber and Goldman, 1979.)

Methodological Alternatives in Fiscal Impact Assessment

In this section, the major methodological alternatives for revenue and cost estimation are examined. Revenue estimation methods are discussed first, followed by cost estimation methods.

Revenue Estimation Methods. Revenue sources of local governments can be broadly classified as own-source revenues (that is, those taxes and charges assessed and collected directly by the local jurisdictions) and intergovernmental transfers (that is, funds received from state and federal levels). Own-source revenues can be further classified according to their primary determinants into those based on property valuation (for example, ad valorem property taxes), those based on income or sales (for example, local income or sales taxes), those based on the level of production of some industry (for example, severance or gross production taxes), and those based largely on changes in population. The techniques which are most appropriate for estimating revenues from these sources will differ depending on the revenue source (Burchell and Listokin, 1978).

Several general factors must be kept in mind when estimating changes in local revenues. An adequate estimation technique must include a mechanism for estimating the change in tax base, a method for estimating (or assumptions concerning) the effective tax rate, and a means of estimating the timing of revenue collections. Estimates of changes in the relevant tax bases (for example, property value and income) are frequently derived from the economic and demographic impact assessment models discussed in previous chapters. Tax rates are frequently assumed to remain at their current levels.[6] Estimating the assessment ratios which will apply to new industrial and residential property is frequently a complex task; this topic is discussed later in connection with specific property tax estimation techniques. Finally, estimating the timing of revenue changes requires careful attention to the prevailing taxation and revenue distribution practices. Frequently, substantial time lags exist between an initial increase in tax base or population and receipt of additional revenues resulting from this change.

Property Tax Estimation. The property tax is by far the most common form of local taxation, accounting for more than half of the own-source revenues of municipal governments and more than 85 percent of own-source revenues of school districts in 1972 (Burchell and Listokin, 1978). The property tax base in a particular state may consist of both real property (land and structures) and personal property. Real property, however,

132

typically represents the bulk of the tax base.

Estimating changes in property taxes involves first estimating changes in the tax base. Major components of the
change in local tax base resulting from a new project include
the taxable value of the project facilities, of additional
business and commercial property resulting from the project,
and of new or improved residential property. Determining the
taxable value of project facilities requires careful analysis
of relevant state statutes and administrative guidelines together with detailed information concerning the investment in
project facilities. Statutes and administrative practices may
differ not only from state to state but from industry to industry and, where local assessors are responsible for valuing
the new facilities, from county to county (Denver Research
Institute, 1979).

Changes in the value of business and commercial property
may be estimated as a function of estimated changes in local
income or sales or as a function of population growth. Changes
in the value of residential property may be estimated as a
function of the changes in population or local income, but
some analysts believe that more precise estimates can be developed through estimating the composition of new residential
development. This approach involves estimating the number of
new housing units by type during the various phases of the
project's life (particularly distinguishing construction and
operation phases) and then estimating the typical values of
each type of unit. An important consideration which is sometimes overlooked, however, is that population growth is likely
to lead to substantial increases in the value and assessed
valuation of existing residential and nonresidential property
(Weber and Goldman, 1979). The relative elasticities of the
assessed valuations of residential and nonresidential property
with respect to population growth will affect the distribution
of tax burdens among classes of property owners (Buchanan and
Weber, 1979). Further, the extent to which these changes in
assessed valuation of existing property are taken into account
may have a substantial effect on the revenue projections.

The possibility that a new project may lead to losses of
tax revenue from certain sources must also be considered. This
issue is particularly relevant if the new project is to be
publicly owned and hence exempt from local taxes.[7] Likewise,
a new mining project may reduce the long-term productive capacity of the mined land for agricultural purposes and hence reduce its anticipated taxable value. Finally, tax concessions
or inducements offered to a new firm may lead to reduced tax
revenues or increased public costs. These effects should be
included in the analysis in order to obtain a complete assessment of the fiscal implications of such projects.

Estimating the assessment ratio which will apply to new
property is often a complex task. Some studies have assumed
that statutory ratios of assessment to market value will be

implemented. The statutory ratio, however, is almost always higher than the effective assessment ratio (that is, the actual relationship between assessed and market values), and so this approach will generally lead to over-estimation of actual tax revenues. In order to estimate the effective assessment ratio, some have utilized the results of published analyses of sales to valuation ratios. Others have collected primary data on sales and assessed values for each jurisdiction being analyzed and/or have interviewed local assessors (Denver Research Institute, 1979). These approaches may, however, lead to under-estimation of the effective valuation ratio for new property. The effective ratio is typically lower for older units than for new property. A sample drawn on a strictly random basis is likely to include a high proportion of older units and thus to provide an estimated assessment ratio lower than that likely to apply to new units. A selective sample including only relatively new units may be the best approach to approximating the effective assessment ratio for impact analysis.

Income and Sales Tax Estimation. In many states, there is a recent trend toward diversification of local governments' revenue sources with reduced dependence on property taxes (Burchell and Listokin, 1978). This trend is particularly evident for municipalities. Sales and income taxes are two revenue sources which are being utilized increasingly.

Estimation of income and sales tax revenues involves application of the prevailing tax rates to the estimated change in taxable income or sales. Income and sales estimates can typically be derived from the economic impact analysis models described earlier (in Chapter 2). Income estimates, for example, can be obtained directly from input-output models or from export base models utilizing income multipliers. Alternatively, given estimates of project-related direct and indirect employment, income estimates can be derived through application of average wage and salary levels to the number of workers by type. Estimates of local sales can be obtained directly from input-output models, or sales can be estimated as a function of the change in local income.

Production and Severance Taxes. Taxes based on the production of specific types of facilities are being utilized increasingly as a source of state and local revenue, particularly in connection with mining projects. In 1978, 29 states had some form of special tax on minerals extraction (Stinson, 1978b). These taxes are usually either gross production taxes (levied as a percentage of the value of the product) or severance taxes (levied as a fixed sum per physical unit of output). Estimation of local government revenues from special minerals taxes requires a detailed understanding of the state's taxation and distribution formulas together with estimates of the facility's production (and in some cases the price of the product) over time. Production estimates generally are easily obtained from the firm developing the facility, but price estimates may be more difficult to obtain. Generalized projections of product prices are usually available at the industry level, however, if project-specific estimates are unobtainable.

Population-Related Taxes and Charges. A number of local taxes and charges are perhaps most easily estimated as a function of population. These include per capita taxes, fees and permits (such as for building or occupancy), and user charges for water, sewer, and sanitation services (Burchell and Listokin, 1978). While it may be possible to develop more accurate and detailed formulas for projecting some of these revenues, simple per capita rates are frequently applied. Alternatively, user charges may be estimated as a function of the number of new households in the jurisdiction, but the number of households is, in turn, usually estimated as a function of population. Particularly if these items account for a relatively minor share of total revenues, simple per capita approaches are often employed.

Intergovernmental Transfers. Intergovernmental revenues are often more difficult to project than own-source funds. These difficulties arise because the allocation formulas are frequently complicated, eligibility for certain forms of assistance changes as local wealth or other indicators change, and frequently, overall community effects must be considered. For instance, state school aid is usually inversely related to local wealth, and so a new project that significantly affects the local tax base would affect the level of state assistance not only for the new students associated with the specific project, but also for all other students in the locality. In such situations, the analyst must take account of this overall net change in order to obtain a realistic estimate of the effect of the project on the community (Burchell and Listokin, 1978).

Intergovernmental transfer programs which provide substantial revenues to local jurisdictions include state educational transfers, redistribution of state-collected sales and income taxes, redistribution of state-levied motor fuels, alcohol, and tobacco taxes, and the federal revenue-sharing program. Educational transfers and federal revenue-sharing typically have some of the most complex distribution formulas, and a detailed simulation subroutine may be required to accurately reflect changes in these revenue sources (Stinson and Voelker, 1978). Because educational transfers often account for a substantial proportion of school district revenues, considerable attention should be devoted to accurately projecting this revenue source (Denver Research Institute, 1979).

To summarize, revenue estimation methods tend to be very

similar in general approach. They differ primarily in the
degree of detail employed in estimating the various revenue
components. The greatest variability is usually found in the
methods used to estimate property tax revenues and intergovernmental transfers. Because the relationships and formulas involved are frequently complex, but generally capable of
determination, revenue forecasting is an area where greater
analytical effort can be expected to provide more reliable
results.

Cost Estimation Methods. A number of approaches can be
employed in estimating the community service costs associated
with growth. Methods for estimating service costs are, of
course, closely related to those used in projecting service
requirements (see Chapter 4). The major difference is the nature of estimates developed. Whereas the objective of public
service analysis is to evaluate changes in requirements for
service facilities and personnel, fiscal impact analysis involves estimating the capital and operating costs of these
services. Cost estimation methods can be categorized by the
nature of the cost estimates they provide into average cost
and marginal cost approaches. The average cost approaches include the per capita expenditures method, the service standard
method, and the use of cost functions derived from cross-
sectional regression methods. Marginal cost approaches include the case study method, comparable city analysis, and
economic-engineering methods. These alternative approaches
are discussed in the following sections.

Per Capita Expenditures Method. The per capita expenditure method is the most widely used of the average cost techniques and is based on the assumption that the average costs
of providing services to current users are a reasonable approximation of the costs to provide services to future users
(Burchell and Listokin, 1978). Using this approach, the additional expenditures of a local jurisdiction are computed as
the product of the present per capita expenditure and the
number of new residents. The major strength of this approach
is that it can be applied quickly and relatively inexpensively
as it involves very simple calculations and utilizes readily
available, historical, local data. The principle weakness of
the technique is that it assumes that there is no excess capacity in local services, that there are no economies of scale,
and that there are no significant threshold effects to be considered. It does not allow for the possibility of changes in
expenditures per capita as a result of changes in income or
other socioeconomic characteristics.
 The per capita expenditure method has a number of variations which involve different methods for calculating or adjusting the per capita expenditure multiplier. Some analysts
adjust the historic per capita expenditure figures judgmen-

tally to account for the effects of changes in income, economies of scale, and other factors in order to arrive at an impact multiplier. The major problem with this approach is its
reliance on the judgment of the analyst. If in-depth interviews with local officials are used as the basis for the adjustments, this approach becomes very similar to the case
study approach discussed in a subsequent section.

Another approach to estimating the per capita multiplier
is to utilize data from a number of jurisdictions. The multiplier may then be derived as a simple or weighted average of
the per capita expenditures of the various jurisdictions or
through a regression of expenditures on population and perhaps
other variables. As more variables are added to the regression, this approach becomes a cross-sectional regression analysis, discussed in a subsequent section.

Service Standard Method. The service standard method,
another average costing technique, involves developing estimates by service category of the work force, equipment, and
capital facility requirements associated with a particular
level of population growth. Given the estimates of work force
and facilities required, cost estimates can be developed. The
standards (for example, police officers per 1000 population)
can be developed from several sources including the community's
current public service personnel and facilities, standards
recommended by state agencies or interest groups, or average
relationships derived from data from state agencies, the U.S.
Census of Governments, or other secondary sources.

The service standards approach has many of the same
strengths and limitations that were discussed with respect to
the per capita expenditure approach. If current local practices are used as the basis for developing standards, the approach should produce the same results as the per capita expenditure approach. Perhaps the principal strength of the
service standards approach is the fact that its outputs (for
example, personnel requirements by service area) are provided
in a form which is quite useful to local planners and decision
makers. Further, the two-step nature of the cost estimation
process (that is, estimate resource requirements, then estimate costs) provides an opportunity for the analyst to take
explicit account of changing labor market conditions and inflation in developing the cost estimates. Finally, the service
standards method can serve as a useful adjunct to the case
study approach, discussed subsequently.

Cross-Sectional Regression Methods. In cross-sectional
analysis, expenditures for each service are compared for different communities with data for the same year. Regression
analysis allows an examination of the relationship between
expenditures per capita and community population, the rate of
population growth, income levels, age distribution, educational

levels, and other socioeconomic characteristics. The development of a predictive formula by use of regression analysis allows the projection of expenditures given local data on each of the independent variables. While such expenditure functions are frequently criticized as lacking an explicit supply and demand framework or behavioral model, a similar criticism could also be made for the estimation methods discussed previously. Because the objective of fiscal impact analysis is to estimate changes in expenditures and revenue resulting from growth and not to estimate cost functions per se, however, the identification problem is not a major concern.

A major strength of the cross-sectional regression approach is its ability to include a large number of variables which may influence local expenditures. The expenditure function which is estimated, however, is a generalized function based on average relationships across a large number of jurisdictions. For this reason some analysts feel that these functions are better suited to regional analysis and to exploration of general trends than to projecting expenditures for a particular jurisdiction (Denver Research Institute, 1979).

Case Study Method. The case study method is a marginal cost approach which may be particularly well-suited to cases in which existing services and facilities may be significantly under- or over-utilized (Burchell and Listokin, 1978). Under these conditions, the average cost of providing services to present users may not accurately measure the cost of providing services to new residents. This method relies primarily on in-depth interviews with officials of local service departments to determine what additional personnel and equipment each department will require to meet the needs created by the proposed development.

A major advantage of this approach is that it encourages participation by service department personnel in the estimation of growth impacts. It allows consideration of such local factors as existing excess capacity (or conversely, current over-utilization of facilities), threshold effects, economies of scale, and any other unique circumstances which may be present. The major problem with this method is judging the accuracy of local officials' responses. In some cases, officials' responses may be influenced by political and budgeting considerations, and this may lead to either over- or under-estimates of actual expenditure requirements. Further, local officials may not always be well-equipped to evaluate potential needs and associated expenditure requirements. For example, if a small rural community is located near the site of a large industrial project, its population could double or triple in just a few years. Under these conditions, local officials may have difficulty estimating additional service requirements as the magnitude of anticipated population growth and the resulting changes in service needs are outside the range of their

138

experience. Finally, an inherent weakness of the case study approach is difficulty in replication. Thus, two research groups using the case study approach could obtain substantially different results for the same community because of differences in interviewing techniques.

Community service standards developed from secondary sources may be quite useful as a supplement to the case study approach. Thus, Burchell and Listokin (1978) suggest estimating the number of additional personnel required based on service standards and comparing these estimates with those obtained from local officials. If the two sets of estimates differ substantially, the officials may be reinterviewed to determine the reasons for the differences.

The case study approach has been used extensively in recent years and may be particularly applicable to impact analysis for large projects in rural areas. It does, however, require considerably more time and effort than some of the average cost techniques described earlier.

Comparable City Method. The comparable city method, another marginal cost procedure, is employed in situations similar to those in which the case study method is used. This method involves use of expenditure ratios calculated by population size and growth rate and is sensitive to economies and diseconomies of scale as well as to expenditure variations which are a function of both the direction and pace of growth (Burchell and Listokin, 1978). It is among the most recent of the fiscal impact analysis methods and has received widespread application only since the mid-1970s.

Economic-Engineering Method. The economic-engineering method may be quite useful in fiscal impact projection. The essence of this approach is to develop a production function for the service in question by specifying the physical inputs required and attaching a cost to each input (Isard and Coughlin, 1957). The economic-engineering approach can be applied either to develop generalized estimates of service production functions (for example, by size of city) or to develop community-specific estimates based on the design and capacity of present facilities and the amount of anticipated growth. The community-specific approach can be very useful as it not only can provide very realistic estimates of additional costs but also can suggest the likely timing of those costs (Denver Research Institute, 1979). Recent examples of application of the economic-engineering approach include studies by Mackey (1977) and Schmidt et al. (1978).

To summarize, a number of distinct techniques can be employed in estimating the local expenditure effects of a new project. Each of these techniques has both advantages and disadvantages. Two major contrasts are apparent when comparing alternative cost estimation techniques. The first is between

the average costing and marginal costing approaches. The
second is the extent to which the different approaches rely on
localized data. Those techniques which rely heavily on localized data may be the most accurate in projecting near-term
changes in local expenditures, but they may be less effective
in projecting expenditures over long time periods or when very
substantial community growth occurs.

FACTORS AFFECTING FISCAL IMPACT ASSESSMENTS

The fiscal implications of a new project are determined
by the interaction of a number of factors including project
characteristics (e.g., the magnitude of investment and the
size and scheduling of the work force) and site area characteristics (e.g., state and local tax structures and the capacity of existing service delivery systems) and by the nature of
the economic and demographic effects resulting from the project. Further, because the fiscal impacts of a project are of
considerable interest both to local officials and their constituents and to developers, decision makers will seek to use the
results of the assessment both to form judgements concerning
the desirability of the proposed development and to design
growth management programs. The fiscal impact assessment
should, therefore, be designed to produce projections in the
form which will be most useful to these policy makers. The
purpose of this section is to summarize the factors affecting
changes in local government revenues, factors affecting changes
in local government costs, and factors affecting the distribution of impacts and to describe the information needs of
decision makers relative to fiscal impacts.

Factors Affecting Changes in Revenues

The effect of a new project on local government revenues is determined in large measure by the characteristics of
the project and its work force, by the extent of secondary
economic activity resulting from the project, and by institutional factors, particularly the state and local tax structure.
Project characteristics which have a very substantial influence
on local revenues include the taxable value of the facilities
and the earnings of the work force. Projects which include a
substantial amount of taxable property can add quite significantly to the tax base of the host jurisdictions. Likewise,
workers whose earnings are relatively high can afford residences with higher taxable values. The extent of secondary
economic activity which accompanies the project will also
affect the revenues of local governments. If the secondary
effects of the project lead to substantial increases in the
sales of local firms, local jurisdictions may experience increased revenues either directly through local sales and income

taxes or indirectly through increases in business property values.

The state and local tax structure can be expected to have a substantial effect on the revenues that local jurisdictions receive from a project. Some states allow municipalities to levy sales or income taxes which are generally more responsive to growth than are property taxes. Property tax assessment and collection practices differ among states with some states taxing major industrial facilities at the state level. The time required for new property to appear on the tax rolls also differs among states. Finally, some states provide special forms of financial assistance to rapidly growing communities.

Factors Affecting Changes in Costs

The effect of development on local government costs is determined by the interplay of a number of factors; the most important of which are the extent of local population growth associated with the project and the extent of excess capacity in local public service infrastructure. The greater the population growth associated with a project, other things equal, the greater will be the associated increase in local government costs. Measures which minimize project-related inmigration, such as recruitment and training of local workers, will tend to lessen the costs borne by local governments. The extent of excess capacity in local public facilities is also a major consideration. Recent estimates of the capital investment in local facilities required in energy-impacted communities of the Rocky Mountain and Great Plains states have ranged from $3,000-$6,000 per capita in 1975 dollars (Gilmore et al., 1976a; Murphy, 1975; Toman et al., 1978). Schools, water and sewer facilities, and streets and roads were estimated to account for the bulk of the capital costs. It is apparent, then, that a community with some excess capacity in its local facilities will experience much lower costs than one whose facilities are being utilized at capacity.

The preferences of local residents can be an important determinant of local public service costs. For example, Gilmore and his associates (1976a) identified substantial differences in service quality and per capita service expenditures among communities with similar populations. These differences were attributed primarily to differing preferences and a resulting willingness in some communities to pay higher costs for better quality services. Differences in preferences regarding public services between project-related inmigrants and long-term community residents can be a source of conflict in rapid growth areas (Auger et al., 1978). Threshold effects can cause substantial increases in the costs of certain services. Likewise, local topographic and geologic conditions can have a substantial influence on the cost of expanding water and sewer systems.

While the factors which determine the magnitude of the
changes in costs and revenues which ultimately result from
development of a new project are important, the timing of
these changes and their distribution among affected jurisdictions are perhaps even more significant. A review of selected
case studies provides insight into the local fiscal implications of large-scale projects.[8] The general conclusion from
these analyses was that the total revenues accruing to local
governments over the life of a project generally equal or
exceed the total project-related governmental costs.[9] However,
virtually all case studies revealed financial problems for at
least some jurisdictions because of the temporal and jurisdictional distribution of costs and revenues. Two major dimensions, then, emerge as the source of local fiscal problems.
These are the timing of additional project-related revenues
in relation to additional costs and the distribution of costs
and revenues among the local jurisdictions.

Factors Affecting Temporal and Jurisdictional Distribution of Impacts

The problem of cost and revenue timing, frequently
referred to as the "front-end financing problem," arises because, although new demands for public services and facilities
begin early in the project construction period, many of the
revenues associated with the project are not available until
the construction phase is completed and production begins.
Project facilities often do not appear on local tax rolls
until construction is completed, and construction populations
typically live in temporary housing with low taxable values.
Under these conditions, local jurisdictions may experience
difficulty in meeting current operating and maintenance expenditure requirements and even greater difficulty in financing new capital facilities.
The timing of additional project-related revenues depends
on the time period required for increases in the tax bases and
on the state and local fiscal structure. The time required
for a project's effects on local tax bases to be fully experienced depends in part on the speed with which the local economy adjusts to the stimulus provided by the project. (Factors
affecting this adjustment were discussed in Chapter 2.) In
addition, for projects with long construction periods, differences in housing patterns between construction and permanent
workers may delay the complete adjustment of the tax base.
Construction workers tend to occupy temporary housing (especially mobile homes) whereas permanent workers are more likely
to occupy permanent housing with higher taxable values (Leholm
et al., 1976b; Wieland et al., 1977).
State and local fiscal structures have very substantial
influences in determining the timing of project-related revenues. For example, states differ substantially in their

142

practices for assessing new plants and related facilities.
In some states a new plant or mine does not add significantly
to local tax rolls until construction is completed.[10] In
others, however, the property is reassessed annually as construction proceeds so that the local tax base increases annually and in proportion to the extent of completion of the project. Some states authorize prepayment of taxes by the developer to local governments or use a portion of state-
collected severance or gross production taxes as a source of
"impact payments" to local governments (Auger et al., 1978).
Finally, some states authorize industrial location incentive
programs whereby new plants may be exempted from local taxes
for a specified time period (Tweeten and Brinkman, 1976).
        The timing of project-related revenues from other sources
also depends substantially on state and local policies. In
some states, local governments (particularly cities) have the
option of levying local sales and/or income taxes while in
others local governments share in state-collected sales or income taxes. Revenues from these taxes are typically much more
responsive to growth than are those from property taxes
(Lamont, 1974). Some local governments have relied partially
on increased public utility user charges to cope with the demands of rapid growth. In some rapid growth communities, substantial tap charges for new utility hookups have provided a
means to rapidly recover the capital costs associated with
expansion of utility systems (Gilmore et al., 1976a; Weber,
1979).   Finally, the procedures and formulas used to allocate
intergovernmental transfers from state to local governments
differ substantially among states, and this can lead to substantial differences in the response of transfer payments to
rapid growth.
        The timing of additional project-related costs depends in
large measure upon the extent and timing of local population
growth induced by the project, the capacity and condition of
local facilities, and the investment strategy employed by local
officials. If the magnitude and timing of population growth
has been estimated, the major considerations become the capacity of present service facilities and the investment strategy of
local officials. As noted earlier, if some excess capacity
exists in the community's service facilities, it may be possible to avoid or at least defer substantial capital costs. Even
if existing facilities are expected to be less than adequate to
meet project-related service demands, local officials have a
range of choices. At one extreme, they could attempt to con-
struct new facilities adequate to meet the peak service demands
(which usually occur during the project construction period),
but this approach could lead to substantial excess capacities
once the construction period has ended. Another approach could
be to build only those facilities which are expected to be
required to meet the needs of the permanent population increase
(that is, the additional population during the project's oper-

ational period). This alternative, however, might lead to a substantial over-crowding of facilities during the peak construction period.

The strategy that will finally be adopted is likely to depend on a number of factors including the degree of uncertainty associated with the project and related growth, the availability of fiscal resources, and the outlook with respect to future developments and related growth. While it is difficult to specify an optimal infrastructure investment strategy under boomtown conditions and probably even more difficult to predict what strategy a given community might choose, it is important to bear in mind that a variety of potentially reasonable strategies exist.[11] One approach to determining what strategy may be used by a given community and what cost implications are likely to result is the case study method discussed earlier.

The interjurisdictional distribution problems may be as severe as those associated with cost and revenue timing. The project facilities that generate new public sector revenues may be located in one county while most of the additional project-related population resides in a different school district, county, or even a different state. In such cases, the jurisdiction receiving the revenues will experience a tax windfall while the area with the influx of new population will be faced with especially severe fiscal problems. Even when the facility and its support population are located within the same county and school district, affected municipalities may experience difficulties as the project facilities are almost invariably located outside city corporate limits and hence do not contribute to the municipal tax base.

The jurisdictional distribution of project-related revenues and costs will be affected in large measure by the settlement patterns of the inmigrating project-related population and by the state tax structure. (Methods for estimating settlement patterns are discussed in Chapter 3.) Aspects of state tax structure which may have a substantial influence on the jurisdictional distribution of project revenues include local sales and income taxes, state redistribution of severance or gross production taxes, and the ability to create special tax districts which allow municipalities or school districts to tax the project facilities.

When the project-related revenues accruing to a jurisdiction are less than project-related costs, local officials have three basic alternatives. First, if the cash flow problem is expected to be only temporary, the jurisdiction may be able to obtain the funds needed to offset the revenue shortfall through bonding or loans. A number of institutional factors may limit the ability of local governments in impacted areas to obtain funds from these sources, however. These factors include constitutional and statutory debt limits, limitations on amortization schedules, and interest rate ceilings. Further, un-

certainty regarding the nature and extent of impacts which
may actually be experienced frequently leads to reluctance on
the part of local residents to incur long-term obligations and
to an unwillingness on the part of lenders to make funds available. (For a more detailed discussion of these factors, see
Gilmore et al., 1976a; and Murdock and Leistritz, 1979.)

If sufficient funds cannot be obtained through various
forms of borrowing, the local officials' options are reduced
to two: (1) to increase rates of local taxes and user
charges; or (2) to reduce the level of services provided.
Under either of these alternatives, equity issues are apparent as long-term residents of the area may be forced to bear
part of the costs associated with the new project, either
through higher taxes or reduced services.[12]

In summary, the intertemporal and interjurisdictional
distribution of project-related costs and revenues are extremely important aspects of the fiscal impacts of large-scale
projects. Accurate assessment of these dimensions requires
reliable estimates of the timing and distribution of the economic and demographic impacts of these projects. Above all, however, a thorough understanding of state and local tax structures and policies is essential to accurate estimation of the
timing and jurisdictional distribution of project-related costs
and revenues.

Information Needs of Decision Makers

The decision making environment associated with the fiscal impacts of large projects has a number of implications
with respect to the information needs of decision makers.
First, because many of the important decisions must be made
by local officials, or sometimes by state agencies acting on
their behalf, projections of changes in costs and revenues
must be provided for individual jurisdictions. Second, because
the timing of changes in costs and revenues may be as important
as their ultimate magnitude, revenue and expenditure projections should be presented annually at least through the period
of project construction and into the operational phase until
costs and revenues become relatively stable. Third, because
future levels of revenues and expenditures without development
may be quite different from current levels, the impact assessment should include specific consideration of the future without development (Weber and Goldman, 1979; Morse, 1980).

The nature of the decisions confronting local officials
indicates a need for fiscal impact assessments to provide
estimates of effects on individual revenue and expenditure
components (Markusen, 1978a). Even more important, however,
is that impact assessment models should be capable of simulating the likely effects of specific local decisions (for example, changes in user charge rates or alternative schedules
for construction of capital-intensive facilities). As in

other aspects of impact assessment, it is important to give
attention to those factors which can be affected by local
decision makers and not merely to the dimensions which can be
most easily measured.

Finally, because the implications of development for local
residents are always a central question in fiscal impact assessment, careful consideration should be given to the format
for presenting the results. Projected revenue and expenditure
changes clearly should be reported for individual jurisdictions
on an annual basis. In addition, however, summary measures
may prove useful to indicate the overall effects of a project
(over its expected life) on a given jurisdiction and to demonstrate the implications of the project in terms of changes in
the fiscal burden on a typical local household.

Comparison of a stream of costs and benefits over time is
typically accomplished through discounting the stream of
annual values to a single discounted present value. The
formula for deriving discounted present value is:

$$PV = \frac{NR_1}{1+r} + \frac{NR_2}{(1 + r)^2} + \ldots + \frac{NR_n}{(1 + r)^n}$$

Where: PV = discounted present value
       NR = net revenue for each year (1, 2, ... n)
       r = discount rate
       n = number of years in the planning horizon

The discount rate employed should be an approximation of the
social rate of time preference.[13] Often the interest rate
which public bodies must pay for borrowed money is used as the
discount rate. If the present value of the future stream of
annual net fiscal balances is positive, it indicates that the
positive fiscal balances occuring during the project's period
of operation are sufficient to offset the negative balances
occuring during the project's construction period, after taking the social rate of time preference into account. The
implication would be that the project is an asset, in fiscal
terms, to the jurisdiction in question. A negative fiscal
balance would have the opposite implication.

Cummulative cash flow analysis is another useful approach
to evaluating the implications of cost and revenue timing for
a given jurisdiction. With this approach, annual net fiscal
balances for the jurisdiction are summed over time, thus providing for any future year a statement of cummulative net fiscal balance from the beginning of the projection period. The
cummulative fiscal balance is typically negative during the
early years of project development but may become positive
later in the projection period. This measure is useful to
local officials as it can be compared with the jurisdiction's
bonding or borrowing capacity to provide an indication of the

need for external fiscal resources. Cash flow analysis also
provides a mechanism for examining the implications of alternative assumptions concerning future inflation rates. Because
some cost and revenue components (e.g., sales taxes and operating costs) are likely to be more responsive to inflation
than others (e.g., property taxes and debt service payments),
alternative inflation rates can have a substantial influence
on projected fiscal balances. This fact should be reflected
in the design of fiscal impact models.

As noted earlier, the fiscal outlook is likely to be much
more favorable for some local jurisdictions (e.g., counties)
than for others (e.g., municipalities). Because the consequences of either adverse or favorable fiscal impacts ultimately are experienced by local residents (through changes in
either tax rates and user charges or changes in levels of
services) and because each local resident is typically a tax-
payer in several jurisdictions (i.e., a county, a school district, and often a municipality), a summary measure which indicates the aggregate change in fiscal burden on a typical household may be useful. An aggregate measure of this type is utilized by Gilmore et al. (1976a). Their index of fiscal burdens reflects the overall influence of a project on a typical
household in the impact area, based on the present value of
the stream of tax and user charge payments required from the
household by each relevant local jurisdiction in order to maintain governmental services at their preproject levels (interpreted as maintenance of preproject levels of per capita or per
pupil expenditure). This present value of future burdens is
then compared to the present value of a constant payment at
the preproject level to form the index. A value for this index
which exceeds 1 (or 100 percent) indicates that a typical
household will have to pay more in taxes and user charges to
maintain existing service levels.

FISCAL IMPACT ASSESSMENT TECHNIQUES

In the actual preparation of fiscal impact assessments,
there is considerable variation not only in the techniques
which are employed but also in the types of costs and revenues
which are considered, in the treatment of cost and revenue
timing, and in the formats in which the results are presented.
In this section the techniques commonly employed in revenue
estimation, in cost estimation, and in evaluating the timing
of revenues and expenditures are described. Before examining
these specific aspects, however, it should be noted that fiscal impact analysis is typically one of the weakest sections
in environmental impact statements (Chalmers and Anderson,
1977). Many statements do not even address fiscal effects and
others treat this topic only with very brief qualitative
statements (Berkey et al., 1977).

When fiscal effects are addressed, the analysis often

covers only a few of the relevant categories of revenues and costs. For example, the revenue analysis may include only property taxes, and perhaps only those increased property tax revenues which can be attributed directly to project facilities. Local government costs are treated in quantitative terms even less frequently than are revenues (Berkey et al., 1977), and, as with revenues, the analysis frequently is limited to only a few services. Public service costs are most frequently projected from present per capita expenditure levels, and capital and operating costs often are not separated (Weber and Goldman, 1979).

The treatment of the distribution of impacts over time and among jurisdictions is also quite variable. Some analyses present only an estimate of the average annual governmental costs and revenues resulting from a project (Shaffer and Tweeten, 1974; Wilson et al., 1979). These analyses provide useful information, but by failing to trace the time path of changes in costs and revenues they also may omit important information. Other studies have presented annual estimates of the aggregate changes in costs and revenues for all affected local units of government (Leholm et al., 1976a). These studies provide a useful overview of the distribution of project-related costs and revenues over time but do not indicate their distribution among jurisdictions. Only a few analyses have provided annual estimates of costs and revenues for individual local jurisdictions.

Overall, the treatment of fiscal impacts in environmental statements and similar studies typically has serious limitations. In the following sections we will examine the practices employed in studies which have attempted a reasonably comprehensive assessment of fiscal effects.

Revenue Estimation Techniques

In this section, the techniques most commonly employed in estimating project-related revenues are briefly reviewed. In general, these techniques differ primarily in the types of revenues included and in the degree of detail incorporated in the revenue estimation process.

Property taxes are the revenue source which is most frequently included. Property tax revenues from project facilities are usually based on the capital investment in the proposed facility, often coupled with information concerning the assessment practices applied to similar projects in the same area (Chalmers and Anderson, 1977). Property taxes from other sources, such as residential and commercial property, are frequently assumed to be proportional to population growth. Other analysts have attempted more detailed evaluations involving estimation of the increased value of commercial property based on changes in local income or sales and estimation of residential property values based on the estimated number and characteristics of inmigrants (Colony Development Operation, 1974; Leholm et al., 1976c). Residential property value estimation frequently involves estimating the composition of new residential development, often differentiating between construction and operation phases, and applying estimates of the assessed value of each type of housing unit. Types of housing typically include at least permanent housing and mobile homes, but permanent housing is sometimes subdivided into single-family and multifamily permanent units (Denver Research Institute, 1979). Most studies have used current tax rates in projecting future revenues.

Other revenue categories, such as income and sales taxes, user charges, and various fees are typically estimated using per capita rates (Chalmers and Anderson, 1977). Some analysts, however, utilize estimates of local income or sales in projecting income and sales tax receipts. Few studies have considered the possible use of locally established fees and user charges as fiscal management tools (Weber and Goldman, 1979), although some analysts have assumed that user charges will be established at rates sufficient to cover the amortized costs of specific facilities.

Production and severance taxes and royalty payments are frequently estimated where applicable. Statutory tax rates and established lease terms generally are the basis for these estimates (Chalmers and Anderson, 1977).

Intergovernmental transfers are usually estimated on a per capita basis if they are even considered. As noted earlier, however, distribution formulas for such transfer programs are frequently complex, and simple per capita estimation techniques may be inappropriate in some cases. A few analysts have employed detailed simulation routines to estimate certain transfer payments, particularly education transfers (Stinson and Voelker, 1978).

Only a few studies have considered possible losses of tax revenues as a result of displacement of other activities by the new project (TERA Corporation, 1976; Toman et al., 1977).

Cost Estimation Techniques

While a variety of techniques have been employed to estimate local government costs, the per capita expenditure approach is clearly dominant in impact assessment reports. The per capita expenditure factors are usually developed from local data although regional averages are occasionally employed. The degree of aggregation in the cost analysis varies substantially with some studies projecting only total costs for a given jurisdiction while others provide a detailed breakdown of costs by service category.

The service standard method appears to rank second with respect to frequency of use. Service standards typically are drawn from state guidelines or from national studies. (A source which has been used extensively is Real Estate Research Corporation, 1976.) Case studies are sometimes utilized as the principal cost analysis technique, and they are often used as an adjunct to the per capita or service standards approaches (Denver Research Institute, 1979).

Economic-engineering and cross-sectional studies have been utilized only rarely in preparing fiscal assessments. Use of the economic-engineering technique has probably been limited primarily by its relatively high cost. When this technique has been employed, it has usually been used to develop generalized estimates of facility costs by size of jurisdiction, rather than to develop community-specific estimates. Cross-sectional studies have been limited by two factors. First, local cost data available from secondary sources are frequently unreliable because of inconsistencies in accounting practices.[14] Second, because cost functions developed through cross-sectional analysis reflect average relationships across a number of jurisdictions, some analysts are reluctant to employ them in near-term analyses for specific jurisdictions. Cross-sectional analysis has been employed most frequently in estimating operating cost functions.

Few analysts have developed explicit projections of revenues and expenditures for the baseline (i.e., without development) situation. Some, however, have projected the fiscal implications of alternative development scenarios, and several studies indicate that capacities of existing facilities and current expansion plans were considered (Hayen and Watts, 1975; National Biocentric, 1977). Other studies, especially those which included a number of jurisdictions, have frequently incorporated the assumption that no excess capacity exists in community facilities. Justifications for this assumption have included the following: (1) existing excess capacity is insignificant when compared to the needs resulting from the project; (2) excess capacity is sometimes difficult to determine -- local and state officials, for example, may provide substantially different estimates of the capacity of a given facility (e.g., a school); and (3) the assumption of no excess capacity should lead to estimates of the maximum costs likely to be incurred by a given jurisdiction (i.e., a "worst case" analysis).

Estimation of Cost and Revenue Timing

Few studies have provided detailed explanations of the assumptions they employ with respect to cost and revenue timing. In general, however, it appears that most analysts who estimate annual changes in costs and revenues assume that costs will be incurred in the same year that project-related inmigration occurs. Substantial time lags may be associated with the receipt of most new revenue sources, with the greatest delays associated with property taxes and severance or

production taxes. Because the timing of revenues can be expected to vary substantially among states based on variations
in assessment and collection practices, most analysts have
tailored their revenue timing assumptions to the tax laws of
a specific state.

Discounted present value has been employed in a number of
analyses including those by Gilmore et al. (1976a) and Leholm
et al. (1976a). In both of these studies, the discount rates
employed were approximately equal to the interest rates which
the local governments in question were paying for borrowed
funds. Cummulative cash flow analysis also has been employed
in several analyses including those by Toman et al. (1978) and
Leistritz et al. (1979b).

SUMMARY AND CONCLUSIONS

The purpose of this chapter was to review the conceptual
bases and methodological alternatives for fiscal impact assessment, to describe the features of the impact process which
influence the information needs of decision makers, and to examine the techniques which are typically applied in fiscal impact assessments for large projects. The basic concepts of
demand, supply, and cost theory provide the basis for fiscal
impact analysis. Difficulty in measuring the output of public
services, however, usually leads to a number of simplifying
assumptions when fiscal impact models are implemented.

The principal methodological alternatives for revenue
estimation are either to assume that revenues will be directly
proportional to population or to employ more detailed models
which involve first estimating the change in the relevant tax
base and then applying an appropriate tax rate. Revenue estimation methods tend to differ primarily, then, in level of
detail rather than in basic form of analysis. It is generally
agreed that more detailed analyses which reflect the unique
characteristics of the state's tax system will provide more
reliable estimates of the magnitude and especially the timing
of revenue changes.

Six general approaches may be employed in cost estimation: (1) per capita expenditures; (2) service standards; (3)
cross-sectional analysis; (4) case studies; (5) comparable
city analysis; and (6) the economic-engineering approach. The
first three methods can be classified as average cost approaches and the latter three as marginal cost approaches. In
general, marginal cost approaches can be expected to be more
reliable if the services being analyzed are subject to substantial economies of scale or threshold effects or if excess
capacity is likely to exist. Average cost approaches, on the
other hand, have the advantage of being quicker and less expensive to employ.

Several features of the impact process are particularly

important in determining the information needs of decision makers and hence in influencing the selection of assessment methods. First, because growth may be both extensive and rapid, demands for local government services also may increase rapidly. Further, the project-related needs for expanded facilities and services may occur as much as several years in advance of the receipt of significant amounts of project-related revenues. Local officials are thus confronted with a number of management decisions relating to alternative strategies for service provision and financing. To be most useful to these decision makers, fiscal impact assessment should, at a minimum, indicate the likely timing of changes in service demands, costs, and revenues. To be of maximum utility to local officials and planners, fiscal impact models should be capable of simulating the effects of different growth management options, both in terms of changes in the magnitude and timing of different categories of costs and revenues and in terms of the distribution of costs and benefits among specific groups in the local population.

A second important factor affecting information needs is that the fiscal implications of a given project can differ greatly among local jurisdictions because of both the settlement patterns of the inmigrating population and the interjurisdictional distribution of project-related revenues. Fiscal assessment techniques should be sensitive to these factors and must provide jurisdiction-specific projections if they are to be useful to local officials. A third consideration is that fiscal impacts are extremely sensitive to a variety of project-specific and site-specific factors. Assessment models must be designed to reflect the effects of such factors. Finally, because considerable uncertainty frequently is associated with the magnitude, timing, and distribution of the economic and demographic effects of a major project as well as with key fiscal parameters, fiscal assessment models should be designed to allow decision makers to cope with these uncertainties through sensitivity analyses and related techniques.

The techniques which have been employed in the fiscal impact segments of most environmental assessment reports have been quite variable. Many of these reports have addressed fiscal effects only qualitatively while others have examined only a few selected revenue and cost categories. There are indications that this situation is changing, particularly for projects which are likely to result in substantial changes in local population and service requirements. Assessments for projects of this type now frequently involve annual projections of costs and revenues by type, sometimes for several jurisdictions. Because fiscal impact assessment methods have been developed primarily in connection with environmental assessments and other applied studies, there is little difference between the state-of-the-art in this area and the techniques employed in the more sophisticated assessments. There

152

is, however, a high degree of variability in the scope and detail of fiscal assessments, and many assessments appear to use rather simplistic techniques.

Future assessments should give greater attention to analyzing the effects of specific local decisions regarding alternative approaches to service provision and financing. The distribution of impacts among groups of local residents (such as long-term residents vs. newcomers, and residential vs. nonresidential property owners) also should receive greater attention. Finally, as with other impact categories, more extensive studies of areas experiencing rapid growth are needed before some aspects of the fiscal effects of such growth can be adequately evaluated.

NOTES

1. For examples of analyses of this type, see Gilmore et al. (1976a), Toman et al. (1977), Krutilla et al. (1978), and Leistritz et al. (1979b). While a recent work (Burchell and Listokin, 1978, p. 2) recommends projecting direct effects only, these authors refer primarily to studies of residential development.

2. For an extensive bibliography of fiscal impact studies, primarily in urban areas, see Burchell and Listokin (1978). For reviews of studies which focus on rural areas, see Murray (1980) and Murdock and Leistritz (1979).

3. Good basic expositions of demand and supply theory are provided in most introductory economics texts; see, for example, McConnell (1969). An extensive discussion of the application of these concepts to public services is provided by Hirsch (1973).

4. It should be recognized, however, that the outputs of many services are measureable in quantitative terms. Emergency service output can be measured in response time, parks and recreation facilities in carrying capacity, and streets and roads in terms of maximum weights and throughput capacity. The difficulty for the researcher is that these managerial/ engineering measures are not normally collected as secondary statistics, and such information is difficult and costly to obtain.

5. Public services can also be usefully classified according to the relative importance of capital and operating (primarily labor) expenditures in their overall cost structure. Some services thus can be classified as capital-intensive (e.g., water and sewer) and others as labor-intensive (e.g., police and social services). Another classification which is often useful in cost analysis is that of fixed and variable costs. Fixed costs are those which do not vary with short-term changes in the level of output of a service (e.g., prorated capital costs and salaries of supervisory personnel).

Variable costs are those which may change with the level of output (e.g., expenses for labor and supplies).

6. When tax rates are assumed to remain at their current levels, the result of the fiscal impact analysis is usually a statement of the net fiscal balance (surplus or deficit) resulting from the project. A projected fiscal deficit is interpreted as an indication that the affected jurisdiction will not be able to maintain both its existing (preproject) service levels and current tax rates, except perhaps through borrowing. A projected surplus has the opposite interpretation. Some analysts then utilize the projected net fiscal balance as the basis for determining the effect of development on tax rates, particularly for local property taxes. For a discussion of this approach and the effects of alternative assumptions on the conclusions, see Weber and Goldman (1979).

7. It should be noted, however, that such projects are often accompanied by some form of transfer payments, often termed "payments in lieu of taxes" or "impact payments," to offset at least in part the additional costs imposed on local governments (Markusen, 1978b).

8. Studies reviewed included both case studies of specific projects or areas (Gray et al., 1977; Krutilla et al., 1978; Leholm et al., 1976a; Toman et al., 1978; Purdy et al., 1977; Shields et al., 1979) and comparative analyses covering a number of impacted areas (Gilmore et al., 1976a; Stinson and Voelker, 1978; and Murdock and Leistritz, 1979).

9. This conclusion may not hold, however, for large public projects whose facilities are exempt from local property taxes unless compensating payments in lieu of taxes are provided.

10. Another factor which can contribute to the lag of local revenues is the administrative capacity of local jurisdictions to add new taxable property to their tax base. In rapid growth situations, the available personnel (often a single and perhaps a part-time assessor) may not be able to assess new property and reevaluate old property as rapidly as would be desireable.

11. An excellent theoretical discussion of community investment strategies is provided by Cummings and Schulze (1978).

12. It should be noted, however, that through judicious use of mechanisms such as user charges and hookup fees, local officials may be able to shift substantial portions of the project-related costs to new residents. For additional discussion and examples, see Gilmore et al. (1976a) and Weber (1979).

13. For a detailed discussion of the rationale behind the discounting procedure and alternative measures of the social rate of time preference, see Mishan (1971).

14. Major concerns include lack of consistency in separation of expenditures by function and failure to separate capital and operating costs (Denver Research Institute, 1979).

6
Social Impact Assessment

The assessment of the social impacts of resource development is an often neglected and ill-defined area of impact
assessment. Social assessments are often not completed at
all and, when performed, they tend to be reported in only a
few short paragraphs in an otherwise comprehensive impact
statement. Equally problematic is the fact that social impacts are often defined as "nonquantitative" or "unmeasurable"
types of impacts, and as a residual category including all
factors not included in economic, demographic, public service,
and fiscal impact assessments. They are also seen as the assessment research performed by sociologists, or as consisting
only of analyses of public service needs and demands. The
limitation of social assessments to such uses is unfortunate
because it deflects analyses from many of the critical social
issues that surround resource developments.

Prevailing social structures and institutions affect the
process of project development and are affected by developments. Key groups in the social structure, such as land
owners, merchants, and new residents, respond to one another
on the basis of social interaction patterns that may be altered significantly as a result of developments. Changes in
structural patterns and in the relative dominance of groups
within such patterns alter the way of life in an area and
often create conflicts between various groups as the relative
importance of various activities is changed. At the same
time, patterns of disorganization may arise as standard social
alignments and controls dissipate. Rates of divorce, delinquency, and drug and alcohol abuse may increase, and the need
for more formal controls over such behavior may increase dramatically.

In addition, many types of social impacts, such as
changes in interaction patterns, social organization, social
structures, social institutions, and social perceptions, are
of vital importance in the project development process.

155

Formal and informal group organizations are, for example, the major focus of social actions both for and against various kinds of developments. Understanding of the dynamics and the issues around which social groups and social movements are formed is a major focus of analysis in the sociology of social movements and the sociology of organizations, and it is clearly of central importance in the process of project development and completion.

Thus, it is obvious that many of the most publicized issues and those of greatest general interest in the initiation of a resource development project and its ongoing process toward completion are social in nature as are many of the effects of such projects. Acceptance or rejection of project proposals, opposition to project siting, and litigation often have their roots in concerns about the effects of projects on community life or ways of life, on people's relations with one another, and on how residents perceive and feel about their communities and project-related changes and new residents likely to result from the development. Although economic effects, such as increased incomes and employment opportunities, are the most often noted positive impacts of development, social factors, such as increased rates of crime, divorce, and other forms of conflict are the most often cited negative factors leading to project opposition (Murdock and Leistritz, 1979). Both in terms of the public and legislative obligations to assess impacts that are of critical importance to residents of impacted areas and in terms of instrumental concerns related to project development, social impacts require careful assessment and consideration.

CONCEPTUAL BASES AND METHODOLOGICAL ALTERNATIVES IN SOCIAL IMPACT ASSESSMENT

Although the significance of social impacts is often acknowledged, the utility of attempting to assess them is not (Chalmers and Anderson, 1977). In part, the difficulty in assessing social impacts has resulted from their having been poorly defined initially. Thus, before attempting to delineate the major approaches in social impact assessment, it is necessary to more clearly define the subject matter of social impact assessments.

The term social generally refers to the processes and products of human interaction. Social impacts can thus be defined as impacts that affect the patterns of interaction, the formal and informal relationships resulting from such interactions, and the perceptions of such relationships among various groups in a social setting (or system) (Popenoe, 1980; Goodman and Marx, 1978). Although such a definition still includes a broad range of subject matter, it avoids the tendency to see the analysis of social impacts as a residual proc-

ess. Rather, it focuses analyses on four broadly accepted
areas of social phenomena. These are:

1. Processes of interaction;
2. Social organization and social structures;
3. Social institutions; and
4. Social perceptions and attitudes.

The first area of analysis examines the forms of interactions between members of social groups that are attempting
to adjust to various environmental, economic, and social conditions. Processes such as conflict, consensus, accommodation,
and cooperation are often the focus of discussion. Such analysis concentrates on the interaction of individuals within
groups and with one another. The emphasis is on the initiation
of interaction patterns, on the first steps in the formation
of social groups, and on the norms, values, and beliefs that
underlie such group structures. In social impact assessments,
analyses of this kind have examined the formation of interest
groups, particularly those involving new residents and the
interactions between new and longtime residents. The analysis
of interactional dimensions is seldom given anything but pass-
ing attention in actual assessment efforts.

The second of these four areas is concerned with patterns
of interactions that have become formalized in identifiable
entities such as informal and formal groups and organizations.
It is also concerned with such groupings as social classes,
with stratification systems and patterns of social dominance,
with patterns of community leadership, and with other phenomena
related to the formation or dissolution of relationships
within and between groups. Such analyses in impact assessments and related research areas thus focus on the origins of
various proponent and opposition groups, on the effects of
development on civic and other community groups, on existing
community leadership and power groups (i.e., farmers, merchants, etc.), and on special groups such as the elderly,
those on fixed income, and minorities. In its broadest dimensions, this area of analysis may even consider impacts on the
total community structure or on the well-being of the total
area.

The third area of analysis is concerned with the effects
of project development on more focused areas of interactions
surrounding given sets of activities such as earning a living,
governance, family life, religion, and training and education.
These regularized sets of activities are ones of paramount
importance in nearly every social setting and are referred to
as social institutions. In all assessments, impacts on these
institutions must be carefully considered. For example, the
effects of project development on educational quality, on
family dimensions such as divorce, child rearing, delinquency,

and similar factors, as well as the effects of the project on churches and church groups are of concern in assessment efforts (Schriner et al., 1976).

The final area of analysis affects and is affected by each of the others. This is the general area of social perceptions and attitudes -- how members of groups come to perceive themselves, their groups, characteristics of their communities, and possible changes in their communities. In impact assessments, this area of analysis includes attempts to measure community and service satisfaction, perceptions of the environment, and community growth and development preferences (Selbyg, 1978; Lopreato and Blisset, 1978; Freudenburg, 1979).

In sum, then, it is essential to understand the context and meaning of the term social impacts. These impacts include effects on: (1) the process by which people interact to form groups; (2) the structures or patterns of interaction resulting from such processes, both generally (social structures and organizations) and in relation to specific functions (social institutions); and (3) perceptions of these processes, structures, and institutions. Social assessment research thus involves analyses of the effects of these social factors on the development process and the effects of the development process on these factors.

The wide range of phenomena that are included under the heading of social impacts reflect equally broad conceptual and methodological bases. The conceptual bases include a broad range of perspectives on social interaction and social phenomena. Although it is not possible to delineate even the basic aspects of or sufficient detail on any of these approaches, it is essential to provide some familiarity with several basic approaches to social phenomena to provide a more complete context for understanding different types of social assessments and the various roles sociologists play in the assessment process.

Conceptual Approaches

Theoretical development in the area of social assessment has been extremely limited (Murdock, 1979), and few impact assessment or research efforts acknowledge that a particular conceptual approach underlies the effort. Since certain paradigms and viewpoints inevitably underlie any research effort (Kuhn, 1970), it is possible from an examination of social assessment research efforts to discern the conceptional bases underlying such efforts. When this is done, characteristics reflecting at least four major theoretical bases appear with some frequency. Because the interpretation of assessment data is often affected by which of these theoretical bases underlie the researcher's perspective, it is essential to

briefly discuss each of these theoretical approaches. These
theoretical perspectives include:

1. The symbolic interactionist perspective;
2. The conflict perspective;
3. The functionalist perspective; and
4. The human ecological perspective.

The Symbolic Interactionist Perspective. The symbolic
interactionist perspective emphasizes the analysis of the
actual processes of interaction, of how persons come to understand and to perceive themselves and others, and how interaction patterns become regularized around activities to form
different types of groups. Taking its emphases from the work
of such sociologists as Mead (1934), Cooley (1909), Blumer
(1969; 1980), and others, the interactionist perspective emphasizes ongoing group actions and interactions and the mutual
effects of individuals and groups on each other. One major
emphasis, then, is on the fluid, ever-changing nature of social
phenomena.

A second major emphasis is on the individual, both as the
individual affects and is affected by group membership. The
individual's perceptions and actions are seen as having substantial effects on group characteristics and, in turn, as
being affected by group characteristics. The perspective
emphasizes what is often termed a social-psychological perspective in sociology.

In the analysis of social impacts, such an emphasis is
particularly evident in those works that stress: (1) the
relatively unique nature of the impacts of each project (Gold,
1974; Cortese and Jones, 1977); (2) the need to establish social impacts by directly observing the patterns of interactions
between groups, such as new and longtime resident groups; and
(3) the effects of developments on individual behavior and
individual perceptions (i.e., delinquency, drunkenness, depres-
sion, etc.). It is perhaps the most individualistic perspective used in assessment activities.

The Conflict Perspective. The conflict perspective on
social life traces its origins to the works of Marx (Avineri,
1970), Dahrendorf (1959), Coser (1967), and similar theorists.
From the conflict perspective, life involves a struggle for
control of limited resources. Individuals come together to
form interest groups to more effectively compete for resources.
The most important social process is conflict and conflict is
assumed to underlie nearly every phenomena. The major groups
between which conflict occurs include social classes and
economic ownership groups.

In assessment research, this perspective is evident in
those efforts which attempt to identify interest groups who

160

are likely to take different stands on development issues and in those efforts that concentrate on the conflicts between new and longtime residents (Massey, 1978). This emphasis is also evident in efforts that examine impacts from a relative costs and benefits perspective (Fitzsimmons et al., 1975; Finsterbusch, 1977). In most cases, such analyses emphasize the potential conflicts that may occur between various interest groups during project development.

The Functionalist Perspective. The functionalist perspective is usually associated with the work of classic social theorists such as Durkheim (1933) and more recent theorists such as Parsons (1951) and Merton (1968). Under this perspective, members of populations are viewed as coming together to form social groups in order to more effectively and efficiently perform certain essential functions. These functions include both those necessary for basic survival and those related to the maintenance of social interaction and group cohesion. In its most elaborated form (Parsons, 1951), society is seen as a system in which such basic elements as culture, individual personalities, and societal factors interactively determine the nature of the social system. These factors seek to perform such functions as adaptation (to the physical and other dimensions of the environment), goal attainment (the meeting of basic social and individual goals), integration (the maintenance of patterns of key interdependencies), and latent pattern maintenance (the maintenance of total societal patterns). Processes of interaction and social structures and institutions are examined in terms of their roles in maintaining such functions.

In impact research, such emphases are evident in analyses that examine the effects of project development activities on key functions or institutions. In fact, a majority of the research on the social effects of the processes of modernization, urbanization, economic development, and industrialization (Applebaum, 1970; Carnes and Friesma, 1974), which are often used in assessment efforts as the theoretical bases for predicting the social patterns that will evolve during a development, utilize a functionalist perspective. Other reflections of such emphases are analyses of the impact-related changes in social patterns that result from an area's change in economic functions and efforts that emphasize the importance of changes in groups' positions and purposes within the area's social system.

Human Ecological Perspective. A perspective that is not widely used in the discipline of sociology as a whole, but which has received increasing use in environmental sociology and impact assessment is that of human ecology (Catton and Dunlap, 1978; Murdock, 1979; Olsen et al., 1977a). Based on the historic work of Malthus (1798), Durkheim (1933), and more recently elaborated by Hawley (1950), Duncan and Schnore (1959), Duncan (1964), Micklin (1973), and others, human ecology takes man's need to adapt to an ever-changing environment as the central human problem. This adaptive process is seen as inevitably leading, through the use of various types of group interdependencies (such as commensalistic and symbiotic relationships), to given types of social interactions and organizational arrangements. Heuristically, the key components of these processes have been termed the POET variables of population, organization, environment, and technology. These four factors encompass nearly all social and demographic phenomena as well as technological and physical environmental factors that affect social phenomena. It is thus perhaps the most holistic perspective used in social analyses and one that emphasizes a wide range of nonsocial as well as social determinants of human behavior.

In impact assessment, the ecological perspective has been suggested as a useful framework from which impact events can be seen as involving changes in population and social organizational factors resulting from the application of technology to various environmental resource bases (Murdock, 1979). In addition, it has been used as a means of conceptually organizing various types of impacts (Olsen et al., 1977a). Substantively, it is reflected in those analyses that concentrate on large-scale social structural changes related to different patterns of resource usage and technology, those efforts that view impacts as resulting largely from changes in population factors, and those which emphasize the effects of differences in project. areal, and other characteristics on the magnitude and distribution of impacts (Krannich, 1978).

These four perspectives, then, form bases for many of the assessment efforts that have been completed. It is clear, however, that a more concerted and definitive use of these and other perspectives is essential if adequate conceptual bases are to be developed for impact assessments and research efforts.

Methodological Alternatives

The methodological approaches used in impact assessment reflect those widely used in the social sciences generally, as well as approaches that have received renewed development within the area of assessment research. Of the most widely used social science methodologies, only the experimental approach has received little use in assessment research. However, the comparative techniques and principles, essential in experimental designs, have been employed (Thompson et al., 1978; Murdock and Schriner, 1978). The major approaches used in assessment efforts include:

1. Secondary Data Methods;

2. Survey Methods, including:
    a. sample surveys,
    b. expert-opinion surveys (delphi-surveys);
3. Participant Observation Methods; and
4. Unobtrusive Research Methods.

Each of these methods has played an important role in different impact assessment efforts. Their major techniques, and the advantages and disadvantages of each, are described briefly below.

Secondary Data Methods. Secondary data methods involve the use of existing data, collected for other purposes, to anticipate the magnitude and distribution of social impacts. The data so used include those from such agencies as the U.S. Bureau of the Census, the National Center for Health Statistics, the U.S. Department of Agriculture, the Federal Bureau of Investigation, the Department of Health, Education, and Welfare, and from such state and local sources as state health departments, state social service agencies, and similar entities.

Such data are extremely important for the description of baseline conditions in an impact area. As such, they provide information that is absolutely essential for the projection of impacts. They are particularly useful in providing a base of historical information on the social, demographic, and cultural context within which project-related social changes occur.

Secondary data methods, however, do not provide a sufficient set of data for completing a comprehensive social assessment. Such methods seldom provide data on social processes, informal organizations, social relationships, social structures and institutions, or residents' attitudes and perceptions. In addition, secondary data are often dated by the time of their publication and unavailable for areas smaller than counties. As a result, secondary data methods must be used in conjunction with other social assessment methods.

Survey Methods. Survey methodologies consist of the direct solicitation of information from individuals via personal interview, mail, or telephone administered questionnaires. A survey method is usually selected when data are not available from secondary sources and when individual or household information is essential. Surveys are often used when perceptual and attitudinal information on impacts or patterns of service usage in impact areas are required. Due to the widespread use of surveys for political and opinion polling, the basic dimensions of surveys are well known. Because of the importance of surveys for the collection of social data, however, it is appropriate to briefly outline the major steps in a survey. The discussion of these steps will also serve to indicate those aspects of survey methods that require careful and critical evaluation.

Although the survey process can be divided into numerous steps, it is convenient to consider six steps as essential in any survey effort. In addition to those steps necessary in the use of any research method (such as decisions concerning which dimensions or research questions should be addressed and the choice of the form of analysis to be used), surveys require that special attention be given to the following steps:

1. Selection of the type and form of survey to be used;
2. Sample design, including:
   a. sampling frame selection,
   b. sample selection;
3. Questionnaire or interview design;
4. Questionnaire pretesting;
5. Questionnaire administration; and
6. Response analysis.

The first of these steps occurs after the decision to use a survey has been made. It requires selection of self-administered versus interviewer-administered or assisted surveys. The most common type of self-administered questionnaire is the mail survey. It has clear advantages in terms of costs and ease of administration, but, in general, response rates are lower than for interviewer-assisted questionnaires and its use requires extensive efforts to insure that an adequate, up-to-date mailing list has been obtained. Mail survey techniques have, however, become increasingly sophisticated in recent years (Dillman, 1978; Heberlein and Baumgartner, 1978; Carpenter, 1977) and were used as the major form in of data collection even for the relatively complex long form in the 1980 census. Mail surveys remain a useful option in impact analyses.

Interviewer-administered or assisted surveys include both the increasingly popular telephone surveys and personal interviews. Telephone surveys have become popular because of their cost advantages over personal interviews and because of the more extensive level of respondent contact they provide in comparison to mail surveys. Their major limitations result from the fact that some households may not have telephones and even those that do may choose to have unlisted numbers. Recent evidence (Groves and Kahn, 1979), however, suggests that such surveys are generally quite representative, and the use of computer-generated random-digit dialing codes insures that even unlisted numbers are included in the sampling frame.

Personal interviews are clearly the most desirable in terms of obtaining complete and in-depth information. Points of uncertainty in the questionnaire items can be clarified and unclear responses probed to insure clarity. Personal interviews are relatively expensive, however, with costs of sev-

eral hundred dollars per interview not being uncommon for a
complex survey. These costs result from the need for extensive
interviewer training as well as interviewer salary, travel, and
similar costs.

The type of survey selected will depend on the nature of
the information required and on time and cost considerations.
If in-depth information is required on a controversial topic,
or if one is relatively uncertain of the critical issues related to a particular dimension, personal interviews may be
necessary. On the other hand, if the subject matter is not
controversial and consists largely of responses describing past
behavior, then either a mail or a telephone survey may be sufficient. The selection of the form of survey to be used must
be made after careful consideration of the subject matter requiring assessment and an evaluation of resource availability.

In addition to the choice of the type of survey to be
used, consideration should be given to the selection of the
form of survey to be employed. That is, it must be determined
whether it will consist of a fixed set of questions structured
in a given order (referred to as a structured form), consist
only of a list of the broad dimensions to be querried without
any fixed question format (referred to as an unstructured survey form), or follow a course between these two extremes, taking a semistructured form. In general, when the context to be
assessed is well-defined, a more structured survey form is
desirable because one can be more certain that responses reflect evaluations of the same dimensions. When the dimensions
to be examined are not well-defined, it may be necessary to
allow the interviewer to vary the context sufficiently to probe
for key dimensions using a less-structured format. Although
structured formats are, of course, required in mail surveys,
the choice of the survey form for other types of surveys must
again be determined by the type of information required
(Dillman, 1978).

Whatever type or form of survey is selected, it is essential that any survey process give special attention to the
selection of the sample of respondents to be surveyed. Since
the major rationale for the use of a survey versus other forms
of primary data collection is usually based on the need for
data from a representative sample, the careful completion of
the sampling process is the key to the success of a survey
(Babbie, 1973). The sampling process is, in turn, dependent
for its adequacy on two factors: (1) the acquisition of an
adequate sampling frame; and (2) the use of a well-designed
technique for selecting a sample from the sampling frame
(Dillman, 1978).

The sampling frame is a list of the population of persons
from which a sample is to be selected (i.e., all of the persons
in a community). Its acquisition is often the most difficult
part of the survey process. Commonly used sources for preparing sampling frames include telephone directories, utility

lists, county agent or similar county officials' lists, lists of licensed drivers, commercial mailing lists, and similar sources. Any list chosen should be carefully examined for possible omissions and supplemented when necessary.

The technique for selecting a sample from a sampling frame may take several forms. A simple random sample selected by numbering items in the sampling frame and choosing a selected number at random may be used when specific characteristics of sample members (age, sex, education, etc.) are not expected to be of significance or data on such characteristics are not available. A stratified or cluster sample is more likely to be selected (Babbie, 1973). In a stratified sample, some characteristic such as the age, residence area, or similar characteristic of population members is chosen, and the sample is selected to be representative of different strata of the characteristic (i.e., rural and urban residence). In a cluster sample, respondents are selected with special attention to their area of residence. Techniques for drawing such samples are readily available in computerized form, and thus this part of the sampling process has become relatively straightforward and much simpler than the acquisition of a sampling frame (Groves and Kahn, 1979).

The step of survey design cannot be described in general form because it varies from one survey effort to another. In all efforts, however, the instrument must be carefully designed with questions that are unbiased, allow for direct and unambiguous responses, and elicit responses related to specific informational needs. The design of a questionnaire requires careful item delineation and analysis (Selltiz et al., 1959).

After the initial design of the survey, it is essential that it be carefully pretested. No matter how careful the construction of the initial survey, the instrument must be pretested to diagnose unanticipated problems in question interpretation and administration. Surveys that have not been pretested should seldom be used. Even a limited pretesting will alleviate many problems.

The administration of the questionnaire or survey form, though seeming to be a straightforward process, requires careful supervision. In mail surveys, this administration should include several waves of questionnaires and post card reminders (Dillman, 1978). In telephone and personal interview surveys, efforts must be made to assure that sample members are recontacted, if the initial contact is not made or the survey is incomplete. Careful supervision of interviewer performance is essential (Groves and Kahn, 1979).

Finally, prior to data analysis, surveys must be checked for completeness and the sample screened to check for obvious response biases or for refusal rates that are sufficiently high to threaten the sample's adequacy. Only if such items are checked prior to the initiation of the analysis and prior to the release of those personnel who were responsible for questionnaire administration and who can most readily assist in the interpretation and alteration of such problems will it be possible to correct potential errors.

These steps, though only some of the key steps in the survey research process, clearly reveal the need for care in the survey process. Proposed survey procedures that do not adequately describe these steps should be viewed with skepticism. The survey process is thus one requiring the use of experienced and well-trained social science personnel.

Sample and Expert-Opinion Surveys. Impact-related surveys use two general forms: (1) the standard sample survey; and (2) the expert-opinion survey. The first of these forms, which involves obtaining information from a representative sample of community residents, is the most common form of social survey, and has received extensive use in impact research (Selbyg, 1978; Thompson et al., 1978; Lopreato and Blisset, 1978).

The second form has been used extensively in community leadership analyses (Hawley and Wirt, 1974), and has received renewed emphasis in the area of impact assessment. In expert-opinion surveys, the sample consists of community decision makers and opinion leaders who are assumed to provide views representative of various interest groups in the community. Such surveys have been popular in impact assessments because they can be done rapidly and may provide the type of information required if that information relates to the actions of various groups. Expert-opinion surveys often use a survey and resurvey format in which leaders' views are assessed and analyzed, responses are reported to them, and their views again surveyed. This technique is commonly referred to as the delphi technique. It is widely used in the evaluation as well as the assessment stage of impact efforts. The obvious advantage of expert-opinion surveys is their ease of application and their relevance for assessing group issues. The disadvantages stem from the frequent misuse of such surveys as substitutes in research efforts which, in fact, require random sample surveys.

The use of survey methodologies requires the completion of a comprehensive and relatively complex research process. The advantages of survey methodologies stem from their ability to obtain data on topics not covered in secondary sources and data from a selected group of respondents that are likely to be representative of the total range of views in a community. Their disadvantages stem from their complexity, their time and financial resource requirements, and their inability to obtain information that cannot be verbalized or that is not consciously recognized by respondents. The use of surveys in assessments is widespread, however, and as noted below, assessment efforts seem likely to make increasing use of this method in the future.

Participant Observation Methods. Participant observation methods have a long and distinguished record in social research (Goffman, 1961; Glaser and Strauss, 1967; Vidich and Bensman, 1958). They consist of methods in which the researcher obtains information through direct observation and possible participation in a social setting (Gold, 1958). Whether or not researchers choose to participate in the social setting and to let their exact purpose be known to local residents will depend on the research questions being examined, but direct observation of the setting (site area) for which assessments will be made is essential. This is a particularly strong method for studying the ongoing nature of social acts and activities, for examining the roles individuals take in participating in activities, for discovering the relationships and alliances that exist in a local area, and for gaining a feeling for the overall context in which activities occur (Lofland, 1971).

In general, the participant observation method requires that the researcher live in an area for an extended period; take careful notes on social activities, persons, and their perspectives; formulate concepts and hypotheses; and test these concepts over time. The time frame for completing such methods may involve several months or even years, and one or several observers may be involved. Whatever its exact form, however, participant observation analyses require the same careful principles of observation, analysis, and reanalysis common to other research methodologies.

The advantages in the use of the participant observation method stem from its ability to more adequately capture the meaning behind and the nature of ongoing activities that may not be fully evident even to the residents of an area and thus not be recorded by them in surveys or other similar forms of data collection. In addition, it is often a cost-effective method requiring a limited number of personnel. Its disadvantages stem from the difficulty involved in assessing the generalizability of the data obtained because of the tendency for observers to be contacted by persons with given, and biased, points of view. For impact assessments, the method possesses the additional disadvantage of requiring relatively extended periods for data collection. The use of participant observation methods is essential for discerning many of the most significant dimensions of change that occur during large-scale developments.

Unobtrusive Research Design. Unobtrusive research designs consist of methods that involve the collection of primary data but do not involve direct contact with area residents. They include such methods as videotaping and tape recording everyday activities (McCoy, 1975), and analysis of the content of newspapers and other written materials describing the

activities of the population of an area (Ludtke, 1978). To
the extent that these methods sometimes fail to provide the
rigor evident in other techniques, they are less desirable
than other research designs for impact analysis. Social analysis based on casual observations, unsystematic newspaper analysis, and similar procedures appear much too often in impact
assessment research. If completed with systematic rigor, these
techniques are, however, valuable research methods capable of
being applied with considerable utility in impact assessments.
Their careful use in impact analysis is clearly advantageous.

The advantages of these techniques lie in their ease of
application and their low resource requirements. Their disadvantages are evident in the difficulty entailed in determining
the representativeness of the information obtained from them
and the direct relevance of such indirect information to
specific impact issues. Given these latter uncertainties, it
is likely that unobtrusive methods will be used largely to
supplement more traditional research methods.

Conclusions Concerning Conceptual and Methodological Alternatives

The conceptual approaches underlying, and the methodological alternatives available for use in, social impact assessments show great diversity, ranging from those that place
strong emphasis on individuals (symbolic interaction) to those
that emphasize total population changes (human ecology), and
from those that see conflict as the key social process (conflict
theory) to those that emphasize consensus (functional theories).
Methods ranging from those that use interpretations of printed
documents as data sources (unobtrusive measures) or secondary
data to those that utilize highly structured questionnaires for
data collection (surveys) can be applied in the assessment process. Such diversity has both positive and negative implications for social assessment efforts. On the one hand, this
diversity provides a flexible knowledge base that is applicable
to a wide range of phenomena. On the other hand, this diversity
allows for substantial differences in the interpretations given
to the meaning of any single set of events. Given the diversity of phenomena to which social analysis must be applied,
however, the use of a wide range of approaches and methods
appears to be necessary if complex social phenomena are to be
adequately characterized and predicted.

FACTORS AFFECTING SOCIAL IMPACT ASSESSMENTS

The process of social impact assessment and the social
factors that it is intended to project are, as with demographic impacts, affected by project, area, and new resident

characteristics as reflected in a large number of historical, cultural, economic-ecological, demographic, and social organizational variables. In addition, the nature of the social assessment process is, in large part, a product of the nature of the overall assessment effort and of the role of the social assessment process within the overall assessment effort. The effects of project, area, and new resident characteristics and of the overall environmental assessment process on the assessment of social impacts are the focus of this part of the chapter and are briefly discussed below.

Project Characteristics

The nature of the project clearly affects the nature of the social impacts experienced in an area. Developments with high levels of employment result in larger numbers of new persons and are more likely to induce significant social changes than those with smaller levels of employment. Likewise, projects with relatively expedited construction periods are more likely to have significant effects than those with extended construction periods. Finally, projects relatively close to large metropolitan areas are likely to have less significant social impacts than those in sparsely settled areas. Variations in project characteristics may thus markedly affect the magnitude of social impacts experienced in an area (Freudenburg, 1979).

Area Characteristics

The predevelopment characteristics of an area also affect the nature of the social impacts in the area. These characteristics involve a large number of factors including historical, cultural, economic-ecological, demographic, and social variables.

Historical Factors. The history of a rural area may have a significant effect on the social environment of the area, particularly that history related to other large-scale resource developments. In many rural areas of the Western and Southern United States, for example, the area's historical experience with large-scale developments, and with various auspices for such developments may play a major role in determining the social nature of the area (Murdock and Leistritz, 1979).

For many rural areas, their recent history has been one of decline. Despite recent patterns of renewed growth in rural areas (Beale, 1976), many of the potential sites for projects, such as energy-related facilities (Federal Energy Administration, 1976), are in areas that have shown little renewed growth and, in fact, have experienced decades of population and economic decline. For such communities, large resource developments will have consequences that they are ill-prepared to manage. Service infrastructures are likely to be poorly developed and services insufficiently professionalized to meet new service demands.

For areas that have been experiencing slow or moderate growth, past expectations may have provided local leaders and decision makers with a useful base of experience that will allow them to more effectively manage patterns of growth. Finally, for areas with histories of extremely rapid growth, a new development may simply compound existing problems and further overload existing facilities.

An area's experience with large-scale developments and developers may also affect the social nature of the area and its desire to support further developments. Thus, for many areas in the West, the boom and bust cycles of the past have made citizens cautious about growth and its expected benefits (McKee, 1974). In addition, since many rural areas have experienced large-scale developments that have significantly altered the level of local control and autonomy (Kraenzel, 1955), many areas may resist developments that are under the control of entities located outside the local area. The history of an area is thus an important determinant of public acceptance and other types of social impacts.

Cultural Factors. The culture -- the total way of life of a population in an area -- may also alter the types of social impacts that are experienced. If the culture is significantly different from that of the mainstream society, the social impacts experienced may be particularly acute. The most evident of such cultural effects are those experienced by Native Americans and other minority groups. Many Native Americans value industrial development less than the maintenance of cultural cohesion, kinship ties, and tradition (Albrecht, 1980), and may be less able to take advantage of the new employment and other opportunities created by developments even when such developments are favored (Schwartz, 1977). Thus, subcultures that place strong emphases on group interaction and cohesion, whether involving minority or majority groups, may find developments less desirable and hence show greater resistance to them than groups in the mainstream of American Culture. When subcultural groups are located within an impact area, special concern should be given to discerning the likely effects of such cultural practices on social impacts and the effects of social impacts on cultural traditions.

Economic-Ecological Factors. The economic and ecological context of an area also affects the social impacts experienced by the population in an area. Areas in which agriculture predominates have distinctively different ways of life than areas dominated by mining and manufacturing. Communities in

which tourism and services dominate are distinctively different than those dominated by extractive industries. In addition,
areas dominated by forests may be distinctively different than
areas in the arid Great Plains (Webb, 1931; Kraenzel, 1955;
McKee, 1974). In fact, the distinctive effects of such ecological and economic context variables are some of the best docu-
mented in the social science literature (Duncan and Reiss, 1956;
Hathaway et al., 1968; Duncan et al., 1960).

The influences of economic and ecological factors are
effected through a number of social structural and processual
relationships. An area's economic activity, for example, will
affect the sequence of social activities and even institutional
and social structures in the area. The economic activities
associated with an agricultural area, for example, will affect
the scheduling of social events (festivals, etc.), the nature
of informal organizations (for example, Grange versus union
halls), and the nature of other enterprises (retail trade and
financial institutions). In addition, whereas agricultural and
other extractive industries have historically been labor-
intensive, making large families advantageous as sources of
additional labor, industrial and occupational structures make
large families a source of additional expenses. In like manner,
the pronounced seasonal variations in northern climates lead to
somewhat different social interaction patterns than are evident
in more temperate climates. Although one must be careful not
to adopt a simplistic form of ecological or economic determin-
ism, ecological and economic differences between areas are
clearly important sources of social variations that require
careful analysis.

Demographic Factors. The size, distribution, and composition of the population of an area also clearly have implications for social effects. The size and distribution of a
social group or population affects the frequency and forms of
social interaction and the nature of social control and similar cultural mechanisms in an area. In smaller areas, social
controls over inappropriate behavior are more likely to be
exercised by family or kinship groups and to be exerted by
peer or group pressures than in larger areas where more
formal controls may be necessary. Similarly, the characteristics, particularly the diversity of characteristics, in a
population may affect the social context of an area. In
areas with a uniformity of age, education, racial, and other
characteristics, new persons with different characteristics
are likely to be more difficult for local residents to
accept than in an area where diversity is common and persons
with different characteristics may be perceived as less unique
and hence more readily accepted. In sum, then, the size,
distribution, and composition of a population are likely to
affect the types of social impacts experienced in an area.
These are factors whose effects have long been the subject of

sociological investigations (Durkheim, 1933; Wirth, 1938), and the assessment of such factors must be an important consideration in any social impact analysis.

Social Factors. Finally, it is evident that predevelopment social conditions will affect the nature of the social impacts experienced in an area. Although these predevelopment social conditions are, in turn, a reflection of many of the factors discussed above, it is evident that their state at the initiation of the project is an essential consideration. Thus, such factors as the forms of predevelopment social structures and social interaction patterns and the prevalent perceptions of residents concerning the area may affect the social impacts experienced. An area with a highly formalized social class structure and highly formalized social interaction patterns may find the placement of new impact-related residents within the social class structure to be more difficult than in areas with less formalized structures. In addition, groups in leadership positions in such structures may become sources of opposition to developments because of the obvious shift in the class structure that may accompany a shift in major economic activities in the area (Murdock, 1979).

The social perceptions of the area's residents may also alter the nature of social impacts. Areas whose residents have high levels of satisfaction with existing community conditions may be less receptive to developments than those that perceive their communities as less desirable. Perceptions of the need for economic development may be critical in causing communities to search for economic development and growth (Lonsdale and Seyler, 1979). Strong attachments to given types of land use and environmental preservation may also alter a population's receptiveness to various types of resource developments (Lewis and Albrecht, 1977; Lovejoy, 1977). The social conditions of an area prior to development clearly affect the nature of the impacts likely to be experienced during development.

The historical, cultural, economic-ecological, demographic, and social characteristics of the site area are thus of key importance in determining the nature of the social impacts likely to be experienced in an area. Although only a limited number of the many factors included in these dimensions can be adequately assessed in any impact situation, a careful consideration of such dimensions is essential in the assessment process.

Characteristics of Inmigrating Populations

A final set of factors likely to affect the substantive nature of social impacts experienced in an area are related to the characteristics of new persons coming to the site area as a result of the development. The historical, cultural, demographic, and social characteristics and experiences of these people will affect the way they react and adapt to the site area, the ease with which they are accepted by local persons, and their subsequent impacts on the site area. Although analyses seem to indicate that resource development-related migrants are similar to migrants in other areas (Murdock et al., 1980b), the general effects of a substantial number of new migrants on an area and on the assimilation process of migrants and longtime residents are well-documented factors of significance to the social context of an area (Price and Sikes, 1975). The potential social effects of the character-istics of new residents on the site area's social patterns must be carefully examined.

The project, area, and new resident social characteristics clearly exert a significant range of effects on the magnitude and the nature of the social impacts experienced in an impact area. As with demographic dimensions, however, it is often the interactive products of these three general sets of factors, rather than their separate effects, that are of greatest signif-icance. The complexity as well as the importance of these dimensions is thus evident and requires concerted attention.

The Effects of the Assessment Context

The context in which the assessment of social factors is completed is not only affected by substantive factors, how-ever, but also by the context in which the actual assessment process takes place. This context often includes extremely limited time frames and financial resources, a misunderstand-ing of the breadth of social phenomena, and a total environ-mental impact assessment mandate for the agency completing the analysis that may lead to the near exclusion of social dimensions.

The time frames for an assessment effort often are limited to only a few months of intensive effort, but many forms of social research, particularly extensive surveys and participant observation studies, may require much longer time frames if the results of the research effort are to be adequate and accurate. Expedited forms of such efforts may simply be impossible. Short time frames may thus eliminate such methods from consideration or lead to efforts that are less comprehensive and less methodologically sophisticated than desired (Freudenburg, 1981). Although different types of social questions require different social research approaches, the time constraints of assessments often limit analyses to second-ary data and other similar research designs.

Financial resources may also place particularly severe constraints on social analysis. As noted above, surveys and similar types of social analysis can simply be too costly for use in such an analysis. Cost constraints are likely to limit any analyses that are dependent on primary rather than second-

ary data. Since social analyses tend to be more dependent on
primary data than many other forms of analyses (such as the
demographic), the effects of cost constraints on social analyses are likely to be particularly evident.

The social assessment is also often affected by a less
than distinct definition of social impacts, as noted above,
and by a resulting paradoxical handling of the social assessment process within the general assessment effort. That is,
the social assessment process is deemed on one hand to include
all factors not included in the economic or demographic
analysis. Thus, the social assessment process is often seen
as the logical place for public service, minority group,
cultural, psychological, as well as standard, social analysis.
Its personnel and financial resource allocations, on the
other hand, may simply be made as if it were a single uniform
area of analysis. As a result, the social assessment analyst
is often required to do an impossible breadth of assessments
with a minimal level of resource commitments.

Finally, because the assessment process is itself often
inclusive of social, physical, biological, political, and other
dimensions and yet restricted in physical length, the discussion of social dimensions in assessment efforts often is reduced to such a minimal length that it is inadequate for the
interpretive types of analyses often necessary in social analyses. In part, then, the format requirements of impact statements (see page limitations in Council of Environmental Quality,
1978) often are especially problematic for the social analyst.

The assessment process is, in sum, often ill-matched to
the requirements of social research. This problem, though unlikely to be solved in the near future, must be recognized and
addressed in assessment evaluations.

Both substantive (project, site, and new resident) characteristics and assessment process factors are likely to
affect the social assessment process and its subsequent
products. The methodological, analytical, and resource requirements necessary to fully address all of these factors are clearly not presently available. Those that can be addressed must
be examined, however, and even those that are difficult to address must be recognized and their affects considered in the
social assessment process.

SOCIAL IMPACT ASSESSMENT TECHNIQUES

The process of social impact assessment is a complex and
diverse process, and the social assessment techniques used in
assessments have often reflected that diversity. The techniques employed in assessment efforts have included those using
secondary and primary data and those using secondary, survey,
participant observation, and unobtrusive methods. In nearly
all cases, however, whatever the method used, the major con-

ceptual and methodological choices surround the three major
processes of baseline profiling and baseline and impact projections. In this section, the most prevalent techniques used
in the completion of these three steps in actual impact assessments are discussed.

Baseline Profiling

As with many other types of impact assessment, one of
the major steps in the assessment process is that of describing
the area prior to development. In social assessments, this
usually involves a description of a large number of variables
derived from secondary data sources. One of the most comprehensive lists of the basic categories measured in social assessments and some of the common indicators of those dimensions is
presented by Fitzsimmons et al. (1975). The aspects listed in
the social well-being account are shown in Table 6.1. For each
dimension, some of the components and a few of the many indicators of each component are shown.

An examination of this table reveals the breadth of
indicators that may be included in a social assessment profile
as well as the tendency for social assessments to include a
large public service component, to rely heavily on secondary
data indicators (that is, public service agency and census
data), and to incorporate standard sociological variables
within a broad sociocultural perspective. Although the specific variables shown in Table 6.1 are influenced by the fact
that the social well-being account is designed for specific
types of developments, the range of expectations it reflects
for the social assessment is not unusual.

Because of the wide range of dimensions usually assessed,
the completion of the social baseline usually involves the use
of secondary data, participant observation, and expert-survey
methods. That is, secondary census and public agency data
are used to describe many of the service and demographic and
context variables. Participant observation analyses, usually
severely limited in scope, are used to describe what
Fitzsimmons et al. (1975) refer to as aggregate social effects.
A limited number of structured or unstructured surveys are conducted with community leaders and other residents in the community to determine the nature of existing institutions and other
community factors. Community-wide random sample surveys may
occasionally be performed, but the norm is for some combination of these three methods to be used (Schriner et al., 1976;
Love, 1978). Although some early assessments relied almost
totally on secondary data, baseline descriptions are seldom
performed using only a single method. This marks a significant increase in the level of realization of the complexity
of and resulting detail necessary for the adequate assessment
of social impacts (Freudenburg, 1981).

TABLE 6.1. DIMENSIONS, COMPONENTS, AND SELECTED INDICATORS
OF SOCIAL WELL-BEING

	DIMENSIONS		
Individual, Personal Effects		Community, Institutional Effects	
Components	Selected Indicators	Components	Selected Indicators
1. Life, Protection, Safety	a. persons served by agencies b. staff size and budget of agencies c. accessibility of agencies	1. Demographic	a. size b. density c. ethnicity
2. Health	a. morbidity levels b. mortality levels c. number of outpatient health facilities d. number of health care personnel e. cost of health care f. satisfaction with health care	2. Education	a. school enrollment b. dropout rates c. number of personnel and facilities d. satisfaction
3. Family and Individual	a. number of families b. number of unemployed c. number of divorces d. family-related services	3. Government Services	a. number of governments b. government budgets c. satisfaction
		4. Housing & Neighborhood	a. persons in substandard housing b. number of units c. costs of housing
4. Attitudes, Beliefs, and Values	a. Expectations of impacts on: ·local environment ·local economy ·local community population characteristics and composition ·local participation in decision-making ·local values and customs	5. Law & Justice	a. number of violations b. number of police officers c. budgets d. satisfaction
		6. Social Services	a. number on welfare b. social service personnel and facilities c. satisfaction
		7. Religion	a. church membership by denomination b. number in clergy c. church stance on community issues
5. Environmental Conditions	a. visual quality b. pollution levels c. accessibility d. land use patterns e. conflict between those desiring alternative uses	8. Culture	a. ethnic composition b. language c. historical sites
		9. Recreation	a. types of facilities b. costs c. satisfaction
		10. Information Organizations and Groups	a. number, size, and membership in groups b. coordination between groups
		11. Community & Institutional Viability	a. change in size, type, location, etc., of services b. change in residents' image of community

Table 6.1. (cont'd.)

Area Socioeconomic Effects		National Emergency Preparedness Effects	
Components	Selected Indicators	Components	Selected Indicators
1. Employment and Income	a. workers by type b. occupation and industry of workers c. persons below poverty level d. satisfaction with employment	1. Water Supplies	a. amount and quality of water
		2. Food	a. amount and type available
2. Welfare & Financial Compensation	a. number of people receiving assistance b. persons below poverty level c. satisfaction	3. Power Supplies	a. effects on power availability
		4. Water Transportation	a. number of miles of waterway
3. Communication	a. households with radios and televisions b. newspaper circulation c. satisfaction	5. Fuels	a. change in different types of fuels
		6. Other factors	a. INR
4. Transportation	a. number of vehicles b. number and quality of highways c. satisfaction	Aggregate Social Effects	
		Components	Selected Indicators
5. Economic Base	a. persons employed by industry b. number and type of establishments c. satisfaction	1. Change in Quality of Life	a. self-development b. quality of interpersonal relationships c. standard of living d. satisfaction
6. Planning	a. level of local planning	2. Changes in Relative Social Position	a. equity of distribution of benefits and costs
7. Construction	a. effects of construction on population, housing, and other factors	3. Changes in Social Well-Being	a. changes in the quantity and quality of services b. changes in income c. economic stability

SOURCE: Fitzsimmons et al. 1975.
INR: Indicators not relevant to present discussion.

The limitations of these practices are that the use of secondary or quickly conducted participant observation and survey efforts often lead to the assessment of those phenomena that can be most easily measured or to the use of those data that are most readily available rather than to the assessment of the most important social phenomena. As a result, the perceptions and perspectives of interest groups, both for and against development, are often included in baseline assessments, but the viewpoint of the general public or the community as a whole remains unreported. Given the time and resource realities of the assessment process, however, such limitations seem likely to remain evident in social impact analysis.

Baseline and Impact Projections

The discussion of baseline and impact projections is presented in one section because the range of methods used in baseline projections is limited and because both projection processes share similar strengths and weaknesses. In fact, of all the aspects of social assessment, it is clearly the projection process which is the least developed and open to widely justifiable criticism. In almost all cases, data obtained by one of the standard social research methods are further expanded by additional iterations of data collection or by the application of conceptual perspectives to existing data bases to project social impacts. Although an extremely large number of methods could potentially be used (Miller, 1977), the most frequently used techniques include the application of:

1. Trend extrapolation techniques;
2. Expert-opinion or delphi surveys;
3. Value forecasting procedures;
4. Social change and development theories; or
5. Scenario forecasting techniques.

Before each of these techniques is discussed, however, it is essential to point out the major inputs that enter into the social assessment process. The most important of these are:

1. Baseline data on social, historical, and cultural trends;
2. Projections of project-related demographic change; and
3. Projections of project-related economic change.

For the social analyst, social projections are and must be made with full recognition of existing social patterns and trends and of the likely magnitude of project-related demographic and economic changes. The size, distribution, and composition of the population accompanying a development and the extent to which the development will alter the basic economic base of the area provide essential inputs into the social analysis. As noted above, such factors are among the most important determinants of social impacts. It is essential, then, to again emphasize that attempts to incorporate measures of the interdependence of the various socioeconomic dimensions, though often not computationally formalized in relation to social factors, is as essential in social assessments as in other parts of the socioeconomic assessment process. This consideration is important in examining each of the techniques that are presented below.

Trend Extrapolation. Perhaps the most widely used technique and, in fact, nearly the only technique used in baseline projections, is that of extending or extrapolating past trends into the future. This method is particularly useful in baseline projections because past trends are nearly the only guide to what will happen in the area in the future without development. In using such techniques, researchers generally take baseline profiles and extend these into the future. Thus, if the area has been dominated by agriculture and shown consistent population decline, these patterns are assumed to continue or to change in some specific manner.

The advantages of this approach are that it is relatively easy to apply and provides projections that are clearly supported by existing data. The major problems with the application of this technique in social assessments have been twofold. Social analysts have tended to use a relatively simplistic model of baseline conditions in rural areas and have failed to recognize that all social patterns change over time. Thus, there has been a tendency to perceive rural areas as at the extreme rural end of the rural-urban continuum and to idealize their predevelopment states. In addition, there has been a tendency to see rural areas as unlikely to change from predevelopment states unless a particular development impacts the area. Although social scientists acknowledge that American society as a whole is changing and seldom fail to extrapolate changes in demographic patterns, the extrapolation of social patterns often consists of simply assuming that past configurations will continue unchanged. Clearly, extrapolations of even baseline social patterns must take into account the ongoing societal patterns of change (such as those related to mechanization, mass communication, etc.) that are affecting rural areas. Techniques failing to do so are unlikely to provide accurate projections.

Expert or Delphi Surveys. Delphi techniques have had a long history of use in a variety of social science fields (Freeman et al., 1978; Pill, 1971; Ament, 1970; Hill and Fowles, 1975). These techniques consist of surveying a group

of experts or knowledgeable community representatives and then
iteratively returning to them with the results of earlier surveys to focus reassessments. By repeating this process, one
can obtain increasingly integrated projections of experts'
views of the future with and without development.

The advantages of this approach are several. It provides
projections by community residents that have intimate knowledge of their community and its residents and projections that
have received concerted and repeated examinations by these leaders. Finally, it is clearly a method likely to receive widespread support among local residents, since it is their projections and their leaders' projections that are used in the analysis. This technique then insulates social researchers from
both the charge that they have failed to include local perspectives or that the researchers are the source of erroneous
projections.

The disadvantages of such techniques include those common
to any survey. In addition, questions about the ability of
local residents to project levels of change and about the extent
to which the experts' (usually community leaders) views represent those of the larger community are areas of concern. Although these dimensions are receiving increasing analyses
(Freeman et al., 1978; Hill and Fowles, 1975), they are clearly factors that require careful attention prior to the use of
delphi methods.

Value Forecasting. Value forecasting is a technique that
uses assessments of baseline values and beliefs to project how
future developments are likely to be evaluated and accepted
by local residents (Miller, 1977). Thus, if the area is one
with patterns of ethnic homogenity, relatively fixed social
statuses and social interaction patterns, and slow acceptance
of change, these "core" values may be projected to lead local
residents to resist the social changes brought about by a
development. The utility and validity of this method depends
on the researchers' levels of knowledge concerning baseline
values and the general state of knowledge concerning the ability
to predict behavior from values.

This method is often used when baseline analyses have been
conducted using participant observation methods. When such
methods have involved long-term observations by well-trained
social scientists, the assessment of baseline values is often
quite accurate (Lofland, 1971). However, if baseline analyses
were completed with limited periods of observation, this method
can lead to dramatic and often questionable predictions (Kohrs,
1974). The ability of even the best assessments to predict
behavior, however, is one that remains a central focus and un-
resolved issue throughout the social sciences generally
(Schumann and Johnson, 1976; Blalock, 1979).

Application of Social Change and Development Theories.
Another technique widely used in social assessment projections
is that of assuming that the impact area will display patterns
similar to developing areas in other settings (Carnes and
Friesma, 1974). Thus, the theoretical premises underlying
theories of social change, and such specialized theories of
social change as those related to economic development, urbanization, and modernity, have formed a major basis for predicting
future social patterns (Applebaum, 1970). That is, such con-
comitants of changes in economic bases as decreases in the
prevalence of extended families, formalizations of social relationships, increased alienation, and greater openness to change
are predicted to occur in impacted areas as they change from
predevelopment economic bases to those represented by the
development.

This technique has the advantage of relying on a wide
body of literature and theory and is, in many cases, the only
form of projection that can be made. The difficulties in the
use of such procedures include those inherent in the theoretical perspectives themselves and those resulting from the difficulties that exist in attempting to place impact areas along
the continua that form the bases for many of the assumptions
underlying such theories. Consensus on the types of changes
that occur for groups and individuals as a result of economic
and social change does not exist and the nature of such changes
form the basis of an ongoing debate in the social change literature (Armer and Schnaiberg, 1972; Inkeles, 1975; Rau, 1980).
In addition, it is unclear where most communities should be
placed on the continua of patterns that underlie such concepts.
Even when these general theoretic patterns may provide useful
projections, where a given impact area should be placed on the
underlying continua and the level of change necessary for
social patterns in the impact area to become more developed,
more modern, or more urban is unclear. The development of this
technique is dependent upon the accumulation of knowledge from
additional basic research on social change as well as the development of the social impact assessment art.

Scenario Forecasting. Scenario forecasting is a specialized form of the methods discussed above (Vlachos, 1977). It
involves systematically formulating a set of logical assumptions about future patterns in various social dimensions and
tracing their likely interactions and trends over time. The
assumptions used can be derived by any of the methods noted
above and from any data collection form. Its unique features
are its clear recognition of the basic assumptions used in its
projections; its recognition of restraints on and dynamic interactions between component factors; and its tendency to examine multiple possible futures. Its logic is similar to that
underlying any basic formalized projection technique.

The use of this technique, except in the most general
sense, has been limited in social impact assessments. Its
attractiveness stems from the conscious attempt to recognize
and include patterns of interaction and dynamic relationships
within a total sociocultural context. Its disadvantages stem
from the fact that its level of utility is dependent on the
level of knowledge concerning the basic patterns of interactions between social phenomena during a resource development. This method is one, in fact, that may be more advanced
than the data available for social analysis. Its utility is
thus likely to increase as the knowledge base concerning social
impacts increases.

Conclusions Concerning Alternative Assessment Techniques

The five methods noted above constitute some of the most
frequently used methods in social projections. In all cases,
these projection techniques are largely nonquantitative, difficult to independently validate, and subject to wide variations
in interpretations. The projection of social impacts thus
clearly requires extensive development if social impact assessments are to gain a more equitable status in the socioeconomic
assessment process.

The techniques actually used in social impact assessment, both for baseline descriptions and baseline and impact
projections, reflect a diversity of conceptual and methodological approaches. They reveal yet again the breadth and complexity of the phenomena to be assessed by, and the underdeveloped
nature of, the social assessment process.

SUMMARY AND CONCLUSIONS

In this chapter, we have delineated the conceptual,
methodological, and assessment process dimensions in the
assessment of social impacts. The conceptual bases as well
as the methodological alternatives for such assessments are
diverse and reflect a broad base of subject matter. On the
other hand, the actual assessment techniques in use tend to
be relatively underdeveloped and require extensive expansion
and basic conceptual and methodological development and
analysis. The discussion suggests that the assessment of social impacts is perhaps the most complex of all the aspects of
socioeconomic impact assessments, but, at the same time, the
least developed and the least used and appreciated. The further development and perhaps even the survival of social impact
assessments will require extensive changes in the substance and
context of social assessments.

One of the first requirements for more effective social
assessments is a clearer delineation of the nature of the

term social as used in assessments and a delimiting of the
phenomena that must be included in a social assessment. This
will require both insuring the inclusion of certain key dimensions and, at the same time, excluding some elements presently
considered as part of many social assessments. Thus, social assessments should include, at a minimum, an analysis of: (1)
the community and social structure of the impact area; (2) the
key social processes and major patterns of interaction in the
impact area; (3) the social institutions in the impact area;
and (4) the attitudes, values, and perceptions of the residents
of the impact area. The assessment of these factors would require analysis of key formal and informal groups, leadership
patterns, patterns of social differentiation, basic values and
norms, basic cultural themes, patterns of influence and social
networks, forms of social organization and disorganization, perceptions of community, satisfaction with community, and similar standard social dimensions. It would, however, eliminate
several dimensions often included in social assessments, including the examination of psychological states and community service demands. At present, the demands placed upon the social
assessment process are often unreasonably inclusive and involve
attempts to assess factors that are neither conceptually nor
methodologically compatible with social bases of knowledge. A
clearer definition of the domain as well as the limits of social
assessments is essential.

Equally important is the need to more effectively integrate the social assessment process with other aspects of the
socioeconomic assessment process. As noted above, the social
assessment process, though utilizing the results of other socioeconomic dimensions, is seldom formally integrated with them.
This integration will require both conceptual and methodological
developments. That is, few social theories effectively integrate social dimensions with economic, demographic, public
service, and fiscal dimensions, and even fewer attempt to integrate social factors with environmental or technological dimensions which form major areas of impact in resource developments.
Although this need has been expressed and some initial suggestions made for effecting such integrations (Murdock, 1979), the
conceptual basis for integrating social dimensions with other
aspects of the socioeconomic assessment process clearly requires
much more extensive attention. Methodologically, also, such
forms of integration are not present. Thus, there is no social
counterpart to the computational linkages that exist between
economic investments and employment requirements or to that between employment change and population growth. Such linkages
must be developed and implemented if the social assessment
process is to become an integral part of the socioeconomic
assessment process.

Perhaps no other single development is as essential, however, as the development of more effective means for projecting

social phenomena. Although one can legitimately argue that many of the projection techniques in other social science dimensions are superior only in form, but not in accuracy, to social projection techniques (Ascher, 1978), the fact that social projections remain descriptive and that they seldom provide assessments of the magnitude or the distribution of impacts often makes them of little utility to decision makers and others involved in local area planning. Although the increases in the level of understanding, provided by such assessments should not be discounted, more definitive projections are essential if the social assessment process is to influence decision making or to gain a more substantial role in the overall assessment process.

The assessment of social impacts clearly shares the need, expressed in the discussion of other socioeconomic dimensions, for a much elaborated data base on the near and long-term impacts of resource developments on social phenomena. Analysis of the actual social impacts of various types of resource developments in different settings and the long-term monitoring of impacted areas and events remain a widely recognized research priority (Murdock and Leistritz, 1979; Freudenburg, 1981). As with other dimensions, then, the social impacts of resource developments requires substantial additional analysis and substantiation.

Finally, it is evident that the social assessment process must be made an integral part of the socioeconomic assessment effort, not merely an addendum or appendix to the demographic or public service analyses. Until the time and resources necessary to complete successful social assessments are provided, the assessment of social impacts will simply not be adequately completed. Although the marginal status of social assessments results, in large part, from the limitations noted above, it should be clear that such limitations cannot possibly be overcome if the social assessment process remains peripheral to the overall socioeconomic assessment effort. Only the acceptance and expansion of the social assessment process can insure its ultimate utility for determining the social impacts and social implications of resource developments.

The conceptual and methodological challenges in the social assessment process are particularly pronounced and require immediate and concerted attention. It is also an analytical area in which the need for accurate and comprehensive assessments is essential both to insure that the impacts of developments are fully and equitably assessed and subsequently mitigated and to insure the successful siting of resource developments.

7
Interfacing Socioeconomic Dimensions

The assessment of the socioeconomic impacts of natural resource developments entails the use of procedures and methodologies from diverse fields including economics, demography, sociology, public service planning, fiscal analysis, and several others. However, unlike many other areas of analysis in which the integration of key dimensions of these fields is largely limited to verbal discussion, in impact assessments actual computational interfacing of the various elements is essential and mandated. Thus, as specified in the National Environmental Policy Act, such assessments must "utilize a systematic, interdisciplinary approach which will insure the integrated use of the natural and social sciences and the environmental design arts..." (NEPA, PL190, 1970, p. 857). The conceptual and methodological bases of the various disciplines must be effectively interfaced in impact assessments.

Unfortunately, attempts to computationally link various socioeconomic components are relatively recent (see Chapter 8 for a history of such developments), and the conceptual and methodological basis of interface procedures relatively undeveloped. The assessment process has, in fact, played a major role in progressing integration procedures from the conceptualization to the implementation stage. Such integration, however, requires substantial conceptual and methodological refinement.

Because the art of interfacing is poorly developed, before initiating our discussion of the conceptual bases underlying interfaces, it is essential to define what the interfacing or integrating of socioeconomic dimensions entails. Although few formal definitions have been developed, the interfacing of socioeconomic dimensions in an impact assessment may be defined as consisting of the use of the output from projections in one content area (i.e., economics) as input into another area of analysis (i.e., demography). This output-input procedure may be single- or multiple-phased and involve two or more content areas simultaneously. It may involve a

185

formal quantitative procedure or the descriptive use of the results from one area in the interpretation of the impacts in another. The delineating features of an interface, then, are its abilities to link two sets of quantitative or qualitative projection procedures either formally or descriptively so that the results of the projections in one of the two areas act upon or interact with the other to influence (or mutually influence) the results obtained in the other projection area. This definition, though admittedly simplistic, makes the interfacing involved in impact assessment an integral part of the systems framework widely used in formal modeling and a part of the broad conceptual process involved in the integration of social science disciplines. As such, the interfacing of socioeconomic dimensions is of central importance to impact analysts in particular and, as a form of tracing interactions between social science dimensions, to social science in general.

CONCEPTUAL BASES AND METHODOLOGICAL ALTERNATIVES IN INTERFACING SOCIOECONOMIC DIMENSIONS

Although most methodological discussions of impact methods present procedures for linking components (Chalmers and Anderson, 1977; Murphy and Williams, 1978; Denver Research Institute, 1979), few provide any discussion of the conceptual rationales underlying the procedures utilized. In fact, the number of conceptual discussions of interfaces are extremely limited, and most consist of little more than discussions of the computations involved in the techniques. In this brief section we attempt to provide initial steps toward the establishment of a more effective conceptual base for the integration of socioeconomic impact dimensions.

In interfacing components from two or more computational sets, principles that reflect impact projection processes, the characteristics of the components to be integrated, the units of the interface, and the interface process are required. Specifically, we suggest that interfaces should have the following characteristics:

1. The use of a common interface procedure for baseline and impact projections;
2. The use of procedures and data that can be effected at the lowest appropriate geographical level;
3. The retention of the maximum number of significant aspects of each of the components being interfaced;
4. The use of multiple interface points; and
5. The use of mechanisms for insuring the feedback of changes from one component to another.

A discussion of the general rationales underlying these characteristics as well as their implications for each of the major substantive areas involved in interfaces in impact assessments appears below.

Baseline and Impact Projections

One of the factors that has caused inconsistency in some impact analyses has been the failure to employ consistent interface methodologies in both baseline and impact projections. The failure to use a common procedure in both major phases of analysis means that differences in results that are due to project effects cannot be differentiated from those that are the result of differences in the interface methods employed. In economic-demographic interfaces, for example, it has been quite common to use simple population to employment ratios for baseline projections but to match detailed economically-derived estimates of required labor with demographically-determined estimates of available labor to complete impact projections (Toman et al., 1976). As a result, baseline and impact projections are not directly comparable demonstrating that the use of a common methodology for both impact and baseline projections is essential.

Geographic Specificity

Interfaces of key components can be completed at a variety of geographical levels. The second characteristic suggests that the areal focus for interfaces should be the lowest possible level of geographical detail. An important trade-off is often involved in the selection of the focal level for interfacing, however. That is, the difficulties of data acquisition increase with the level of geographic detail required. The use of national or regional data may thus be advantageous if time and other resources are limited or if local data are not available (Stenehjem, 1978). On the other hand, the interfacing of components at lower levels of geographic detail is suggested by the need to adequately characterize differences between impact areas. If these differences are substantial and likely to alter the nature of interface dimensions, relatively small areas are the preferred level for interfacing.

In interfacing computations, this premise points to the desirability of performing computations at the county level or below rather than at the regional or other higher levels of geographical aggregation. When regional interfaces are involved, allocation functions are generally required to obtain values for county and municipal areas. In many cases, these allocation procedures are simplistic and do not allow the characteristics of smaller areas to be taken into account.

For example, if the interface of demographic and service dimensions occurs at the regional level, then the important differences between service availability in the region and in smaller areas (which may be substantial if the region is a functional economic area and the local area is a small rural community) may not be adequately measured. In general, to the extent that the characteristics of small areas accurately reflect those of the larger areal unit, the accuracy of projections for small areas will not be affected by completing interfaces at larger areal unit levels. In nearly all other cases, some inaccuracies will be introduced. Even the use of characteristic-specific functions, showing the smaller area's proportion of a larger unit's dimensions (such as the percent of the region's population 15-19 years of age accounted for by a county's population of that age), may not allow cylical flows in the patterns (such as age structure changes) for smaller areas to be accurately predicted.

Finally, the application of rates at the lowest possible level of geographical aggregation is suggested by the need to insure the greatest possible accuracy at those levels for which the data are most likely to be used. Increasingly, impact assessments are being employed not for region-wide planning but for county, community, and school district analysis because these areas are those that are the most likely to experience negative socioeconomic impacts (Murdock and Leistritz, 1979). To the extent that the use of small area data improves the accuracy of projections of changes for small areas (a premise that admittedly requires additional verification), the use of small area data is desirable. These considerations, together with the fact that the accuracy of projections varies directly with the size of the unit for which projections are made, has led to a compromise which has made the county the standard unit of analysis. Although the utility of this level of focus has yet to be fully established, its use appears to be gaining acceptance in impact assessments (Chalmers and Anderson, 1977; Denver Research Institute, 1979).

Retention of Component Characteristics

The need to retain the essential aspects of each component is an evident, but often neglected, factor in interfacing projections from different substantive areas. In many impact interfaces, simplifications of each component often occur prior to the interfacing of the components. Thus even though an economic model may be utilized which provides sector detail on gross output and employment for economic projections, many of the most commonly utilized interface techniques simplify such data prior to their use in the economic-demographic interface by summing across employment types by sector to get one estimate of required labor. At the same time, the demographic

analysis may produce age and age and sex-specific data, but
these data are often simplified to a single estimate of available labor for interfacing with economic components or aggregated to produce a total population figure for interfacing with
service or other components. When this is done, the advantages
entailed in the use of detailed data are lost. For each of
the major components, such simplifications can entail a significant loss of information that should enter the interface.
It is necessary, then, to delineate the general features that
should be included in all interfaces and to specify the elements that must be included in each interface component.

Although many of the individual factors that should be
retained are specific to a given component (for example, economic, service), at least two features are sufficiently general to suggest the conceptual utility of including them in all
interfaces. These are the need to insure that interfaces include: (1) measures of the magnitude of the impacts; and (2)
measures of the distribution of impacts across key dimensions.
For example, total employment demands as well as employment
demands by sector, total available labor as well as available
labor by type, and total revenues as well as revenues by type
should be included if at all possible. The distributional
component is the most often neglected of these two factors.
For example, an economic and demographic interface function
that matches total required and total available labor to determine migration may project a need for little or no inmigration because total available and required labor are nearly
equivalent. However, because both labor availability and demand are, in actuality, differentiated, significant inmigration
may be necessary to fill specialized labor demands. Clearly
some of the available local labor will not be at the appropriate skill level to address the demand and could not be
employed at the development site. Unless interfaces include
such distributional dimensions, substantial projection errors
may result.

In addition to these general considerations, it is essential to suggest at least some of the aspects that should enter
the interfaces between each component and other components.
In the economic component, for example, it is necessary that
each of the types of employment demands created by the project
enter as separate components of the interface. At a minimum,
it is essential that construction, operational, and indirect
types of employment be included because these types of employment require different types of skills, involve different population subgroups, and have different public service, fiscal,
and social impacts. Unless employment types are differentiated, subsequent projections will also be unable to provide an
adequate level of differentiation. In addition, economic interfaces should include data by at least broad individual
economic sectors. One of the major advantages of sector detail

is that it provides a more flexible base for interfacing with
other dimensions. Thus, because data on the demographic characteristics of persons by occupation are available, sector-
specific detail allows for more detailed projections of the
demographic implications of given levels of employment change.
Employment and sector differentiation are essential.

In the demographic component, the key factors appear to
be the inclusion of not only total population but also population by age and sex. Although other demographic indicators
may be desirable, such as those on household composition, the
close association between age and sex characteristics and nearly all other sociodemographic variables, such as economic,
public service, and fiscal variables, suggests that age and
sex detail provide an adequate level of differentiation. The
substantial differences between subgroups within populations
are often masked in total population values (see Chapter 3)
and clearly suggest the need for age and sex detail.

For service interfaces, the essential features not only
include indicators of the level and distribution of services
but also indicators of service quality and of existing service
infrastructures in impact areas. As noted in Chapter 4, this
latter dimension is particularly important because it is often
neglected in actual assessments. The assumption of "no excess
capacity" or the projection of service demands on the basis of
new impact population only is seldom justified. In projecting
different types of services, then, it is essential to consider
existing service bases.

Projections of the quality of services are also seldom
included in impact projections (see Chapter 4) or interface
computations. If included at all, they are often only verbal-
ly described in discussions of the assumptions underlying a
set of projections or noted as qualifiers of the validity of
such projections. The operationalization of the concept of
service quality, except as indicated by the magnitude of service personnel per unit of population, is extremely difficult,
but this difficulty does not negate the necessity of using
quality of service indicators in interface procedures. When
interfacing service demands with projected population and
other factors, it is essential to adjust the interface results
in terms of service quality factors.

In the assessment of fiscal impacts, it is important to
include several basic dimensions. Foremost among these is the
need to include separate indicators of different types of revenues and expenditures (see Chapter 5). Because the characteristics of different types of new residents and different
types of resource developments have quite different taxation
implications, it is essential to differentiate between types
of revenues and expenditures. The use of a single per capita
indicator of public revenues or expenditures fails to take into account that different types of residents will generate

different levels of revenues and expenditures. Those living in mobile homes, for example, will generate significantly less revenue than those living in single-family dwellings. Although the exact number of categories of revenues and expenditures that should be used in any given situation will vary with the tax structure of the area being considered, some differentiation is essential.

When social components are involved, the interfaces are seldom quantitative in nature. Whatever the manner in which social interfaces are effected, however, it is evident that, at a minimum, patterns of interaction, and institutional, structural, and perceptual phenomena should be interfaced to trace their effects on: (1) the patterns of interaction between various groups of residents; (2) the major social institutions -- the family, religion, education, politics, and the social aspects of economic structure; (3) the social structure of the area (i.e., the effects on such factors as roles, statuses, social class, and the social organization of the community); and (4) the values, attitudes, and perceptions of people in the area. Although quantitative interfaces between such factors and others have yet to be developed, these four dimensions should form basic aspects of any such interface.

It is essential in all interface components to develop not only a means of interfacing them but also a means of insuring that the interfaces effectively merge the major components of each dimension. Unfortunately, this assertion clearly remains an ideal that is far from realization.

Multiple Interface Points

A majority of the interfaces between socioeconomic components utilize a single factor interface. For example, public expenditures are often obtained by the application of a single per capita rate of expenditures to total population values, and the interface points for economic and demographic models and for demographic and service modules are often single-faceted. Few components are simultaneously interfaced either with more than one other component or with more than one variable within each component. Fiscal components tend to be the exception in that income (to determine income tax revenues), housing demands (to determine property tax revenues), and population (to determine per capita revenues or expenditures) are all interfaced with fiscal factors. In an ideal conceptual design, all components would be interfaced with all others at multiple points to take the mutual interdependence of socioeconomic dimensions into account.

The importance of these multiple linkages is as apparent as the interdependencies that are known to underlie such dimensions. The specific dimensions of each component interact in numerous and complex ways. Thus, both employment and indus-

try characteristics affect population size, distribution, and
composition; population size, distribution, and composition
affect the magnitude, nature, and quality of services; and
service quality affects employment, population size, and numerous other factors. Few dimensions are interrelated through
only a single factor. If actual conditions are to be accurately simulated, the full range of interdependencies that exist
between socioeconomic factors must be included in interfaces.
Although it is clearly impossible to fully simulate all of
these interdependencies, existing interface techniques (as
noted below) require extensive supplementation to include multiple interface points.

Feedback Mechanisms

The need to insure that changes in the conditions of one
factor for one time period are fed back into (used in) the calculation of related factors for subsequent time periods is
closely related to the design of multiple interface points. If
interrelations between items have not been linked conceptually
and computationally, it is impossible to trace feedback relationships between factors. The need to carefully determine
those relationships that should be treated iteratively must be
given special emphasis. The very nature of the interactive
relationships that exist between socioeconomic components
points to the need for such emphasis. Although the presence
of such feedback mechanisms in actual impact events has been
thoroughly discussed in the impact literature (Gilmore et al.,
1976a; Murdock and Leistritz, 1979; Albrecht, 1978; Cortese
and Jones, 1977) and, at least partially, included in the
structure of several computerized models (Ford, 1976; Cluett
et al., 1977), insufficient attention has been given to tracing the most influential of such mechanisms and to including
them in impact projection methodologies.

The need for feedback mechanisms, if long-term projections are to be made, cannot be overemphasized. It is essential to trace the effects of factors at one point in time on
other factors at later periods. Thus, it is essential to examine such relationships as the effects of employment opportunities on indigenous residents' employment and migration patterns in subsequent periods. It is important to assess the
effects of changes in area income levels on service demands
and on perceptions of the local community and the quality of
life in the community. It is essential to evaluate the effects
of community perceptions on migration patterns and the effects
of fiscal structures on the quality of services. It is important to measure the effects of employment growth on population
growth, population and employment growth on service quality,
and the interactive effects of service quality on employment,
population growth, and retention (the problem triangle).

Finally, it is important to assess the effects of changes in business volume on the subsequent retail service mix and of this mix back on business volume. These interactive effects must be established, quantified, and included in impact projections. Substantial additional research is essential because most of these relationships have yet to be fully identified and even fewer have been quantified. The need to establish and methodologically implement feedback mechanisms should receive priority in the development of impact methodologies.

Conclusions Regarding Conceptual Bases

The delineation of the five dimensions noted above provides only an initial step in the formation of a conceptual base for interfacing socioeconomic impact components. These dimensions are not inclusive of all those that might be delineated nor are they premises without exceptions. They require supplementation and further specification. It is essential that impact scientists more carefully consider the goals they wish to achieve in interfacing model components rather than allowing established methodological techniques to determine their conceptual goals. The development of sound conceptual bases for the interfacing of impact projection components must be initiated and pursued with resolve.

FACTORS AFFECTING MODEL INTEGRATION

The integration of socioeconomic model components is affected by two sets of often difficult to reconcile factors. Extensive integration is necessitated by the nature of socioeconomic phenomena, but the methodological implementation of such interfaces is often limited by the nature of the impact assessment process and by the limits of existing techniques and data. The factors underlying these dimensions are discussed below.

The need to examine the interrelationships between economic, demographic, public service, fiscal, and social impact dimensions is evident to anyone familiar with social science literature or with the impacts of major resource developments. Because it is neither possible nor appropriate, given the focus of this book, to chronicle the many individual interactions that occur between social science dimensions in impact situations and because elements of these interactions are described in several other chapters (for example, see Chapter 1) and in numerous places in the impact literature (Gilmore and Duff, 1975; Gilmore et al., 1976b; Albrecht, 1978; Cortese and Jones, 1977; Murdock and Leistritz, 1979), it is not necessary to list all of the interactions in each individual area. It seems appropriate, however, to discuss some of the broad impact events that necessitate an integrated social science approach by examining key interactions between each dimension and all others. The intent is thus to exemplify rather than to comprehensively delineate the interactions that underlie the need for component integration.

Although impact events involve a large number of dimensions (Murdock and Leistritz, 1979), they are, in large part, the result of an initial economic stimulus to the local economy. As such, economic dimensions require careful integration with all other social science dimensions. The effects of increased employment, income, and business activity, as well as a likely shift in the overall economic structure of an entire area as a development proceeds, will affect other socioeconomic dimensions (see Chapter 2 and Leistritz et al., 1980a). Employment-related growth means that the total population of the area will become larger, that more children will enter the population, and that persons with more diverse needs and desires will enter the area. Increased business activity also leads to indirect population growth as new service industries arrive to provide additional services to project-related populations. In addition, a larger proportion of young adults who might otherwise have left the area may remain in the area and obtain project-related employment. Economic changes lead to significant demographic changes in population structure and composition and affect present and future population patterns.

Economic impacts also affect service functions directly, by increasing the public and private potential for purchasing services, and indirectly, through population and fiscal effects. Increases in purchasing power lead to increased demands for more and better quality public services. New persons brought in by the increased economic activity increase the numerical level of demands on public services and may demand service levels comparable in quality to those in their former areas of residence. The income generated by new persons and the increased incomes of many longtime residents as a result of the project will, in turn, increase both public revenues and expenditures and the availability of funds to support public services.

Expanded economic activity affects fiscal factors through growth in local area personal income and business volume and hence in tax revenues (income, sales, and property taxes). Economic growth is also likely to lead to increased expenditures particularly if a significant number of inmigrating employees are needed to meet the demands of an expanding labor market. Thus, both fiscal revenues and expenditures show numerous areas of interaction with economic activity.

Social dimensions are also closely related to and interrelated with economic dimensions. Increases in business activity often lead to increased demands on private and public leadership, to subsequent shifts in leadership patterns and to

the emergence of new more growth- (or nongrowth-) oriented
leaders. Increased costs for housing and other services may
adversely affect those on fixed incomes and other disadvan-
taged groups. Changing income situations may alter the social
class structure of the local area, causing increased social
mobility for some residents and decreased mobility for others
(Murdock and Schriner, 1978). As new employment-related groups
move into the area, interaction patterns in the area may be
changed, friendship patterns may be altered, and perceptions of
the community may change rapidly (Albrecht, 1978).

In short, economic impacts have ramifications throughout
all other socioeconomic dimensions. They provide a major
impetus to impacts in other dimensions and must be systematically interrelated with each of the other dimensions.

Demographic impacts also have close interrelationships and
require careful interfacing with each of the other dimensions.
In addition to those relationships with economic dimensions
already noted, the demographic structure of the area may be a
major factor in determining even the feasibility of initiating
a resource development. The existing demographic structure
will, in large part, determine the size of the local labor
force (Easterlin et al., 1978); and the characteristics of
that population (for example, its levels of education) will
determine the quality of that labor force. Both of these factors may affect the developer's decision to initiate a project.
After a development is initiated, local demographic structures
and economic conditions continue to have reciprocal effects.
As young people reach employment age, economic opportunities
will affect their decision whether to remain in the area or to
migrate from it, and these decisions, in turn, will affect the
labor force available for the development.

The demographic growth resulting from development inter-
acts in numerous ways with service and fiscal factors. Its
size affects the magnitude of new service demands and the
characteristics of those involved in that growth will affect
the type of demands. The size of the new population will influence local revenues and expenditures and its characteristics
will affect the relative magnitude of each. For example, if
the project-related population growth involves the inmigration
of very young adults, it will lead to greater demand for apartments and mobile homes but to less demand for single-family
dwellings than if the inmigration involves older groups. Since
the per capita revenues generated by apartments and particularly mobile homes are less than for single-family dwellings,
the younger inmigrating population is likely to generate less
new revenue than an older population of migrants. Fiscal patterns and the services dependent on them are thus closely related to demographic patterns.

The effects of demographic factors on social phenomena
are especially significant. The size and distribution of the

new project-related population will determine the magnitude of the effects on local social structures and whether new persons dominate or are dominated by the existing structure. In turn, the composition (age, ethnic, and regional background) of the new population may determine the acceptability of the new population to the indigenous population and the extent to which new residents seek and obtain leadership and other positions of dominance in the area.

Overall, demographic phenomena are interrelated with each of the other dimensions. As with economic dimensions, demographic factors require interfaces with all other components.

The interfaces of fiscal and service factors have already been extensively described, but it is necessary to emphasize that they are not only affected by other components but, in turn, affect the nature of economic, demographic, and social factors. Continued economic growth in a region is affected by its tax structure and the existence of local services (Lonsdale and Seyler, 1979). Overtaxed service capabilities and negative fiscal impacts may lead to shifts in labor force residence patterns. Inadequate services or decreases in services due to insufficient public revenue growth are major determinants of community satisfaction (Christensen, 1976). Such social impacts as leadership changes and community conflict often result from controversies over local revenues and expenditures and from inadequate service provision. Fiscal and service dimensions are interrelated with other factors as both causes and effects.

The social dimension is the most comprehensive and the most poorly understood of the socioeconomic impact dimensions (see Chapter 6). Despite extensive descriptive and empirical analyses that establish the significance of such factors (Gold, 1974; Freudenburg, 1980; Albrecht, 1978; Cortese and Jones, 1977; Murdock and Schriner, 1978), few have been systematically linked with other social science dimensions in impact projections. Social factors, such as resistance to developments, however, often affect the very likelihood of a development being accepted in an area. They affect the local levels of employment availability through their effects on career preferences, and they affect local revenues and expenditures through their effects on public acceptance of tax increases and revenue distribution formulas. Social dimensions must be integrated with economic, demographic, public service, and fiscal dimensions if effective and comprehensive projections are to be made.

These are only some of the many interrelations between socioeconomic dimensions. It is clearly impossible to adequately simulate the impacts of resource developments without taking these interrelationships into account, and this simulation is impossible without the development of effective procedures for interfacing the socioeconomic dimensions in impact projections.

The realities of the impact assessment process as well as
the stage of development of existing methodological techniques,
however, have resulted in interfaces that seldom approach the
levels of detail necessary to adequately simulate the interactions noted above. Most impact assessments must be performed
with severely limited time and financial resources. As a
result, the nature of the impact assessment process often
leaves little time and provides few resources for the conceptualization or implementation of interfaces. Such limitations
have meant that many of the conceptual ideals noted in the
last section, such as the use of local level interface procedures and multiple interface points, have required data and
conceptual approaches that could not be developed.

Even more limiting, however, has been the lack of adequate
baseline data and integration procedures. It is essential to
note that we simply do not have the necessary data or procedures for interfacing numerous dimensions that are known to
be interactively and iteratively related. Thus, the data and
procedures have not been developed for interfacing such factors
as: (1) income change with outmigration rates; (2) changes in
age and sex composition with tax revenues; (3) service quality
with local employment retention; (4) service provision with
public revenues; (5) changes in migration rates for indigenous
young adults with increased service demands; and (6) if quantitative procedures are desired, for social dimensions with
virtually any of the other dimensions. The conceptual basis
for implementing, the data necessary to implement, and the
procedures for implementing socioeconomic interfaces have yet
to be adequately developed.

To summarize, there is little doubt that the realities of
impact events require that interfaces between socioeconomic
dimensions be established. Unfortunately, it is equally evident that among the most important factors affecting the use
of interface procedures in impact assessments is the underdeveloped conceptual and empirical state-of-the-art of impact
assessment. Until these conceptual and empirical bases are
adequately developed, severe limitations will continue to be
evident in impact interfaces.

TECHNIQUES FOR INTERFACING SOCIOECONOMIC ASSESSMENTS

The interface techniques used in actual impact assessment
procedures are presented in this section. Although some variations may appear in individual impact assessments, as a whole,
there are relatively few deviations from the general procedures noted below. Additional discussion of these procedures
can be obtained from several excellent reference sources
(Chalmers and Anderson, 1977; Denver Research Institute, 1979;

Murdock et al., 1979a; Murphy and Williams, 1978; Burchell and Listokin, 1978).

The discussion emphasizes quantitative interfaces and the most established techniques in each interface area. The interfaces between economic, demographic, public service, fiscal, and social dimensions will be discussed in turn beginning with descriptions of economic and demographic interfaces with other dimensions. Because these interfaces involve a limited number of combinations, this approach decreases the discussion of interface procedures from the perspective of the fiscal, service, and social dimensions. It is important to recognize, however, that this is only a product of the mode of discussion and does not reflect the relative importance of these dimensions. Effective interfaces must involve the merging of co-equal factors from multiple dimensions. Because of the extensive description of some interfaces (such as the economic-demographic) in other chapters, the discussion of some interfaces is limited in this section.

The economic dimension is generally interfaced with the demographic and fiscal dimensions and seldom directly interfaced, at least quantitatively, with either the service or social dimensions. As a result, only its interfaces with the demographic and fiscal components are discussed here.

The economic-demographic interface is the most thoroughly developed of all interface procedures. It has received extensive attention (Denver Research Institute, 1979; Murdock et al., 1979a; Cluett et al., 1977), and similar forms are becoming evident in most impact assessments. The two procedures most commonly used are population to employment ratios (either a total ratio or separate ratios for different types of employment) and techniques which match available and required employment. Since each of these is described in considerable detail in Chapter 3, only the general form and characteristics of these procedures are noted below.

The use of single or employment-specific population to employment ratios was the first technique widely used to interface employment growth with population growth in impact analyses. It was nearly the only procedure used in early impact assessments (Dalsted et al., 1974) and may still be the most widely used technique (Denver Research Institute, 1979; Murphy and Williams, 1978). The technique involves a direct projection of population assuming that each employed person will have a given number (such as 1.9 or 2.5) of persons associated with them.

The disadvantages of this technique stem from its almost total dependence on the economic component. The demographic structure of and changes in the site area affect the result of the interface only as they affect the population to employment ratio. There are no mechanisms for taking other demographic factors into account and so a constant ratio or a ratio with a fixed pattern of change must be used. The technique is also usually single-faceted, noninteractive, and noniterative. Its advantages are its ease of use, ready data availability, and clarity. Its utility appears limited except in circumstances in which only limited data are available.

The second form of economic-demographic interface involves a matching of employment demands from the economic model with estimates of labor availability from the demographic model (see Hertsgaard et al., 1978; Murdock et al., 1979b; Cluett et al., 1977, and Chapter 3). The unique characteristic of this procedure is in the projection of labor availability (labor supply). The supply factor is estimated by applying a labor force participation rate (or a set of rates) to a projected base of population. If demographic detail is provided in the participation rate or rates used (such as age or age and sex detail), then the characteristics of the demographic structure of the area are taken into account. These estimates of available labor are matched with labor demands to produce a projection of the extent to which labor demand either exceeds or is less than the labor supply. The excess or deficit of labor demand in comparison to labor supply is, in turn, used to project migrating labor. Finally, the demographic impacts of in- or outmigrating workers are determined by applying a set of employment-related demographic characteristics (i.e., family size, age of dependents, etc.) to the projection of in- or outmigrating workers.

The advantages of the procedure are that it allows both economic and demographic characteristics to affect the results of the interface. Through the inclusion of demographic as well as economic characteristics, both changes in population and employment structure affect the level of expected new employment and population. In addition, if the technique includes a procedure for differentially matching different types of employment demands to different types of available labor, the procedure may more effectively simulate the actual effects of increased employment opportunities on shifting employment patterns in developing areas.

The disadvantages of this technique lie in the relatively large data bases that are required for its use and in the relatively large number of projections and explicit assumptions that underlie the matching procedure. Data must be obtained on labor force participation rates by detailed characteristics, the extent to which various types of available labor may be able and willing to fill different kinds of labor demands, the demographic characteristics of various types of labor, and numerous other factors. These data items are often simply not available without extensive primary data collection. Explicit assumptions must be made not only about employment demands, but about future labor force participation rates, about future labor supplies and their compatibility with various types of

demands about the characteristics of workers in the future,
and about the demographic patterns that underlie the base to
which the assumed labor force participation rates are applied.
The detail used in this procedure thus requires extensive
data bases.

Whatever procedure is used, the economic-demographic interface is logically the first performed and, in a sequential
assessment procedure, its accuracy and its level of detail will
affect the accuracy and level of detail of subsequent procedures. Its design requires careful elaboration and systematic
analysis.

The economic-fiscal interface is a multifaceted interface
in which public sector revenues are either directly interfaced
with economic factors or indirectly interfaced with economic
factors through population, and expenditures are indirectly
interfaced through the demographic component. Although some
authors delineate up to six major interface procedures
(Burchell and Listokin, 1978), most existing techniques appear
to be derived from two basic procedures.

The simplest of these is an indirect procedure involving
the use of per capita rates. Given that an economic-
demographic interface has been completed, this procedure uses
projections of new population and, by application of per capita
revenue and expenditure values, projects total public sector
costs and revenues. Single per capita revenue and expenditure
ratios or ratios that are specific to different types of revenues and expenditures may be used but in each case population
as determined by economic factors forms the basis of the interface.

The advantage of this technique lies in the simplicity of
its data inputs and its ease of computation. Its disadvantages
are similar to those for population to employment ratios in
that differences in the nature of different types of fiscal
events are not adequately simulated.

The second general procedure is more direct. It involves
interfacing data on project-related personal income and gross
business volume with appropriate data on tax rates and assessment ratios to determine tax revenues and the application of
costs per capita or per unit of service to determine expenditures. In this procedure, income, sales, and other corporate
tax rates are applied directly to the estimated project-related
increases in personal income and business activity. Other
major tax revenues, such as property taxes, are usually obtained by the application of average tax levels per capita or
per type of unit (for example, apartment, single-family dwell-
ing). Expenditures are derived from the application of either
per capita costs by type of expenditure or costs per unit
of service. In this latter procedure, the units of service
required are based on rates per unit of population. The application of these rates to projected population values determines

total units required, and an average cost per unit is applied to the number of units to determine total expenditures for the service. For example, hospital costs per hospital bed might be used to determine total hospital costs.

This second procedure uses a wider range of economic inputs in the projection of public revenues. Its advantages lie in the greater level of differentiation it allows in the specification of the forms of inputs that enter into the economic part of the interface. As such, it allows differences in these inputs by areas to be taken into account and avoids the assumption of an average mix of economic changes in impact areas. This can be particularly important because the patterns of distribution of employment-related impacts may be quite different from those for the business activity associated with a project. Its disadvantages stem from the greater complexity it demands in the economic forecasting procedures and the greater detail it requires in the application of tax rates and cost schedules.

Overall, the economic-fiscal interface procedures demonstrate the complexity of interactions involved in socioeconomic impact events. Economic activity, demographic patterns, and service demands as well as revenue and expenditure patterns operate interdependently, and their interfaces require multiple-level conceptualization and methodological development.

Although demographic interfaces with economic dimensions have been discussed, the interface between demographic and fiscal components requires further explication, and demographic and service interfaces must be described. Each of these interfaces is discussed below.

As noted in the discussion of the economic-fiscal interfaces, the most frequent means for projecting the fiscal impacts resulting from a resource development are: (1) on the basis of per capita rates applied to new populations; or (2) on the basis of per unit revenues and costs with the number of units having been determined on the basis of population projections. The procedures underlying these techniques have been described above and require little further explication, but both the advantages and disadvantages of these procedures should be specified.

The major elements of the procedures delineated above are as follows: (1) a set of per capita revenue and cost rates; (2) a set of rates or units required per unit of population; (3) estimates of costs per unit of service; and (4) a set of projections of future population levels. This latter element involves the limitations inherent in the demographic projection process, and these limitations affect the accuracy of fiscal projections. The use of per capita rates rather than characteristic-specific rates involves an averaging over various population types that can mask significant differences in the

revenue generating and expenditure patterns of different population groups. The use of costs per unit of service has the
advantage of providing cost estimates on the basis of different types of services, but requires the use of difficult to
confirm assumptions about service to population ratios. In
addition, none of the interfaces provide effective feedback
on the economies of scale or other factors that may arise from
the larger service bases accompanying increased populations
(Lansford, 1980). Finally, the assumed linearity of the relationship between expenditures and revenues and population has
not been adequately evaluated.

The advantages of these techniques lie in their simplicity
and data availability. Per capita costs can easily be dis-
cerned from censuses of governments and capital and operating
costs from a variety of engineering and other widely available
estimates (Intermountain Planners, 1974; Stenehjem and Metzger,
1976; Murphy and Williams, 1978). These characteristics seem
likely to insure the continued use of these procedures.

Interfaces between demographic and public service functions show relatively little variation from one assessment
to another, as noted in Chapter 4. Population, either total
or characteristic-specific (usually age or age and sex-
specific population values), is used as a base to which rates
of service demands per unit of population, such as hospital
beds per 1000 population or police officers per 1000 population, are applied. The major variation in the use of such procedures is in the extent to which the interfaces take existing
service levels into account. The inclusion of a means of taking existing service bases into account is highly desirable in
demographic-service interfaces and is often completed by com-
piling an inventory of existing services. This inventory is
then compared to established standards (Intermountain Planners,
1974; Murphy and Williams, 1978), and the net deficit or excess
of baseline services by type is determined by comparing projected and existing capacity.

The demographic-public service interfaces described above
are easy to use and are based on relatively easy to obtain
data. Few, however, take quality or distributional characteristics of services into account. They provide quantitative indicators only and require considerable interpretation and description when employed.

The last of the major quantitative interfaces is that between the fiscal and the public service dimensions. This
interface normally involves, as noted earlier, the merger of
per unit costs with estimates of service demands. Given the
extensive description of this interface earlier in the discussion of economic and fiscal interfaces, it is necessary here
only to note the relative advantages and disadvantages of this
interface procedure.

Foremost among the advantages of this procedure are the

ready availability of the data required to effect it and the
ease and wide range of circumstances under which it can be
applied. Its disadvantages include its dependence on the
underlying assumptions of the techniques used to project the
service and fiscal inputs and the fact that the procedure
provides a relatively simplistic perspective on the complex set
of interactions that actually take place between fiscal and
service factors.

The last set of interfaces to be discussed are those
between social and other dimensions. Such interfaces have
received little attention, and those that have been used have
been qualitative in nature. The majority of these interfaces
have involved two approaches -- qualitative evaluations by researchers of the social implications of a given impact in
another dimension or solicitations of experts' (or random
samples of residents') perceptions of the social meaning of a
given type of impact. The latter techniques most closely
approximate interfacing procedures while the former are forms
of data interpretation.

Although discussions of the pros and cons of expert versus
random sample surveys are discussed in Chapter 6, it is essential to point out that even these techniques tend to make the
social dimension a product of, rather than an active aspect in,
the interface procedure. For example, when respondents' evaluations of the implications of a given level of population
growth on community leadership are analyzed, the interactive
effect of community leadership on population growth is seldom
taken into account. In the poorly developed interfaces that
have been designed between social and other dimensions, then,
social factors tend to be treated as reactive rather than interactive.

The interfaces between social and other dimensions that
have been developed are largely qualitative. Of these, the
two most often discussed are the demographic-social and
the economic-social interfaces. The relationship most often
drawn upon in the discussion of social impacts is that between
population growth and social change. Whether conceptually or
heuristically, the effects of population growth are used to
project social events during impact situations. Coupled with
this technique has been the examination of the effects of economic growth on social factors. Demographic and economic
changes have become the mainstays for explaining social impacts. Thus, the social factors associated with population
growth and economically induced processes -- such as ecological
expansion (Murdock, 1979), urbanization, modernization, and
economic development (Carnes and Friesma, 1974) -- form the
major theoretical basis for explaining social impacts. In fact,
although social conditions are sometimes discussed in relation
to service or fiscal factors (Gilmore and Duff, 1975; Gilmore
et al., 1976b), it is only the economic and demographic inter-

faces with social dimensions that have received sufficient attention to merit discussion as interfaces.

Because of the lack of development of social interfaces, none are sufficiently developed to merit a discussion of their strengths and weaknesses. It is, in fact, sufficient to simply point out that social interfaces must be developed. Until this is done, the role of social analysis within impact analyses will remain largely a peripheral and ineffectual one.

SUMMARY AND CONCLUSIONS

The conceptual and methodological bases for interfacing socioeconomic dimensions have received insufficient development. No clear conceptual premises have been developed to form a basis for interface development, and existing procedures have evolved from only a few basic techniques developed largely on the basis of convenience. Although the development of conceptual bases for interfaces requires further attention, an initial evaluation suggests that the use of common procedures for both baseline and impact interfaces, the employment of such interfaces at the lowest appropriate geographical level, the retention of the most significant aspects of each component in the interface procedure, the use of multiple interface points, and the use of interfaces with feedback or iterative mechanisms are desirable features in the design of interface procedures. At present, most interfaces are single-point, single-dimension, and noniterative and thus require extensive development.

Of the interface procedures most widely used, the economic-demographic interface is the most developed and complex and may be multifaceted, multidimensional, and iterative. Nearly all other interfaces involve the application of rates or ratios from one dimension to the outputs of another dimension. The interfaces so designed include the economic-fiscal, the demographic-fiscal, the demographic-service, and the service-fiscal interfaces. The interfaces of social and other dimensions are the least developed and are largely qualitative.

The status of socioeconomic interfaces reflects both problems and promises. The fact that relatively few of the necessary interfaces have been designed and that many of the existing ones lack the breadth and complexity necessary to adequately simulate the interactions that take place between social science dimensions in impact situations points to the primitive stage of development of interfaces. It indicates the need for concern about the extent to which socioeconomic assessments do, in fact, provide the integrated assessment mandated by NEPA and believed essential for interdisciplinary research. There is little to lessen this concern in the existing methodologies used or in the conceptual basis underlying impact interfaces.

On the other hand, there is also promise in the socio-economic interfaces that have been used in impact assessments. These interfaces represent some of the first attempts to systematically and quantitatively integrate dimensions from several disciplines and to combine the methodological strengths of the various disciplines. They attempt to combine the economists' methods for characterizing and differentiating parts of an economy, the demographers' techniques for demographic projections, fiscal analysts' knowledge of tax structures, public service analysts' methods for projecting service demands, and the sociologists' techniques of social assessment. Although substantial additional development of these techniques is essential, the progress to date represents a major first step in the formal integration of social science dimensions.

The future development of interface procedures is likely to be demanding and exciting. There is substantial work to be completed to bridge the conceptual gaps between, and to design the techniques necessary to combine, elements that span several disciplines. If impact researchers are careful to insure that scientists from all the appropriate disciplines play an equitable role in the evolution of these interfaces, then the tasks to be done may also be among the most creative and successful of those undertaken by social scientists in the coming years. The interfacing of socioeconomic dimensions provides a challenge and an opportunity for social scientists to attain the often enunciated goal of producing a truly integrated approach to social science analyses.

8
Computerized Impact Projection Models

As indicated in the preceding chapters, each of the aspects of socioeconomic impact assessment may require a large number of very precise calculations. Because the sheer volume of these computations may become quite burdensome, it has become increasingly attractive to systematize the computational procedures. In addition, the usefulness of techniques for economic, demographic, public service, and fiscal impact assessment may be quite limited unless important interactions among these impact categories can be taken into account (see Chapter 1). In response to the need to more systematically account for interrelationships among the various impact dimensions and to provide for integration of impact assessment techniques, many analysts have attempted to develop comprehensive models which incorporate a number of impact categories and provide for specific linkages among these impact dimensions.

Another important factor influencing the development of socioeconomic impact assessment techniques is the needs of decision makers. Local decision makers in particular not only want specific answers; they want timely ones. Despite the growing number of impact assessments, such analyses are often difficult to understand and too outdated to meet local needs. The frequency of changes in development dimensions, such as changes in facility size, location, and other factors, often negate the validity of the assumptions on which the formal impact assessment of a project may have been based. As a result, many impact statements tend to be outdated before they are published, and the differences between the effects they predict and those that may occur as a result of altered project structures may be impossible for local decision makers to discern. As a result of such problems, local decision makers and planners have increasingly demanded impact assessments and impact assessment methods that provide local area projections for a wide range of socioeconomic factors under a variety of possible sets of development scenarios and that do so with only a limited time delay in the production of such projections.

207

In response to these demands, a substantial number of computerized socioeconomic impact assessment models have been developed. These models all provide a relatively wide range of outputs and do so in a timely and flexible manner. Further, they provide a valuable mechanism for systematically accounting for interactions among the various impact dimensions. These models, however, differ widely in input data requirements, computational procedures, outputs, and in many other respects. The criteria that should be used in choosing such a model and the relative advantages of the various models under different circumstances are often difficult to discern. As a result, decision makers may avoid using such models despite their obvious advantages or may use an inappropriate model because they have no means of evaluating the relative merits of different models.

The purpose of this chapter is threefold. First, the history of the development of computerized socioeconomic impact assessment models is briefly reviewed. Then a number of such models which have been employed extensively in impact assessment and policy analysis are briefly described. Finally, criteria for the evaluation of impact assessment models are discussed, and selected models are evaluated in terms of these criteria. The intent is to present information which will be useful to environmental decision makers in evaluating and selecting alternative modeling techniques. The intent is not to suggest which are the best models, for the models have counterbalancing strengths and weaknesses, but rather to provide a basis for choosing models to meet specific needs.

HISTORICAL BACKGROUND OF COMPUTERIZED MODELS

The basic techniques for economic and demographic impact assessment have been developed and refined over a considerable period (see Chapters 2 and 3). Public service and fiscal impact analyses have a shorter but still substantial history (see Chapters 4 and 5). During the decade of the 1960s, however, there was growing recognition of the interdependence of various forces and hence an increasing interest in finding ways of taking such interdependencies into account. During the same period, the capability for developing more complex models which would integrate multiple dimensions was greatly enhanced by the increasing power and availability of electronic computers. Early work emphasized both developing more complete, detailed models for single dimensions (e.g., economic, demographic) and attempting to integrate various dimensions (e.g., economic activity and population, population and land use). Early activity in social science modeling was concentrated in the areas of national econometric models and urban land use models.[1] By the end of the decade, however,

some attention had been given to both: (1) integration of
the economic and demographic areas of study; and (2) application of integrated economic-demographic models in rural areas.

The development of integrated economic-demographic models
also was stimulated by an increased interest in alternative
economic development strategies for lesser developed countries.
Because analysis of alternative development strategies in such
settings appeared to require explicit consideration of interactions among diverse phenomena in the economic and demographic systems, substantial resources were devoted to the
development of integrated economic-demographic models for a
number of countries.[2]

One regional economic-demographic model which was developed during the late 1960s had a substantial influence on subsequent socioeconomic modeling efforts. The Susquehanna River
Basin Model differed from most earlier models in that it provided for a specific linkage of the economic and demographic
sectors and that it included nonmetropolitan areas whereas
previous models had generally focused only on a single large
city (Hamilton et al., 1966; Hamilton et al., 1969). The
model made extensive use of feedback loops to link its various
components, a structure which was inspired at least in part by
the earlier work of Forrester (1961).

The research group at Battelle Laboratories which developed the Susquehanna Model subsequently constructed similar
models for the city of San Diego (San Diego Comprehensive Planning Organization, 1972) and for the state of Arizona (Battelle
Columbus Laboratories, 1973). The Susquehanna Model also influenced the structure of a regional forecasting model developed by the Tennessee Valley Authority (Bohm and Lord, 1972).
These models in turn influenced subsequent model development
efforts (see Figure 8.1). Noteable among these were the series
of economic-demographic models developed by the states of
Arizona and Utah (Bigler et al., 1972; Anderson et al., 1974;
Reeve and Weaver, 1974; Beckhelm et al., 1975; Anderson and
Hannigan, 1977), the MULTIREGION Model developed at Oak Ridge
National Laboratory (Olsen et al., 1975; Olsen et al., 1977b),
the North Platte River Basin Model (Matson and Studer, 1975;
Carlson et al., 1976), and the CPE Model developed at the University of Colorado (Office of State Oil Shale Coordinator,
1974).

These models all provided for linkage of the economic and
demographic sectors through a submodel which simulated the
operation of the labor market and provided for in- or outmigration from the study area in response to changes in labor
market conditions (i.e., if the demand for labor increased
more rapidly than the "natural increase" in labor supply, inmigration would occur). The models differ somewhat in the
degree of sectoral disaggregation within the economic module,
however. For example, while the Susquehanna Model utilized
only three employment categories, the ATOM-3 Model included

210

FIGURE 8.1. PARTIAL GENEALOGY OF SOCIOECONOMIC IMPACT
ASSESSMENT MODELS, 1960-1979

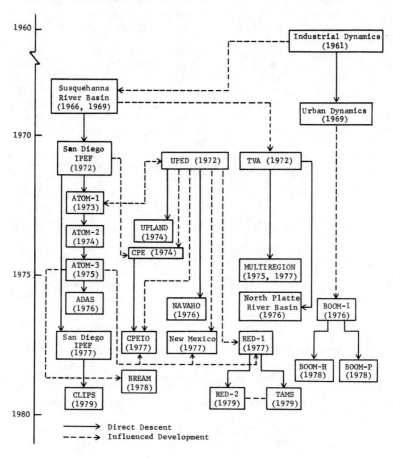

88 employment sectors. The models also differ in the degree
of spatial detail of their outputs with some providing employment and population projections at the county level (e.g.,
ATOM, UPED, CPE), and others providing projections only at the
multicounty regional level (e.g., Susquehanna, MULTIREGION).
Finally, these models differed significantly in the time increments associated with their projections. While a few
models provided projections annually (e.g., ATOM-3), several
produced estimates only at five-year intervals (e.g., UPED,
MULTIREGION).

Socioeconomic projection models developed during the late
1960s and early 1970s were employed primarily as tools for
state and regional economic planning. As interest in evaluating community-specific impacts of major projects grew, however,
these models were found to have substantial limitations as impact assessment tools. The two principal limitations were
failure to include a number of significant impact dimensions,
particularly public service requirements and fiscal effects,
and insufficient spatial and temporal disaggregation of outputs. Thus, in the mid-1970s, attention turned to developing
models which incorporated additional impact dimensions and
provided outputs at county and subcounty levels. A number of
models were developed to meet these needs, including the RED-1
and RED-2 models (Hertsgaard et al., 1978; Leistritz et al.,
1979a); the BREAM Model (Mountain West Research Inc., 1978);
the BOOM Models (Ford, 1976; Monts, 1978; Rink and Ford, 1978);
the SEAM Model (Stenehjem, 1978); the WEST Model (Denver Research Institute, 1979); and the SIMPACT Model (Huston, 1979).

These "second-generation" models differ from the earlier
economic-demographic projection models primarily in the number
of impact categories included and in the degree of spatial and
temporal disaggregation of their outputs. Thus, several of
these models address public service requirements and public
sector cost and revenue effects as well as economic and demographic impacts (e.g., RED, WEST, SIMPACT); some provide projections for individual cities, school districts, or other
subcounty areas as well as for counties and regions (e.g.,
BREAM, RED, WEST); and most provide yearly projections of key
impact indicators. The specific characteristics of a number
of these models are described and compared in the sections
which follow.

MAJOR COMPUTERIZED PROJECTION MODELS

Several factors were considered in selecting the specific
models to be examined. First, attention was focused on models
that address multiple dimensions of economic and social impacts
and that provide projections at the county or subcounty levels.
Second, those models which have been applied extensively in assessing impacts of resource development projects or which were

designed for such applications have been given greatest attention. After models had been identified, we attempted to
obtain complete documentation materials for each. In some
cases, lack of available documentation materials precluded detailed examination of a model.

The models which were selected for detailed examination
include the following:

1. ATOM-3 (Beckhelm et al., 1975)
2. BOOM-1 (Ford, 1976)
3. BREAM (Mountain West Research Inc., 1978)
4. CLIPS (Monts and Bareiss, 1979)
5. CPEIO (Monarchi and Taylor, 1977)
6. HARC (Cluett et al., 1977)
7. MULTIREGION (Olsen et al., 1977b)
8. NAVAHO (Reeve et al., 1976)
9. NEW MEXICO (Brown and Zink, 1977)
10. RED (Hertsgaard et al., 1978; Leistritz et al., 1979a)
11. SEAM (Stenehjem, 1978)
12. SIMPACT (Huston, 1979)
13. WEST (Denver Research Institute, 1979)

Each of these models is briefly described in the following
sections.

ATOM-3 Model

The ATOM-3 (Arizona Trade-Off Model) was developed by re-
searchers at Arizona State University with sponsorship from the
Arizona Office of Economic Planning and Development and the
Four Corners Regional Commission (Beckhelm et al., 1975). It
represents a substantial refinement of the earlier ATOM-1 and
ATOM-2 models. The model has been utilized extensively by the
State of Arizona as a state and regional planning tool.[3]
ATOM-3 consists of three major submodels: demographic,
employment, and labor market. The demographic submodel incorporates a cohort-survival routine utilizing 172 single-year
age-sex cohorts. Two subgroups of the population are identified, the Indian community and the military population; and
these subgroups are accorded special treatment in the demographic calculations. The employment submodel incorporates an
88-sector input-output model for the state. Employment for
most sectors is projected at the state level and then allocated
among the state's 14 counties. The labor market submodel links
the other two modules by evaluating the consistency of the output from the demographic submodel with that from the employment
submodel. If there is an excess of jobs relative to the size
of the labor force (i.e. if the implied unemployment rate falls
below some lower bound), it is assumed that inmigration will
occur to reestablish the balance between the supply of and demand for labor. Conversely, if there is an excess supply of

labor, it is assumed that outmigration will occur. Thus, the basic interrelationship between economic and demographic activity in ATOM-3 is the same as that found in a number of socioeconomic simulation models that have a common ancestry going back to the Susquehanna River Basin Model (Beckhelm et al., 1975).

BOOM-1 Model

The BOOM-1 model was developed by personnel at Los Alamos Scientific Laboratory and has been utilized in a number of policy analyses. The model employs simulation techniques to estimate interaction between construction of a large-scale energy facility and secondary growth, migration, housing, and public service consequences (Ford, 1976). It emphasizes systems dynamics features which allow projection of important variables by simulating multiple interactions among sectors.[4] Some 48 parameters are incorporated in model relationships with the values of most of these parameters being drawn from other studies or based on "expert opinion and individual intuition" (Ford, 1976). Little site-specific data is employed in the model.

BOOM-1 contains five major subsectors: power plant, housing, retail and service, migration, and public. The model incorporates numerous interactions among these subsectors. For example, population may grow at levels higher than originally anticipated because adverse boomtown conditions induce high rates of construction worker turnover and reduce productivity, prompting expansion of the construction work force. The model provides projections for a single community only, and in the original version of the model the outputs were quite aggregated (e.g., total population, aggregate public sector revenues and costs for all jurisdictions). The housing sector has subsequently been refined by Los Alamos personnel (Rink and Ford, 1978), and the public sector has been substantially disaggregated by researchers at the University of Texas (Monts, 1978).

BREAM Model

The Bureau of Reclamation Economic Assessment Model (BREAM) was developed for the U.S. Bureau of Reclamation by Mountain West Research, Inc. The model is employed by the Bureau in preparing impact assessments of water development and other resource development projects in the western states. The model's structure and data sources are described by Mountain West Research, Inc. (1978).

The model contains five major submodels. The model evaluates the consistency of the labor supply projections obtained from analysis of the area's population (demographic submodel) with labor demand implied by analysis of the area's economy (economic submodel). In the event that the supply and demand for labor are not in balance, adjustments are assumed to occur (labor market submodel). The principal adjustment mechanism is migration, although changes in the local unemployment rate also are assumed to occur. The fourth submodel (construction worker submodel) is used whenever a project is expected to require inmigration of construction workers. This submodel estimates the number of construction workers who will in-migrate, the demographic characteristics of these workers and their families, and their settlement pattern. Once employment and income are established for each county in the local impact area, the model disaggregates the county population projections and allocates them to the communities within the county (community allocation submodel).

CLIPS Model

The CLIPS (Community Level Impact Projection System) Model was developed by the Center for Energy Studies at the University of Texas at Austin under sponsorship of the Texas Energy Advisory Council (Monts and Bareiss, 1979). It was developed primarily to evaluate the local socioeconomic impacts of lignite coal development in Texas, but information regarding specific applications of the model was not available.

The CLIPS Model provides baseline and impact projections of employment, population, public service requirements, and associated costs for a designated impact region and for selected counties and cities within the region. Employment projection is accomplished using an export base technique whereby changes in export (basic) employment are determined by exogenously specified growth rates, changes in business-serving (indirect) employment are determined by changes in export employment, and changes in household-serving (induced) employment are determined by changes in the region's population. The population submodel is based on a cohort-survival routine using five-year age-sex cohorts. Regional baseline population projections are used as control totals for the community population projections. A gravity model is used to allocate project-related workers and their families to communities of residence. The CLIPS Model relies heavily on the per capita cost approach in projecting public service costs, and the cost coefficients are drawn primarily from Murphy and Williams (1978).

CPEIO Model

The Colorado Population and Employment (I-O) Model was developed by the Business Research Division of the University of Colorado with sponsorship from the Colorado Department of Local Affairs (Monarchi and Taylor, 1977). The model has been employed as a state and regional planning aid and also has been utilized in several energy development impact assessments.

The model consists of two linked submodels. The population submodel incorporates a cohort-survival routine using single-year cohorts. Four types of migration are considered in the population submodel: (1) retirement, (2) military, (3) college, and (4) employment-related. The population submodel is linked with the employment submodel through employment-related migration. The employment submodel utilizes an input-output framework in which employment rather than dollar value of output is the unit of measurement. The model can accommodate up to 25 employment sectors, and each sector can have basic, business-serving, and household-serving employment components. Assumed exogenous growth rates for basic employment in each relevant sector drive the economic submodel. The CPEIO Model provides annual projections of employment and population for a specified area of interest (i.e., region, county, or city), but it does not project the distribution of effects within the area (Monarchi and Taylor, 1977).

HARC Model

The Battelle HARC Model was developed by a team of researchers at the Battelle Human Affairs Research Centers. The model provides projections of demographic and public service indicators under both baseline and impact conditions for a selected site county. Projections are available at five-year intervals over a 35-year planning horizon (Cluett et al., 1977).

The model utilizes a cohort-survival routine to project baseline population in the affected area on the basis of the initial age-sex composition of the population and recent patterns of net migration. The population estimates are transformed into labor force estimates through the use of national labor force participation rates. The total employment requirements of a new development project are estimated by applying employment multipliers to the construction and permanent work force requirements of the facility (supplied exogenously). The proportion of the direct and indirect work force requirements which can be met by the indigenous population is then computed, and the remainder of the new jobs are assumed to be filled by inmigrants.

Migrating workers and their dependents are allocated to the site county and to adjacent counties with a gravity model which takes account of distance to alternative places of residence, housing availability at those locations, and the area's initial population distribution. Migrants who take up residence in the site county are then projected, separately from the baseline, throughout the projection period. Projections for this project-related population include consideration of employment turnover and replacement and relocation of workers

216

formerly employed at the project (Cluett et al., 1977). Additional requirements for selected public and social services associated with the inmigrating workers and their dependents are estimated by applying state or national standards to the projections of project-related population. Services considered include health, education, sanitation, fire and police, recreation, social problems (e.g., crime), and government (administrative staff).

MULTIREGION Model

The MULTIREGION Model was developed by researchers at the Oak Ridge National Laboratory with sponsorship from the National Science Foundation and the U.S. Energy Research and Development Administration (now U.S. Department of Energy). The model provides projections of employment by 37 industry groups, population by 32 age and sex cohorts, and labor force by 16 age and sex cohorts for 173 BEA (Bureau of Economic Analysis) economic areas at five-year intervals. The model consists of employment and population subsectors linked through a module which simulates labor market conditions. Each of the BEA areas is treated as a labor market area. Labor demand in each area is affected by the area's attractiveness as a location for natural resource-based industries, manufacturing, and local service industries. Labor supply for a region is affected by its patterns of labor force participation, fertility, and mortality; and migration occurs to balance the supply of and demand for labor. Interregional interdependence is incorporated in the model through the inclusion of measures of access to markets via truck transportation. The model is intended for a variety of regional analysis applications (Olsen et al., 1975; Olsen et al., 1977b).

NAVAHO Model

The Navaho Economic-Demographic Model was developed through a cooperative effort between the Navaho Nation and the State of Utah, Office of State Planning Coordinator. The model was designed for use as a tool for economic planning and policy making for the Navaho Nation (Reeve et al., 1976). Its basic structure is quite similar to that of the Utah Process Economic Demographic Model (UPED) which had previously been developed by the State of Utah.

The Navaho Economic-Demographic Model has three major components: an economic module; a demographic module; and an economic-demographic interface module. The economic module uses the economic base employment multiplier technique to project future levels of secondary employment, given initial projections of basic employment. The demographic module utilizes the cohort-survival technique to develop estimates of future population and potential labor force. The interface module

consists of a routine for matching jobs and workers by occupational group and equalizing the supply of and demand for
labor through migration and commuting of Navaho workers and
migration of non-Navaho workers. Model outputs are provided
at five-year intervals and include Navaho and non-Navaho population by age and sex, population by broad occupational
classes, number of households, school age population, Navaho
labor force by age, sex, and broad occupational group, and
basic and residentiary job opportunities by industry and occupation.

NEW MEXICO Model

The New Mexico Economic-Demographic Model was developed by
the Institute for Applied Research Services of the University
of New Mexico with sponsorship from the Four Corners Regional
Commission. The model provides projections for each of the
state's seven planning districts at five-year intervals for
the following variables: population by five-year age and sex
cohorts, school age population by age and grade level, gross
output for 40 industrial sectors, employment for each sector,
labor force by five-year age-sex cohort, net migration by
five-year age-sex cohort, average unemployment rate, and average per capita income (Brown and Zink, 1977). The model is
reported to have been used by several Federal agencies, but no
specific information regarding the nature of this use was
available.

The economic component of this model utilizes a multiregional input-output model with 40 sectors and 12 regions. The
regions are the seven New Mexico planning districts, the
neighboring states of Arizona, Colorado, Utah, and Texas, and
the rest of the United States. The demographic component is a
cohort-survival model using single-year cohorts. The economic
and demographic components are linked through migration. In
this model, economic migration is determined by changes in a
region's unemployment rate (reflecting changes in the supply
of and demand for labor), and the age-sex distribution of migrants is industry-specific. Other (i.e., noneconomic) migration may be specified by the user during scenario development.

RED Model

The REAP Economic-Demographic Model (RED) was developed by
researchers from North Dakota State University, the University
of North Dakota, and Arthur D. Little, Inc. under the auspices
of the North Dakota Regional Environmental Assessment Program,
a state-funded program created to aid planning efforts and to
inform policy making at the local and state levels (Toman et
al., 1979; Hertsgaard et al., 1978). The model consists of six
basic components or submodels: (1) economic input-output mod-

ule; (2) cohort-survival demographic module; (3) economic-
demographic interface module; (4) residential allocation module; (5) service requirements module; and (6) fiscal impact
module.

The input-output module is used to estimate gross business volume by economic sector for a specified level of final
demands. Employment requirements by sector and development
phase are then derived from the estimates of gross business
volume. The demographic module provides projections of population by age and sex and an estimate of the available labor
force. The interface component links the projections of required employment from the input-output module with the projections of available labor force from the demographic module
to determine the level of employment needs that can be met by
the indigenous population and those that must be met by the
inmigration of new workers. The residential allocation module
estimates the settlement patterns of new workers and their
families. The service requirements module develops projections of needs for selected public and quasi-public services
based on changes in population and population composition.
The fiscal impact module provides projections of the expected
costs and revenues resulting from the associated economic and
demographic changes. Outputs are available at the regional,
county, and municipal levels and include such variables as
employment by type, population by age and sex, school enrollment by age, housing requirements by type, public sector costs
and revenues by type, and net fiscal balance.[5]

SEAM Model

Developed at the Argonne National Laboratory, the Social
and Economic Assessment Model (SEAM) contains data on, and has
the capability of being used in, any or all counties in the
continental United States (Stenehjem, 1978). It has been used
by the laboratory staff in conducting several regional assessments and national policy analyses.

The SEAM model consists of four major components. First,
a demographic projection model provides county-level population projections by age, sex, and up to three population
subgroups. Second, an impact projection model forecasts annual changes in employment and population as a result of any
given new energy or industrial project and superimposes these
estimates on the population projections for the subject
county. Third, a spatial allocation model is used in specialized applications when detailed information on housing demands
and settlement patterns of inmigrating workers are required at
the community level. Fourth, a public costs projection model
utilizes population projections from the preceding models in
estimating annual costs of constructing and operating public
facilities and services necessary to accommodate the additional population.

SIMPACT Model

The SIMPACT Model was developed by personnel of Arthur D. Little, Inc., in conjunction with an environmental impact assessment for a large steel manufacturing facility (Huston, 1979). The model has seven major components: (1) an economic-demographic block; (2) a private infrastructure block; (3) a social infrastructure block; (4) a utility infrastructure block; (5) a physical impact block; (6) a fiscal expenditures and finance block; and (7) a fiscal revenue block. The model provides annual projections over a 12-year planning horizon for a region and 11 subareas (e.g., cities or townships).

This model emphasizes detailed disaggregation of projected impacts. In the economic-demographic block, employment, payroll, gross business volume, investment, and land area requirements are projected for 18 sectors using multipliers from regional input-output tables. Population effects are computed from assumed demographic characteristics of inmigrating workers with demographic projections disaggregated by 20 occupation groups, seven income categories, six age groups, and six household size categories. Infrastructure requirements are projected in the areas of housing (10 categories), health facilities (3 categories), schools (4 categories), fire protection, law enforcement, streets, and water, sewer, and solid waste facilities. The physical block includes projection of air pollutant emissions (5 categories), wastewater (by economic sector), and run-off water. Public service costs for each of the local jurisdictions are estimated in the fiscal expenditures and finance block while changes in the revenues of these governmental units as well as for state government are estimated in the fiscal revenue block.

WEST Model

The WEST Model was developed by researchers at the Denver Research Institute under contract with the Council on Environmental Quality (Denver Research Institute, 1979). The model is designed primarily for use by state and local officials and includes employment, population, income, public finance, and housing forecasting components. The employment component uses export base employment multipliers to estimate the levels of secondary (residentiary) employment likely to be associated with an initial increase in project-related basic employment. The population component estimates the magnitude of population growth associated with increased employment through a multi-step process which involves first estimating the proportion of each type of workers who will be inmigrants to the area and then assigning household characteristics to each type of inmigrating worker (e.g., energy facility construction, other energy, secondary). The inmigrating workers and their families are allocated to places of residence using a judgemental approach which emphasizes interviews with community and company officials and local housing developers.

The public finance component includes routines for estimating both revenues and costs of local jurisdictions. The revenue and cost estimation procedures provide for the use of considerable local data regarding effective assessment ratios, tax rates, and per capita expenditure levels. The housing component provides a detailed analysis of the housing preferences of various types of workers, their ability to pay for housing, and the expected costs of various types of housing units. Model outputs are available annually and include employment by type at the county level, population at county and city levels, school enrollment by district, revenues and expenditures (capital and operating) for counties, school districts, and cities, housing by type, and income.

COMPARISON OF FEATURES, STRENGTHS, AND WEAKNESSES OF COMPUTERIZED MODELS

These brief descriptions of different computerized impact assessment models indicate both the similarity of their basic objectives and substantial differences in their input data requirements, computational procedures, and outputs. Without criteria for evaluating such models, the task of choosing an impact model may be quite difficult. In this section, criteria that may be used to evaluate the relative strengths of such models are examined, and the models described above are evaluated in terms of these criteria.

Although the needs of clients and thus the criteria for evaluating models are likely to vary greatly, several model characteristics should be common regardless of the background circumstances. Model evaluation criteria should include: (1) information requirements; (2) methodological forms and validation; and (3) use characteristics. Each of these factors is discussed briefly, followed by a comparison of the models using these criteria.

Informational Requirements

The information needs of the user are clearly the starting point in selecting a modeling system -- what information is needed, for what area, and for what periods of time. Environmental impact assessments are requiring an increasingly large volume of socioeconomic data. These data usually include, at a minimum, information on the economic, demographic, public service, fiscal, and social changes likely to occur under both baseline and impact conditions and for both construction and operational phases (Council on Environmental Quality, 1978).

The economic data usually include changes in income, employment, business activity, and industry mix. Demographic information usually includes data on population increases and, increasingly, information for particular age, ethnic, and other groups and for small geographic units such as municipalities as well as for total impact areas. Public services data include information on new service facilities and personnel required to serve inmigrating populations, while fiscal information emphasizes the costs of such increased services and the public sector revenues likely to be generated by new populations. Social changes are usually measured by the population's perceptions of development, goals for their community, community satisfaction, and likely changes in social structures. Because the costs of acquisition of single data sets (social, economic, etc.) are likely to require investments that may exceed those for an entire modeling effort, the inclusiveness of a model may be particularly significant. Those models that provide larger proportions of the necessary data items are clearly of greater utility.[6]

Equally important is the need to ascertain the levels of geographic output provided by the model and its ability to provide outputs for alternative time periods. Many of the available models provide output only at the total impact area level or for counties, but not for individual cities or other government districts. Such models, though useful for those involved in regional planning and decision making, are likely to be of little utility to the decision maker charged with allocating resources or assessing impacts for school districts or other local units of government.

At the same time, it is essential to insure that models provide results for the necessary temporal periods. Impact periods, particularly construction phases, often show rapid changes from year to year, and these changes often require careful planning and resource allocation. Models providing results for only five-year periods will not reveal year to year changes.

Finally, it is essential that the model provide separate outputs for baseline and for construction impact and operational impact periods. Because impact assessment involves comparing impact induced changes to a projection of baseline changes over time, data for both baseline and impact conditions are essential. In summary, the temporal as well as geographical specificity of model outputs should be carefully considered.

Methodological Considerations

Several aspects of model methodology should enter into evaluations of alternative models. First, some methods are generally more adequate than others. Although, under any set of circumstances, several alternative techniques may be of

equal utility, general assumptions about the utility of specific techniques can be made. For example, even a brief examination of information on demographic projection techniques
will suggest that techniques using age cohorts are generally
more useful than those with less detail (Shryock and Siegel,
1973). A short consultation with experts in the appropriate
fields will generally provide similar information in regard
to other model dimensions. Secondly, it is essential to
evaluate the extent of submodule integration in such models.
Most such models involve a major premise that economic and
demographic aspects of development require careful integration
(see Chapter 7). Some, however, make no attempt at effective
integration of key components but simply apply separate methodologies to a common situation instead. Finally, the
methods employed in such models must be evaluated in terms of
their dynamic capabilities, including: (1) their ability to
project changes in the structure of model relationships over
time (e.g., differential productivity changes in various economic sectors, changes in fertility patterns); (2) their incorporation of the key structural dimensions of the phenomena
of interest; and (3) their incorporation of feedback loops for
updating computational bases.

In general, models that allow the use of multiple rates
for various factors during different phases of the projection
period (such as changes in labor force participation rates or
fertility rates), that utilize factors that most closely differentiate between key dimensions (such as industries or age
cohorts), and that incorporate procedures that feedback
changes, such as alterations of population age structures or
changes in economic structures, are superior to those lacking
such features.

Finally, an overriding factor in model selection must be
an evaluation of a model's accuracy in predicting impact and
baseline conditions. Although most of the models have been
developed recently and relatively little evidence has accumulated for evaluation of their validity, evidence concerning
the validity of some models has been accumulated or can be
derived by using available data sources. In addition, given
samples of model projections for various areas, several types
of evaluations can be made quite easily. For example, estimates of economic factors such as income and employment at the
county level and population levels for counties and incorporated areas are published periodically by the Bureau of Economic Analysis and the Bureau of the Census. These estimates
can be compared to those from the various models, and some
idea of their accuracy can thus be gained. Such analyses provide an essential step in model analysis and model selection.

Use Characteristics

An important use characteristic is the availability and

cost of obtaining the input data required for a model's implementation. For example, some models incorporate input-output economic modules that require the availability of state or regional input-output interdependence coefficients. These are available in many areas, but if an appropriate set of coefficients does not exist, then the implementation of such models is likely to be quite expensive, requiring extensive data collection (see Chapter 2). Similar consideration must be given to other data dimensions.

It is essential to note that models that reduce data collection costs by utilizing national data bases may accentuate problems in projecting local level conditions that depart markedly from national patterns. The trade-off between the need for locally-oriented data inputs and the costs of collecting local data must be carefully evaluated.

The flexibility of use of the model should also be considered. Impact assessments and impact events involve numerous factors that are difficult to evaluate and predict. The range of potential impacts should be examined under widely varying assumptions for such factors. Models that provide easy alterations of these factors and rapid outputs for alternative development scenarios are desirable. In evaluating models, the options provided for altering key assumptions such as the number of projects, size of the project, location of the project, inflation rates, birth rates, per capita service usage rates, and other factors should be closely examined.

Yet an additional factor to be considered is the availability and adaptability of the computerized form of such models. Some models can be accessed only through the agency that implemented the model, while in other cases cooperative agreements can be established to provide the model code for a user agency. In general, efficient use of the model is facilitated by the ability to acquire the model code. In addition, however, it is essential to insure that appropriate computer facilities and computer compilers are available if the computer code is to be obtained. Lack of compatability in hardware configurations and the lack of appropriate language compilers can make model adaptation very costly.

Model Comparison

In this section the models which were described earlier are compared in terms of the criteria noted above. The comparison of these models is presented in three tables; Table 8.1 addresses Criterion 1, the Informational Characteristics of the models. The impact categories included in the model, the project phases, the geographic units, and the time periods for which projections are made are discussed. Impact categories considered as possible components of such models are the economic, demographic, interface, distributional, public service, fiscal, and social components.

224

Table 8.2 compares the methodological characteristics of
the models. These include the methods used in each of the
major model components, the form of integration, the dynamic
capabilities of each component, and the extent of validation
of each model. Characteristics of the economic, demographic,
interface, distributional, service, and fiscal components of
each model are described.

Table 8.3 addresses Criterion 3 and provides information
on use characteristics. In particular, it compares the data
inputs and the computerization requirements of the models and
the extent to which each model allows user input through parameter alteration and the use of interactive programming.

Information provided in available reports for each model
limits the comparisons. In cases where such reports do not
discuss a particular item, the designation INP, information
not provided, is used. Users should conduct careful analyses
of models that appear appropriate for their particular informational needs. Although it is impossible to discuss the data
in Tables 8.1-8.3 in detail, even a brief description of the
items in these tables indicates how diverse the models are in
overall capabilities and characteristics.

As is evident from Table 8.1, only four models (BOOM-1,
RED, SIMPACT, and SEAM) contain as many as five dimensions.
None address social factors, and few contain the potential for
such an expansion. All provide projections for each of the
three vital project phases, but areal coverage varies widely.
Only six models analyze both county and city impacts. Most
provide yearly outputs, but many are limited in the total
number of units that can be included in the model.

In terms of methodological characteristics (Table 8.2),
the differences are less pronounced. Only five systems utilize an input-output approach, and only three do not use a
cohort-component demographic projection technique. Almost
all use an interface procedure that involves the matching of
available and required employment to determine migration
levels. Nearly all are dynamically programmed. None have
received adequate validation, but some have been subjected to
sensitivity and historical simulation analyses.

The use characteristics (Table 8.3) again show great diversity from one model to another. The RED model requires the
greatest amount of primary data while the SEAM model requires
little local data (except for the interface procedure where
local data is necessary for nonwestern areas). All other
models tend to have intermediate data requirements. Only five
of the models are interactive (allowing users to alter various parameters) and, of these, the RED model appears to allow
the alteration of more parameters than other models. Nearly
all of the models are programmed in languages likely to be
available at major computer installations. The use of interactive languages (GASP IV, SIMSCRIPT, and APL) is likely to
decrease the core storage necessary for the use of such

models, and thus models using these languages are likely to be more adaptable to smaller computer systems. On the other hand, at small and medium size installations, compilers for such languages may not be readily available. Finally, in almost all cases, the adaptability of such models is untested. Although several models (including BREAM) incorporate aspects of the ATOM-3 model, and the BOOM-1 and RED models have been adapted by various groups in Texas, the adaptability and transferability of such models remain largely untested. (For an evaluation of one such effort, see Murdock et al., 1980c.)

Overall, the comparisons in Tables 8.1-8.3 suggest that available socioeconomic assessment models are least different in the methods employed and most different in the extent of information provided and in use characteristics. Since these latter two factors are ones central to decision makers' concerns, careful evaluations of individual models are an essential first step in model selection.

SUMMARY AND CONCLUSIONS

An increasing demand for environmental impact assessments has stimulated the development and use of computerized socioeconomic assessment models. The results of the discussion here suggest several considerations related to that use.

First, it is clear that such models cannnot address many of the issues relevant in environmental decision making. Questions related to social phenomena presently are not included in such models. These models provide a large part, but not all, of the data requirements necessary for a complete socioeconomic impact assessment.

Second, the methods employed in such models require extensive and continued development. The unknown validity of most such models requires careful attention. The similarities in the modeling techniques employed may simply indicate that the enthusiasm and the need for such models has led to the development of similarly configured models before the utility of such configurations has been adequately assessed. One of the major tasks of model developers in the early 1980s should be the assessment of the validity of their models in comparison to the data provided by the census of 1980. Until such assessments are made, the unanimity of methods may simply indicate how little is known about socioeconomic impacts. In addition, more attempts to adapt such models to other settings are essential.

Finally, the results suggest that, if properly selected, such models can meet a wide range of data needs and that such selection can, in large part, be done with only limited technical expertise. For example, using criteria such as those in Tables 8.1-8.3, it is possible to select models that assess a wide range of dimensions or those that provide only basic

TABLE 8.1. INFORMATIONAL CHARACTERISTICS OF SELECTED SOCIOECONOMIC IMPACT ASSESSMENT MODELS

Model	Dimensions Included							Project Phases Analyzed			Geographic Areas Included	Time Increments and Total Projection Periods	Total Number of Areal Units
	Economic	Demographic	Interface	Distribution	Public Services	Fiscal	Social	Baseline	Construction	Operational			
ATOM-3	X	X[1]	X					X	X	X	State and County	Yearly; NLS	14 counties in Arizona
BOOM-1	X	X	X	X	X	X[2]		X	X	X	City only	Yearly; NLS	any given city
BREAM	X	X	X	X				X	X	X	Region, County, Cities	Yearly; NLS	2 counties maximum
CLIPS	X	X	X	X		X[3]		X	X	X	Region, County, Cities	Yearly; 20 years	INP
CPEIO	X	X	X		X[4]			X	X	X	Restricted to one area, any level	Yearly OAD; NLS	one areal unit
HARC	X	X[1]	X	X	X			X	X	X	Project and County	Five Year; 30 years	INP
MULTIREGION	X	X	X	X				X	X	X	BEA Regional	Five Year; NLS	ALL BEA Regions

	X marks (left group)	X marks (right group)	Geographic levels	Time frame	Regions
NAVAHO	X X X	X X X	Reservation Districts	Five Year; NLS	9 Reservation Districts
NEW MEXICO	X X X	X X X	State Planning Regions	Five Year; 20 years	7 State Planning Regions
RED	X X X X X	X X X	State, Region, County, Cities	Yearly-OAD; 25 years	8 Regions, 53 cos., 350 cities
SEAM	X X X X X X[3]	X X X	County, Cities	Yearly; 30 years	INP
SIMPACT	X X X X X	X X X	Region, County, Cities	Yearly; construction, 10 years operation	Region and 11 subareas
WEST	X X X X[4]	X X X	Region, County, Cities	Yearly; NLS	INP

Abbreviations for Items

NLS = No Limit Specified
OAD = Or As Desired
INP = Information Not Provided

[1] Demographic Model includes special population submodules
[2] Costs are aggregated
[3] Revenues are not calculated
[4] Only two services projected

TABLE 8.2. METHODOLOGICAL CHARACTERISTICS OF SELECTED SOCIOECONOMIC IMPACT ASSESSMENT MODELS

Model	Methodological and Integrative Forms by Component						Dynamic Capabilities by Component						
	Econ	Dem	Interface	Subarea Distribution	Service	Fiscal	Econ	Dem	Interface	Subarea Dist.	Ser	Fis	Validation
ATOM-3	I-O	CC-S	E-M-1	% Share	NA	NA	Yes	Yes	Yes	Yes	NA	NA	Historical
BOOM-1	E-B	E-P	E-P-1	NA	P-B	Per Capita	Yes	Yes	Yes	NA	NA	NA	Sensitivity
BREAM	E-B	CC-S	E-M-1	%Share and Gravity	P-B	NA	Yes	Yes	Yes	Yes	NA	NA	INP
CLIPS	E-B	CC-S[1]	E-M-1	% Share and Gravity	NA	Per Capita	Yes	Yes	Yes	Yes	NA	Yes	INP
CPEIO	I-O	CC-S	E-M-1	NA	NA	NA	Yes	Yes	Yes	NA	NA	NA	Some, Forms Unspecified
HARC	E-B	CC-S	E-M-1	Gravity	P-B	NA	Yes	Yes	Yes	Yes	Yes	NA	Sensitivity
MULTIREGION	E-B	CC-S	E-M-1	NA	NA	NA	Yes	Yes	Yes	NA	NA	NA	Historical
NAVAHO	E-B	CC-S	E-M-M	Gravity	NA	NA	Yes	Yes	Yes	Yes	NA	NA	INP
NEW MEXICO	I-O	CC-S	E-M-M	NA	NA	NA	Yes	Yes	Yes	NA	NA	NA	INP

RED	I-O	CC-S	E-M-M	% Share and Gravity	P-B	Per Capita	Yes	Yes	Yes	Yes Yes	Sensitivity/Historical
SEAM	E-B	CC-S	E-M-M	LP	P-B	Per Capita Facility	Yes	Yes	Yes	Yes Yes	Sensitivity/Historical
SIMPACT	I-O	E-P	E-P-1	% Share	P-B	Per Capita Facility	Yes	Yes	Yes	Yes Yes	INP
WEST	E-B	E-P	E-P-1	% Share	P-B	Per Capita	Yes	No	Yes	Yes Yes	Sensitivity

Abbreviations for Items

Econ
I-O = Input-Output
E-B = Export Base

DEM
CC-S = Cohort Component Survival
E-P = Employment - Population Ratio

Interface
E-M-1 = Employment - Migrations - One phase
E-P-1 = Employment - Population - One phase
E-M-M = Employment - Migration - Multiphase Procedure

INP = Information Not Provided
NA = Not Applicable

Subarea Distribution
% Share = Distribution to subareas on bases of Employment or Population ratio
Gravity = Gravity Allocation Model
LP = Linear Programming Model

Service
P-B Population Based Projections

Fiscal
Per Capita = Per Capita Costs and Revenues
Facility = Projections of facility requirements also completed

[1] Cohort Component Survival Method used at Regional level only.

TABLE 8.3. USE CHARACTERISTICS OF SELECTED SOCIOECONOMIC IMPACT ASSESSMENT MODELS

Model	Input Data Requirements			Flexibility		Computerization	
	Source	Geographical Level	Form	User-Alterable Parameters	Degree of user Interactivity	Model Language	Transferability
ATOM-3	State and Local	State and County	Primary I-O other Secondary	None	None	FORTRAN	Other Models closely related (BREAM)
BOOM-1	State and Local	County and City	Secondary, Judgmental	None	None	GASP IV	Yes-Texas
BREAM	State and Local	Region and County	All Secondary	None	None	FORTRAN	Untested
CLIPS	State, Local Western U.S.	Region, County, City	All Secondary	SD,PC INP	Interactive	FORTRAN	Untested
CPEIO	State and Local	The given level of analysis	Primary I-O other Secondary	SD,PC AE, UNEMP. Output	Interactive (Knowledgable User)	SIMSCRIPT	Untested
HARC	National, State and Western U.S. Judgmental	County	All Secondary	None	None	INP	Untested
MULTIREGION	National and Regional	National and Regional	All Secondary	None	None	FORTRAN	Untested

Model							
NAVAHO	National and Reservation	Reservation & District	All Secondary	None	None	FORTRAN	Untested
NEW MEXICO	State and Regional	State, Region County	Primary I-O other Secondary	None	None	INP	Untested
RED	State, Region, Local	State, Region, Local	Primary I-O Primary Labor Force Other Secondary	SD,PC BR,IR TR,GM Output	Interactive	APL	Yes-Texas
SEAM	National & Regional	National & Regional	All Secondary	SD, PC Impact Area	Interactive	INP	Untested
SIMPACT	Regional, State and Local	Region County and Local	INP	INP	Interactive	FORTRAN	Untested
WEST	State and Local	State and Local	All Secondary	None	None	FORTRAN	Untested

SD = Starting Date
PC = Project Characteristics
AE = Available Employment
UNEMP. = Unemployment Rate
OUTPUT = Type or form of Output
BR = Birth Rate

IR = Inflation Rate
TR = Tax Rate
GM = Gravity Model Coefficients
IMPACT AREA = Selection of Impact Area
INP = Information Not Provided

economic and demographic outputs. Given that choice, the user can eliminate those models that do not cover the geographical units or time periods or that do not have the capacity (total areal unit coverage) they desire. Methodological considerations can largely be left to a second and more intensive level of evaluation following this initial screening. The user can then select models on the basis of: (1) their ease of use, eliminating those with costly primary data collection if desired or using such models to provide greater sensitivity to local conditions; (2) their degree of user interactivity; and (3) their likely adaptability to available computer systems. If the selection of such models can be done with care, this analysis suggests that computerized socioeconomic assessment models may provide a valuable tool for use in the decision making process.

NOTES

1. It should be noted that econometric modeling has a long history with the first development of national models occurring in the 1930s. These activities were greatly accelerated, however, when computer systems became readily accessible.

2. For example, see Obermiller et al. (1975). A review of such modeling efforts is provided by Sanderson (1978).

3. The state has subsequently developed another model incorporating many of the features of ATOM-3 but utilizing an export base model in the economic sector. For a complete description of this model, see Anderson and Hannigan (1977).

4. The BOOM-1 model thus has its conceptual roots in the earlier work by Forrester in the areas of industrial dynamics (Forrester, 1961) and urban dynamics (Forrester, 1969). The formulations of key interactions in this model were based in large part on a case study by Gilmore and Duff (1975).

5. The basic model structure incorporated in the RED-1 and RED-2 models was also used as the basis for the Texas Assessment Modeling System (TAMS). For a complete description of the TAMS Model, see Murdock et al. (1979c).

6. Models which address a larger number of impact categories and provide projections in a more disaggregated form can address a broader range of user needs. Such models also impose greater costs for data collection and updating, however, and estimation of the relationships embodied in them can become statistically complex. Trade-offs are inherent in designing impact models.

9
Use of Assessments
in the Policy Process

As indicated in the preceding chapters, growing awareness
of the need for thorough analysis and comprehensive growth
management planning in rural areas affected by major development projects, coupled with increased legal requirements for
impact assessment and mitigation, has led to an increased demand for procedures which provide timely and accurate impact
information. As a result, socioeconomic impact assessment
techniques have received increasing attention. Computerized
socioeconomic impact models have become particularly popular,
as noted in Chapter 8, because of their wide range of outputs,
flexibility, and quick response times.

As the number of examinations of the forms and uses of
assessment systems increases (Murdock and Leistritz, 1980;
Leistritz et al., 1980b), it becomes increasingly evident that
development of such systems can be quite expensive and that,
in most cases, these systems have received insufficient validation. It is also apparent that the adaptability of
models and other assessment techniques to settings other than
the areas for which they were originally designed has received
relatively little attention.[1] Further, other more general examinations of the use of assessment systems and related forecasting techniques in the policy process suggest that they
often have failed to achieve their intended purposes and that
their utilization by policy makers has been less frequent than
anticipated (Hoos, 1972; Fromm et al., 1975; Greenberger et
al., 1976; Ascher, 1978).

In light of these difficulties, an examination of the
factors affecting the credibility and usefulness of impact
assessment systems appears desirable. The purpose of
this chapter is to examine factors influencing the usefulness
of socioeconomic impact assessments in policy development and
planning for areas affected by resource development projects.
The examination is from two vantage points: (1) that of the
social science analyst who wishes to make an effective contri-
bution to the policy process; and (2) that of the decision
maker who has questions concerning the usefulness of these

assessments and the ways in which they can be effectively utilized in policy making. Specifically, our purpose is:

1. To describe the major functions of socioeconomic
   assessments in planning and policy development;
2. To evaluate the factors affecting the usefulness
   and acceptability of such assessments to decision
   makers; and
3. To delineate those conditions critical to the successful development and utilization of such assessments.

FUNCTIONS OF SOCIOECONOMIC IMPACT ASSESSMENTS

Impact assessments fulfill three important functions in
the overall impact assessment/policy development process:
(1) to project the social and economic profile of the study
area under "baseline" and "impact" conditions; (2) to sensitize decision makers to critical problem areas and key relationships; and (3) to provide direction to future research.
The first function, projection of socioeconomic profiles,
produces conditional forecasts of the levels of various economic, demographic, public service, fiscal, and social variables. These projections are critical to decision makers as
a basis for evaluating potential problems which may emerge and
for evaluating the efficacy of alternative policy options.
Specifically, decision makers frequently utilize impact projections in three distinct types of applications: (1) facility and program planning; (2) project evaluation; and (3) policy
analysis. In the first application, impact projections are
often used as the "best available forecast" of future conditions, and the projected levels of critical variables are used
as target values for facility and program planning. In project evaluation, interested parties frequently utilize impact
projections -- particularly the comparison of baseline (i.e.,
without the project) and impact projections -- in determining
whether the proposed project is acceptable and what types of
impact mitigation measures will be required. Finally, impact
projections may be utilized to evaluate the likely effects of
various growth management policies. As a projection tool,
computerized assessment models are often particularly valued
because of their capacity to deal with complex analytic situations and large data sets (i.e., involving large numbers of
variables and interrelationships), their ability to provide
quantitative answers (even though these may be approximations), the replicability of the results, and the rapidity
with which the implications of alternative policies or assumptions can be assessed (Fromm et al., 1975). It must be emphasized, however, that impact projections are conditional forecasts -- they are contingent on the actions which policy

makers will take and also on the validity of the basic assumptions concerning factors such as the level of development which will occur.

The second function of impact assessments, enhancing the perceptions of policy makers, provides these decision makers with a frame of reference for assessing the effects of alternative actions. Because a model provides an abstracted and explicit representation of the real world phenomenon being studied (often termed the model's "reference system"), it offers a means of portraying essential relationships and isolating critical problems. Even if the policy maker does not utilize an assessment directly in decision making, it may provide useful insights concerning the probable consequences of alternative courses of action. Because they provide an explicit representation of a real world system, formalized assessment procedures provide a focus for differing opinions. Even when controversial, however, assessments can provide a framework for discussion, and such discussion may improve the probability that key decisions will receive concerted attention (Greenberger et al., 1976). While assessments may serve to increase decision makers' awareness of key relationships and critical issues, however, they cannot be expected to resolve policy differences which are basically philosophical in nature. Likewise, models cannot and should not be expected to replace the decision maker's role of considering all available information in arriving at a final decision (Low, 1980). Neither should the existence of assessment projections remove the decision maker's responsibility for those decisions.

The role of assessments in stimulating and guiding research, their third major function, is widely recognized.[2] The process of developing assessment methods consists essentially of conceptualizing relationships among variables, seeking empirical evidence to quantify and/or refine these relationships, and providing a computational structure (model) which portrays the system under investigation. The absence of data to quantify certain relationships which are believed to be important suggests that these relationships constitute a priority area for further analysis.

A guide for such research design is provided if the model is subjected to sensitivity testing. In this process, the model is tested with the key coefficients for each of the relationships under investigation being specified at alternative values. The results of these simulations will reveal those relationships whose precise specification is most important in influencing the values of the output variables.

Not only does the process of methodology development and utilization provide direction for future research, but it may also serve to promote communication between decision makers and technical specialists (Fromm et al., 1975).

Public and private sector officials who sponsor the development of impact assessment methodologies may recognize the benefits which arise from the role of such methods as educational tools for decision makers and researchers. Their decision to support the development of a modeling system, however, typically hinges on whether they believe the model will provide information useful in specific planning and policy contexts. Thus, a consideration of major factors which influence the usefulness of assessments to policy makers follows.

FACTORS AFFECTING USEFULNESS AND ACCEPTABILITY OF IMPACT ASSESSMENTS

Numerous factors influence the extent to which an assessment methodology can or will be utilized by decision makers.[3] It appears, however, that two considerations are of overriding importance in this regard: (1) the compatibility of the assessment's focus with the needs of decision making; and (2) the decision makers' confidence in the methodology. In this section, the key dimensions of these two major considerations are explored.

Compatibility With Needs of Decision Makers

It has become axiomatic in treatises on policy-oriented modeling and methodology development to stress the importance of interaction between the analysts who develop the model and the policy makers who are expected to use it (House and McLeod, 1977; Greenberger et al., 1976). In the case of socioeconomic impact methods, it appears particularly important to carefully define the types of decisions which are to be made and the types of information which are needed. Such methods may be used for several types of decisions and possibly by several distinct groups of decision makers, each having different information needs and levels of resources. While different needs do exist, however, it may not be possible, given time or resource constraints, to implement a system that is "all things to all people." Frustration and superficiality are likely to result from an overly comprehensive approach to methodology development. Priority uses and users will exist, and these priorities must be identified and addressed.

Four groups which may be expected to be frequent users of socioeconomic impact assessments are local governments, state and federal policy makers, state and federal action agencies, and private sector managers. Local officials will naturally be most interested in the implications of development for their specific jurisdictions. They will likely be concerned with the implications under alternative conditions, as they will need this information in their facility planning and capital budgeting decisions and possibly as a basis for negotiation with the developer. They also are likely to be interested in the prospective effects of alternative local

growth management strategies (e.g., different rates for utility user fees and hookup charges, infrastructure investment
options, and local zoning alternatives) on the various impact
categories.

State and federal policy makers should be very interested
in the socioeconomic implications of alternative resource development patterns. They may be confronted with decisions concerning financial assistance to impacted areas, including
justification for such assistance, the level of assistance required, and the most appropriate form of such assistance
(e.g., grants vs. loans).

State and federal action agencies are most interested in
the implications of development with respect to their specific
programs. These entities frequently have information needs
which closely parallel those of local officials, but on a region-wide basis, and they may utilize impact projections as
target values in their program planning.

Private sector managers also have questions regarding
socioeconomic impacts. From their perspective, however, the
key questions may relate to the relative severity of impacts
that may be anticipated at alternative project sites and the
effects of various construction management strategies (e.g.,
extent of local hiring, use of bachelor quarters or company-
subsidized transportation, and staging of construction activities) on the magnitude and distribution of impacts.

Because the various potential users of the assessment may
differ in the types of information they desire and in the exogenous variables they consider important, as well as in the
level of resources at their command, it is generally necessary
that decision makers be involved early in the development process.

Input from decision makers is needed with regard to a
number of major output features. These include: (1) the impact categories (e.g., economic, demographic, public service,
fiscal, social) to be addressed; (2) the specific socioeconomic profile characteristics to be projected; (3) the level
of aggregation of model outputs (e.g., total population or
population by age category); (4) the geographic units for
which outputs are to be projected; and (5) the temporal periods for which results are reported. The intended mode of use
(e.g., direct access by users vs. indirect access through
programers and analysts) may influence the format in which
outputs are reported. Likewise, the users' definition of an
acceptable period of time for completion of the assessment may
influence the choice of methodology.

The specific uses which are contemplated also may influence the analytical methods to be employed, the data requirements, and the procedures for interaction between the methodology and its users. If, for example, some intended uses of
the methodology will require the projected population to be
disaggregated by age and/or sex, then the method's designers

likely will employ the cohort-survival technique in the demographic analysis. This decision will in turn determine the
types of data needed as input to the model. Similarly, if the
procedure is to be utilized to assess the implications of
alternative taxation and impact assistance policies, provision
may be made for convenient user alteration of selected tax
rates and other fiscal variables.

At the stage in methodology development when user needs
are specified and the overall design is established, a number
of trade-offs must be carefully considered. Decisions regarding the scope of impact categories to be addressed, level
of detail of projections, and other related factors may often
have a substantial impact on the resources required to develop
and maintain the model as well as on the time period required
for its development. More detailed projection techniques may
impose greater costs for development and also may lead to
greater requirements for computerization and to higher costs
for each use of the method. Similarly, techniques which utilize substantial amounts of local data may be more reliable in
projecting local level conditions that depart markedly from
state or national patterns but may also imply substantial
costs and extensive time periods for data collection. The
model design phase, then, requires active participation from
both decision makers and modelers in assessing the benefits
and costs of various design alternatives.

Factors Affecting User Confidence

If impact assessment systems are to play a major role in
shaping important decisions, users must understand their capabilities and inherent limitations and must have confidence in
their reliability in simulating the behavior of the reference
system. In this section, the factors which are important in
determining whether decision makers will develop confidence in
an assessment methodology are examined.

Description and Explanation of the Assessment Methodology.
The quality of a method's description is likely to be critical
in determining the degree of confidence with which decision
makers will view its results. Without knowing something of
the purpose, logic, and capabilities of the method, one cannot
decide whether it applies to a particular problem. Similarly,
an explanation of the premises and assumptions of the method
is necessary to adequately interpret or act upon the results.
Reviews of socioeconomic impact assessment methods and models
(Murdock and Leistritz, 1980) and of policy analyses in general (Fromm et al., 1975) suggest that the quality and completeness of assessment methodology description and model
documentation varies considerably. Further, representatives
of sponsoring agencies tend to be less satisfied with the
adequacy of model documentation than are the directors of

modeling projects (Fromm et al., 1975). This divergence in
views suggests a substantial gap between impact analysts and
users -- a gap which may seriously limit the usefulness of the
assessments.

While written documentation is necessary to the understanding and use of a model, it may not be a sufficient means
of communicating the model's purpose, logic, capabilities,
and limitations to decision makers. Rather, it will probably
be necessary to at least conduct a series of briefings for
policy makers. (Of course, decision makers and their aides
should ideally be involved throughout the assessment process.)
Communication between analysts and decision makers is likely
to be more effective if the analysts are recognized by the
decision makers as having both expertise in relevant subject
areas and knowledge of local conditions. If some members of
the analytical team have previous experience in interacting
with the relevant decision making entities, communication may
be established more readily. It also is very useful for the
sponsoring agency to have staff or trusted associates who are
capable of assessing the validity of the method used. Finally, decision makers may be more receptive to assessment
efforts which are perceived as timely (i.e., the need for the
information is recognized and the assessment effort has the
potential to provide this information within a time frame consistent with pending decisions).

Methodology Validation. Validation is a test of whether
a method provides an adequate representation of the elements
and relationships of the reference system that are important
to the uses which are planned for the technique. Validation
is not a general seal of approval; rather it is an indication
of the level of confidence in the method's accuracy under
limited conditions and for specific purposes (Shapiro, 1973).
Because all methods are designed to be abstractions of their
respective reference systems, they can never by entirely valid
in terms of being fully supported by objective truth. The
various techniques of validation are aimed more at invalida-
ting rather than validating a method, and they can only reveal
the presence (not the total absence) of problems. Thus, it is
suggested that "useful" or "convincing" are more appropriate
descriptive terms to apply to methods or models than "valid"
(Greenberger et al., 1976).

Confidence in a given method can be enhanced: (1) by
critically examining its theoretical basis, assumptions, data
sources, and computational procedures; (2) by investigating
its response to perturbations; and (3) by testing its ability
to reproduce historical data. (For more detailed discussion
of these validation techniques, see Ascher, 1978; Pindyck and
Rubinfeld, 1976; and House and McLeod, 1977.) Most impact
methods or models have undergone at least one of these forms
of validation to some degree, but no computerized socioeco-

nomic impact assessment model of which we are aware has been subjected to extensive validation of all three forms.

The first form of validation (review of theoretical basis and analytical procedures) consists of a review of the technical description/documentation materials by persons with expertise in impact assessment. Some impact models have received increasing attention in professional literature, which is an indication that they are gaining credibility. It should also be noted that one way for decision makers to begin with confidence is to employ recognized socioeconomic impact researchers in model development and evaluation efforts.

The second form of validation (investigation of response to perturbations) involves altering selected input variables or model parameters in a manner consistent with intended uses and evaluating the resulting outputs in terms of their consistency with expert understanding of key relationships and with evidence regarding the actual behavior of the same variables under similar circumstances. Most impact models likely have been subjected to this type of validation by their developers. The strength of this form of validation is that the model's behavior is being examined under circumstances similar to those that may be encountered in actual use. Its limitation is that the evaluation may be somewhat subjective.

The third form of validation (testing the ability to reproduce historic data) is frequently termed "historical simulation".[4] This form of validation involves choosing a past period for which the values of the output (endogenous) variables are known. The method is then supplied with the known starting values of the input (exogenous) variables and simulated over the period.[5] The values of the output variables estimated by the model are then compared with the actual values; a variety of statistical tests can be applied to evaluate the similarity between the two series (estimated and actual) for each variable of interest.[6] In addition to evaluating the degree of correspondence between estimated and actual values, another important criterion is how well the method predicts turning points in the historical data.

Of the three general forms of model validation, the comparison to historical data appears to be particularly appealing because it provides objective measures of performance. Further, such measures are easily understood by decision makers and their constituents. A method which closely reproduces historical data on the variables of interest gains credibility and wins the acceptance and trust of potential users (Greenberger et al., 1976). This approach to validation may require substantial effort in assembling historical data series for the key input and output variables, however, particularly for intercensal years and in rural areas. Because such efforts are time-consuming and expensive, historical simulation has been utilized less frequently than the other approaches. The historical simulation technique also has limitations because, although it offers a test of the ability to reproduce past changes, shifts in the structure of the reference system or major changes in values of key system variables could adversely affect the model's future performance. Ideally, all three of the forms of validation should be employed. It is unfortunate, therefore, that most existing methodological descriptions contain little or no information on the results of attempts to test their validity. Historical simulation evaluations are most frequently absent in computerized model descriptions (see Chapter 8). In defense of the research groups that have developed computerized impact models, however, it should be noted that most of these models have been developed quite recently so that the time available for extensive validation has been limited. Further, because many areas where these models have been applied have relatively recent histories of rapid growth (Murdock and Leistritz, 1979), the data available for testing the validity of these models under impact conditions have been sparse. Rigorous empirical evaluations of the validity of assessment methods should be given high priority over the next few years. Although some efforts have been made to assess the accuracy of economic and demographic projections for small rural areas (Klindt et al., 1972; Hertsgaard et al., 1977; Glickman, 1977; Ascher, 1978), such assessments have been infrequent. Additional analysis is clearly essential.

CONDITIONS FOR SUCCESSFUL IMPACT ASSESSMENT

Those who conduct impact assessments will find it necessary to develop criteria of method acceptability, whether as a basis for choosing among alternative methods or as a guide in deciding whether a given technique can be used with confidence. While many factors may enter into such decisions, we suggest that three considerations should predominate:

1. The method must provide the types of information needed by the user. Increased communication between analysts and decision makers will be required to achieve better congruance between assessment capabilities and user needs. It must be recognized, however, that determination of information needs is not a trivial task. Decision makers frequently experience difficulty in articulating their needs in terms that are meaningful to impact analysts. Similarly, analysts often appear to be insensitive to the imperatives confronting decision makers. It may be necessary for the decision makers and analysts to jointly simulate a typical decision process before a final prioritization of needs can be developed.

242

2. The assessment should use tested, state-of-the-art techniques to provide the most realistic possible representation of the real world system being analyzed. To date, lack of empirical validation has been one of the major shortcomings of socioeconomic impact assessments. Analysts should give more attention to empirical validation of their products with emphasis on the ability to replicate actual outcomes in rapid growth areas, and potential users should demand objective measures of validity.

3. Impact assessment methodologies are at best a simplification of the system being studied; decision makers must evaluate them not in terms of an ideal but unobtainable "perfect model" but rather in terms of available alternatives (Forrester, 1968). While the present computerized models are by no means approaching perfection, they may well be superior to the manual or mental models which are the alternatives to their use.

For those that contemplate sponsoring impact assessments, a number of questions frequently arise. While these questions may take different forms in different settings (e.g., use of inhouse staff vs. outside consultants, development of a new method or model vs. transfer of an existing one), their focus is on defining the conditions necessary for a successful impact assessment effort. While there is certainly room for differences of opinion in this area, we would suggest the following as important conditions:

1. Early planning involvement of potential information users -- Participation of potential users in the methodology design effort not only improves the chances that the resulting methods will be compatible with their needs but also can provide the developers with easier access to local data bases. User involvement through the development period allows for correction of initial model inaccuracies based on information about local conditions. Further, the meaningful involvement of users in the development process increases the likelihood that they will use the assessment.

2. Appropriate timing with respect to information needs -- Awareness of upcoming decisions and the need for the information the assessment can provide and timely provision of information to meet those needs are also essential. If assessment efforts are pursued before decision makers feel the need for the information they can provide or if the development process is so extended that the important issues have been addressed prior to the assessment's

completion, the effort is unlikely to be highly utilized or well received.

3. Knowledge of study area conditions -- Socioeconomic impact analysis requires a detailed understanding of the economic, demographic, public service, fiscal, and social conditions of the study area. If the researchers do not possess such knowledge, they must be willing to commit a significant effort to thoroughly understanding local conditions and relationships.

4. Knowledge of impact assessment techniques -- Socioeconomic impact analysis generally and impact modeling in particular requires a variety of skills, including thorough knowledge of economic, demographic, public service, and fiscal impact assessment methods and expertise in computer systems/programming. Because it would be highly unlikely to find this combination of skills in one individual, a multidisciplinary team must usually be assembled. Further, if such a team is to function effectively, attention must be given to developing an adequate project management structure.

5. Continuity of professional and technical support -- Once the assessment methodology has been completed, there is a continuing need for competent analysts both to assist users in various applications and to update various data bases and coefficients. There is also a continuing need for advice from persons with expertise in the use and interpretation of assessments in determining when use of a method is appropriate and in interpreting its outputs. In addition, as the method is applied to a variety of problems, needs for refinement are often identified. Determination of the institutional setting (e.g., mission agency, research institute, etc.) which can best provide a continuity of support will be important to the long-term usefulness of any methodology.

6. Resources commensurate to the task -- Impact methodology development, like other research and development endeavors, is not inexpensive. For example, it is estimated that more than $2 million have been invested in development of the SIMPACT computerized assessment system (Huston, 1979). Development of some other regional impact modeling systems has involved costs of several hundred thousand dollars, not including background data collection and analysis. Transfer of an existing system may be possible at a cost substantially lower than that required to develop a new system

(Murdock et al., 1980c). This option is attractive,
however, only if an existing model appears to
meet information needs and if questions relating
to documentation and computer system compatibility
can be satisfactorily resolved. (The active involvement of the developer may be the best way to
assure the success of a transfer effort.) In any
event, the costs of the effort must be realistically
assessed and adequate resources allocated.

CONCLUSIONS AND IMPLICATIONS

     Rapid growth resulting from large-scale development pro-
jects has created growing interest in developing integrated
socioeconomic impact assessment systems. A number of such
systems have been developed, and they appear to have considerable potential for providing information useful to decision
makers. These systems will be most useful, however, if their
inherent capabilities and limitations are thoroughly understood. Like other methodological systems, they are more appropriately regarded as sophisticated calculating mechanisms
than as the modern day equivalent of the crystal ball. When
properly designed, impact assessment systems provide an efficient mechanism for organizing our assumptions and for projecting the implications of these assumptions into the future.
     There are some things, however, which these methods can-
not be expected to do. No matter how sophisticated their
design, they cannot provide certainty in an uncertain decision
environment. Neither can they be expected to resolve policy
differences which are basically philosophical in nature.
Finally, they cannot and should not be expected to replace the
decision maker's role of considering all available information
and applying judgement in arriving at a final decision.
     Whatever their limitations, however, it is clearly as an
aid to policy analysis that impact assessments gain their
significance. Their refinement, expansion, and evaluation
must remain a priority area for social scientists who wish to
play an important role in the policy process.

NOTES

     1. An exception is the discussion by Murdock et al.
(1980c) of the adaptation of the Texas Assessment Modeling
System (TAMS) from the RED-1 and RED-2 Models.
     2. For example, Fromm et al. (1975) reports that, when
directors of modeling projects were queried concerning benefits of their model, the most frequent response was "educated
the model builders."

3. For extensive discussions of these factors, see House
and McLeod (1977) and Greenberger et al. (1976). A more general discussion of the influence of forecasts is provided by
Ascher (1978).

4. Some authors refer to this approach as "backcasting"
while others define backcasting as the situation in which the
model is run backward in time. We follow the terminology of
Pindyck and Rubinfeld (1976, p. 314) who distinguish historical simulation (where the model runs forward in time over a
historical period) from backcasting.

5. Two basic variations of the historical simulation approach are possible. One alternative is to supply the (known)
values of the exogenous variables to the model throughout the
period. The other is to supply the model with exogenous variable values which were "estimated" using the same techniques
employed to estimate these variables in forecasting applications.

6. Statistical measures which are frequently applied include the Thiel U_2 Coefficient, Mean absolute error, Mean
error, and R^2 coefficients. For further discussion, see
Pindyck and Rubinfeld (1976) and Senechal (1971).

10
Summary, Implications, and Conclusions

Our intent has been to provide an overview of the conceptual bases and alternative techniques available for use in assessing the economic, demographic, public service, fiscal, and social impacts of development projects. In this final chapter, we wish to briefly summarize our conclusions with respect to the need for additional development and refinement of impact assessment methods and supporting data bases.

SUMMARY -- STATE-OF-THE-ART IN SOCIOECONOMIC IMPACT ASSESSMENT

Our intent in this section is to summarize our impressions of the current state-of-the-art in socioeconomic assessments for large-scale projects, and to point out those areas where additional conceptual and/or empirical effort is needed to allow for more adequate assessments. In so doing, we are admittedly being evaluative and expressing views the empirical validity of which have yet to be clearly established.

When the techniques which are most commonly employed in socioeconomic impact assessment are evaluated, one immediate conclusion is that current methods and approaches leave much to be desired. Many assessments are based on inadequate methods, utilize inappropriate data bases, and frequently achieve only a partial analysis of the relevant impact dimensions.

Examples of such shortcomings are abundant in recent assessments. In the area of economic impacts, they include the use of techniques which provide only aggregate measures of economic effects and which are insensitive to key differences in project characteristics. Even more serious, secondary economic effects have been ignored altogether in many assessments (Berkey et al., 1977). Demographic impact assessments provide similar examples, including use of simple population to employment ratios which ignore the structure of the population and the dynamics of population growth and decline. Demographic analyses also provide numerous examples of the use of

247

inappropriate data bases. For example, many analysts have used an area's average family size derived from census data as an estimate of the demographic characteristics of inmigrating construction-related populations, even though extensive data bases concerning these characteristics are available from recent surveys.

The integration of the various impact dimensions is, as noted in Chapter 7, an assessment area where conceptual development has been especially deficient. It appears that adequate integration requires use of common procedures for both baseline and impact interfaces, employment of interface procedures at the lowest possible geographic level, retention of the most significant aspects of each impact dimension in the interface procedure, and use of feedback or iterative mechanisms. Most integration procedures in current use, however, are single-point, single-dimension, and noniterative. Further, in many cases, analysts fail to consistently apply common interface procedures in both baseline and impact assessments.

Evaluation of changes in public service requirements has been similarly limited. Such assessments often have been based on the application of national service standards to total population changes. Such approaches not only ignore unique local conditions, such as the service expectations of local residents and the capacities of present facilities, but they also ignore the effects on service requirements that may result from differences in key socioeconomic characteristics (for example, income and age structure) between inmigrants and the resident population. Further, many assessments have been very limited in the types of services examined, with some including only a small subset of the services provided by local governments and others making no explicit attempt to examine service requirements (Berkey et al., 1977).

Fiscal impacts of major projects are one of the major concerns of local decision makers. Fiscal assessments, however, frequently have been subject to limitations similar to those noted previously with respect to public service evaluations. In many cases, only a few of the cost and revenue components have been examined. In others, only the public sector costs and revenues directly associated with the proposed project have been evaluated while the indirect and induced fiscal effects have been ignored. Finally, few fiscal analyses have adequately addressed the temporal and jurisdictional distribution of costs and revenues, although it has become increasingly apparent that these distributional aspects are frequently a source of problems for local jurisdictions (Murdock and Leistritz, 1979; Gilmore et al., 1976a).

In the area of social impact analysis, the limitations are equally evident. A failure to properly define the content of social impact analyses and subsequent unrealistic expectations for them, the use of impressionistic data based on short-term observations, the analysis of only public services or of only those dimensions that can be derived from secondary data are some of the most common limitations. It is essential for social impact analysts to develop, and be provided with an adequate set of resources to develop, more comprehensive and definitive assessment techniques.

A general weakness of the impact assessment methods in current use is their tendency to focus on the demand side of the local economy. Thus, impact assessments typically emphasize a projects' effects on the demand for labor, housing, and private and public sector services. Much less attention has been given to the supply side of the local economy (for example, supply of labor, private sector retail and service capacity, capacity of the local housing industry, and public service capacity). Because the key issue in impact assessment is the ability of local systems to accommodate change without undue strain, assessments should place more emphasis on supply factors.

Overall, it is apparent that past impact assessments have frequently suffered from inadequate conceptualization and from a failure to utilize the most appropriate techniques and data sets that were available. It must be recognized, however, that socioeconomic impact assessment is a relatively new and rapidly developing research area. While regional economists and demographers have long been interested in developing a better understanding of the forces affecting rural economic and population changes, it is only within the last decade that NEPA requirements have stimulated concerted efforts to provide integrated assessments of a broad range of economic, demographic, and social impacts. Further, as has been indicated in previous chapters, significant advances in the sophistication and hopefully the realism of these assessments have occurred in recent years. Thus, in the next section, an evaluation of the most advanced methods which are being employed in assessments is presented.

The state-of-the-art in impact assessment (that is, the most advanced techniques that have been operationalized and employed) clearly represents a substantial advance over the techniques previously employed. These methods, however, still appear to have substantial limitations. The more salient deficiencies of impact assessment techniques appear to be in the following areas: (1) insufficient conceptualization of key dimensions and interactions; (2) inadequate data bases; (3) inappropriate levels of analysis; (4) insufficient orientation to the needs and concerns of decision makers; and (5) inadequate validation.

Inadequate conceptualization of key relationships, while apparent to some degree with respect to all major impact assessment dimensions, is most evident in the integration of major components. As noted in Chapter 7, no clear conceptual premises have been established to provide a basis for inter-

facing socioeconomic dimensions. The lack of attention to
this issue may result in part from the traditional isolation
of disciplinary specialties. Thus, the development of economic impact concepts and techniques has been the realm of the
regional scientist, and population analysis that of the demo-
grapher, while fiscal impact evaluations have been the concern
of an equally specialized group of public finance analysts and
planners. Only recently has the need for integration of concepts from these and other diverse disciplines become apparent.

The traditional organization and reward systems of some
major research institutions (for example, universities) may
act to discourage the intense and sustained levels of interdisciplinary interaction required to achieve substantial advances. Segregation of the relevant disciplines into several
different departments, often in different colleges, tends to
limit interactions, except during those periods when the researchers are drawn together to conduct an "interdisciplinary"
project. Because such projects often are of relatively short
duration, effective interdisciplinary interaction may be difficult to establish, as differences in conceptual bases and
specialized disciplinary phraseology often impair communication (Swanson, 1979). Existing reward systems, which often
place heavy emphasis on publication in the leading professional journals of the researcher's discipline, also may discourage substantial commitments to integrative efforts. If
interdisciplinary analyses are less acceptable to major
journals than more discipline-specific efforts, researchers
may be reluctant to commit substantial resources to these activities, especially during their formative years (Swanson,
1979).

Whatever the underlying causes, conceptual bases and
specific techniques for interfacing socioeconomic dimensions
have not received sufficient attention. The economic-demographic interface appears to be the most highly developed,
but even here the specific procedures employed are often ad
hoc in nature and their reliability under a variety of contextual conditions has not been adequately assessed. Methods
for integrating other impact dimensions have received substantially less attention, and attempts at quantitative interfacing of social and (physical) environmental dimensions with
other socioeconomic categories appear almost nonexistent.[1]

Insufficient data bases pose limitations to socioeconomic
impact analysis which are at least as severe as those resulting from inadequate conceptualization. Whatever the limitations in model conceptualization, it still appears to be true
that our capacity to design highly sophisticated regional
models has far outrun our ability to implement them, given
the primitive nature of available data and data-gathering
techniques (Miernyk, 1976). These limitations are applicable
to nearly all aspects of socioeconomic impact assessment.

Thus, in each of the socioeconomic areas discussed in the preceding chapters, limitations in data bases are major barriers
to the development of more comprehensive and reliable assessment models.

The scarcity of data available for estimating many of
the relationships which are central to impact assessments has
had several effects. One is the tendency of impact analysts
to rely heavily on "expert opinion and individual intuition"
(Ford, 1976) in quantifying many key relationships. A review of numerous impact statements and model descriptions
leads us to conclude that virtually all analysts have relied
heavily on this approach. A second result of data limitations
has been a willingness of analysts to utilize certain data
sets in settings where their applicability appears questionable. The widespread use of data on worker characteristics
and settlement patterns for energy facilities in the Great
Plains and Rocky Mountain states (Mountain West Research,
Inc., 1975; Wieland et al., 1977) in projecting such patterns
for a wide variety of facilities in diverse environmental
settings is a case in point.

Many impact assessment efforts appear to involve levels
of analysis which do not allow critical questions to be adequately addressed. Some of the most important questions to
be addressed in impact assessments relate both to the aggregate changes in various socioeconomic variables and to the
distribution of those effects -- among groups in the affected
population, among jurisdictions, and over time. For example,
assessment approaches which examine only fiscal effects resulting from the expected changes in total revenues and total
costs of a typical local jurisdiction for a typical year
after the facility is in operation fail to address some of
the most important issues related to fiscal impacts. Similarly, demographic analyses which fail to give sufficient
attention to the likely settlement-commuting patterns of project workers will be of limited utility to local planners and
decision makers. Overall, it appears that the level of
analysis frequently has been based more on that which is most
convenient for the analyst than on the needs of those who
will utilize the information as a basis for decisions.

Another limitation which appears to be pervasive in impact assessments is an insufficient orientation toward and
sensitivity to the needs of decision makers. In general, impact analysts must give greater attention to the production of
results that have meaning to policy makers and which can be
acted upon by them. This requires not only the development
of more adequate research techniques and conceptual specification but also a clear identification of key policy issues
and a delineation of the critical questions at the beginning
of an assessment effort. More specifically, if impact assessments and particularly computerized assessment models are
to achieve their full potential in guiding impact management

and mitigation efforts, they must become increasingly oriented to the evaluation of the effects of specific impact management strategies. Thus, impact assessment models should be capable of addressing the likely implications of alternative approaches by the developer (such as alternative project construction schedules, expanded local recruitment, and provision of bachelor quarters or subsidized transportation for workers) and by public officials (such as alternative approaches to service provision and financing). Finally, such evaluations must be provided in a timely fashion, with many potential users expecting initial results within a three to six month time period and subsequent updates and analyses of alternative strategies in even shorter time frames (Coddington and Gilmore, 1980).

A final consideration which has been noted with respect to every major impact category is the requirement for much more extensive validation of impact assessment models. As noted previously, published descriptions of the most widely used models give little indication of the extent to which their accuracy and reliability has been evaluated or of the results of those evaluations. Even when such evaluations have been reported (Thompson et al., 1978; Leistritz et al., 1979a), they typically have been based on a very small number of observations, and hence, the conclusions which can be drawn from these evaluations are similarly limited.[2] In general, it is evident that the evaluation of the accuracy of impact assessments must become a more systematic area of research.

IMPLICATIONS -- NEEDS FOR FURTHER REFINEMENT AND DEVELOPMENT

Our purpose in this section is to point out implications of our findings in terms of future needs in impact assessment and to discuss those research and analysis emphases which must be altered in order to improve the quality of impact assessments. Our remarks are directed specifically to three groups with vital interests in the impact assessment process: (1) impact researchers; (2) sponsors of impact studies; and (3) policy makers who attempt to utilize the results of these efforts. Overall, we attempt to delineate aspects of impact assessment which require additional emphasis and to suggest possible mechanisms to strengthen impact assessments.

A review of current impact assessment practices reveals a need for additional conceptual and analytical refinement within each major impact assessment category. The need for improved conceptualization and refined analytical approaches is even more apparent when the integration of various impact dimensions is considered. If such conceptual and analytical refinements are to be achieved, it is essential to increase the levels of interest among social scientists in pursuing

impact research as a legitimate research area with scientific
merit. If the impact assessment research process is viewed
as pursuing questions tangential to the major interests of the
various disciplines, social scientists will be reluctant to
make substantial and continuing commitments to this area of
research.

It is our contention that impact-related studies allow
researchers to address a broad range of questions which are
basic to economics, sociology, and several related disciplines.
The manner in which many impact research efforts have been
supported, however, has tended to deter pursuit of these more
basic questions. Support for impact-related research has come
primarily from agencies charged with preparing impact statements. Short time periods and, to a lesser extent, limited
funding for these efforts frequently have left analysts with
no choice but to rely on established techniques and existing
data bases. To encourage significant advances in the quality
of impact assessments, sponsors must give greater attention
to initiating studies which will lead to the refinement of
analytical techniques and the development of expanded data
bases. At the same time, researchers must be innovative in
devising approaches by which some contributions to analytical
refinement and data base expansion can be achieved within the
time and budget constraints commonly associated with impact
assessment projects. Provision for continuity of research
efforts beyond the assessment process, such that techniques and
data bases can be developed in incremental fashion over the
span of several sponsored projects, is a particularly crucial
consideration (Murdock et al., 1976).

Further development of impact assessment techniques will
also require researchers and research administrators to address a number of questions concerning the organization and
management of such research efforts. While a number of researchers and administrators have discussed alternative mechanisms for organizing interdisciplinary research projects
(Ellis, 1974; Rossini et al., 1978; Swanson, 1979), most projects involving several disciplines have failed to achieve the
level of systematic integration which is desirable in such
efforts. Certainly most impact assessment efforts to date
suffer from lack of adequate interdisciplinary integration.

It is imperative, then, that greater emphasis be placed on
developing more effective approaches to the organization and
management of interdisciplinary efforts and on establishing institutional mechanisms that encourage continuity in such efforts beyond the time span of any single sponsored project.[3]
For example, research administrators need to examine whether
creation of special institutes or centers with personnel from
a variety of disciplinary backgrounds will be a more effective
means of encouraging productive interdisciplinary efforts than
other, less formal, structures involving committees or interest groups focusing on specific topics of multidisciplinary

interest. Similarly, the effect of present reward structures in encouraging or deterring long-term commitments to interdisciplinary efforts must be carefully examined.

Finally, there may be a need to provide new avenues of communication for researchers and practicioners involved in impact assessment. Impact-related research, and particularly its interdisciplinary aspects, are often regarded as being outside the mainstream of the major contributing disciplines (e.g., economics, sociology). The provision of alternative mechanisms for the communication of new techniques and findings could enhance the development of this field.

In terms of providing more adequate data bases, it is readily apparent that more longitudinal and comparative analyses of the impacts of resource developments are essential. Longitudinal analyses are clearly necessary in order to address many of the specific impact-related issues identified in previous chapters. For example, the determination of how local economic interdependencies or social structures change over time as a result of development requires longitudinal data from developing areas. The need for comparative analyses is equally apparent. These studies are particularly important in discerning the effects of various contextual factors. Although most impact analysts assume that contextual conditions influence the various socioeconomic consequences of development, there is little evidence concerning which of these conditions has the greatest influence on impact events or on how important their relative influences may be.

The importance of longitudinal and comparative analyses in impact assessment lies not only in their scientific merit but also in their clear pragmatic significance. If such studies reveal contexts in which impacts are particularly severe and others where they are less problematic, this information could be very critical in the formation of future decisions concerning project siting or impact assistance. These studies thus offer important pragmatic, as well as methodological, advantages.

Future impact assessment efforts must give greater attention to the information requirements of decision makers. Impact analysts must give higher priority to identifying those individuals or groups who will be the principal users of the assessment and discerning their information requirements, including impact categories to be addressed, specific variables of interest, and most useful levels of analysis. While it must be recognized that determining information needs is not a trivial task and that the expressed needs of decision makers may require substantial interpretation by analysts, a greater commitment to tailor impact assessments and assessment models to the needs of user groups is essential (Edwards, 1980). Furthermore, impact assessments should be viewed not as a mechanism for developing a one-time projection but as an impact management tool to be utilized throughout the project

planning and development process. Such a use of assessments
will require greater commitments by both analysts and decision
makers but, if completed, should result in the development of
assessments which are increasingly relevant to the needs of
their users.

Finally, it is an often-noted, yet still highly applicable, conclusion that greater attention to the validation of
impact assessment models and techniques is necessary. Despite
the extensive resources devoted to impact assessments and the
development of increasingly sophisticated assessment techniques, the validity and reliability of different assessment
methods has not been adequately evaluated. A major task for
analysts in the early 1980s should be the evaluation of the
performance of their methods in comparison to data provided
by the census of 1980, as well as data from other reliable
sources. Until such assessments are completed, impact analysts will have little guidance concerning the relative
validity or reliability of alternative methods or the effect
of various contextual factors on their performance, and decision makers will have little basis for evaluating the
reliability or validity of the information provided through
the impact assessment process.

CONCLUSIONS

It is apparent that the future development of socioeconomic methods for assessing the impacts of resource developments will provide significant challenges for the social
science practitioner. Techniques that uniquely reflect the
impact assessment process must be developed while at the same
time major questions not yet fully resolved by the social
science community as a whole must be examined. Thus, socioeconomic impact analysts must not only design techniques that
can be completed in short periods of time, with limited resources, and that can readily be understood by a diverse set
of users but must also arrive at tentative answers to such
broad questions as: (1) how economic structures change as a
result of a major economic stimulus; (2) what factors determine
migration and settlement decisions; (3) how rural service
structures respond to increased demands; (4) how taxation policies will be applied during a period of rapid development; and
(5) how social structures respond to patterns of rapid growth.
These are clearly complex and difficult to address socioeconomic issues. In addition, the analyst must answer such questions not only for the present but often for several decades
into the future. If they are to be effective, impact analysts
must thus not only be specialists in impact analysis techniques
but conceptually and methodologically sophisticated social
scientists as well. Clearly then, the years to come will be
challenging ones.

It is apparent at the same time, however, that they will
be exciting and potentially rewarding ones for impact analysts
and the social sciences. The laboratory of research opportunities for both conceptual and methodological refinement
of social science concepts and methods provided by impact
events and the assessment process must not be allowed to es-
cape the attention of concerned and policy-oriented social
scientists. To avoid the problems and challenges that will
arise in the development, refinement, expansion, and evaluation of socioeconomic impact assessment techniques in the
coming years will entail missing a significant opportunity to
contribute to the development of the social sciences as well.
Even more important, it will mean that the information needs
of residents in impact areas will not have been adequately
addressed. The pragmatic and professional necessity for the
further development of the socioeconomic impact assessment
art is thus apparent. It is a challenge that must be met.

NOTES

1. A few initial efforts to incorporate environmental
dimensions into socioeconomic models have been noted, including
Huston (1979) and Hite and Laurent (1972).

2. One research project which is currently underway has
as one of its major objectives an expanded evaluation of the
accuracy of impact assessments. This project, sponsored by
the Electric Power Research Institute and conducted by the
Denver Research Institute, involves retrospective evaluation
of thirteen electric power plant sites (Coddington and Gilmore,
1980).

3. For a review of alternative approaches to organizing
and managing such efforts, see Swanson (1979) and Rossini et
al. (1978).

Bibliography

Adams, F. G., C. Brooking, and N. J. Glickman. 1975. "On the Specification and Simulation of a Regional Econometric Model: A Model of Mississippi". Review of Economics and Statistics 57: 286-298.

Albrecht, Stan. 1978. "Socio-cultural Factors and Energy Resource Development in Rural Areas in the West". Journal of Environmental Management 7: 78-90.

Albrecht, Stan. 1980. "Unique Effects of Rapid Population Growth Upon Different Cultural Groups: The Native American Experience". Paper presented at the Seminar on the Social and Economic Impacts of Rapid Growth, Scottsdale, Ariz., February 27-29.

Almon, C., M. Buckler, L. Horowitz, and T. Reimbold. 1974. 1985: Interindustry Forecasts of the American Economy. Lexington, Mass.: D.C. Heath and Company.

Alonso, William. 1968. "Predicting Best With Imperfect Data". Journal of the American Institute of Planners 34 (4): 248-254.

Ament, R. H. 1970. "Comparison of Delphi Forecasting Studies". Futures 2: 35-44.

American Statistical Association. 1977. Report to the Conference on Economic and Demographic Methods for Projecting Population. Washington, D.C.: American Statistical Association.

Anderson, E., and B. Hannigan. 1977. Arizona Economic-Demographic Projection Model: A Summary Report and Technical Description. Phoenix: Arizona Office of Economic Planning and Development.

Anderson, E., J. Chalmers, D. Schmidt, G. Yaquinto, and M. York. 1976. Analysis of Development Alternatives: Technical Report. Cheyenne: Wyoming Department of Economic Planning and Development.

Anderson, E., J. Chalmers, T. Hogan, and T. Beckhelm. 1974. ATOM 2: Part I of Final Report. Phoenix: Arizona Office of Economic Planning and Development.

258

Anderson, Theodore R. 1955. "Intermetropolitan Migration: A Comparison of the Hypotheses of Zipf and Stouffer". American Sociological Review 20 (3): 287-91.

Applebaum, Richard P. 1970. Theories of Social Change. Chicago: Rand McNally College Publishing Company.

Armer, M., and A. Schnailberg. 1972. "Measuring Individual Modernity: A Near Myth". American Sociological Review 37: 301-16.

Ascher, William. 1978. Forecasting: An Appraisal for Policy Makers and Planners. Baltimore: Johns Hopkins University Press.

Auger, C. S., B. Udis, R. Maurice, D. Brunt, and R. Hess. 1976. In the Development of a Standard Method for Socioeconomic Forecasting and Analysis of Energy Related Growth: Socioeconomic Impacts of Western Energy Development. Washington, D.C.: Council on Environmental Quality.

Auger, C. S., E. Allen, S. Blaha, V. Fahys, L. Low, R. Maurice, C. Vestal, and C. Walker. 1978. Energy Resource Development, Socioeconomic Impacts, and the Current Role of Impact Assistance: An Eleven State Review. Boulder, Colo.: Tosco Foundation.

Auger, C. S., and Martin E. Zeller. 1979. Siting Major Energy Facilities: A Process in Transition. Boulder, Colo.: The Tosco Foundation.

Avineri, Shlomo. 1970. The Social and Political Thought of Karl Marx. New York: Cambridge University Press.

Babbie, Earl R. 1973. Survey Research Methods. Belmont, Calif.: Wadsworth Publishing Company, Inc.

Barclay, George W. 1958. Techniques of Population Analysis. New York: John Wiley and Sons, Inc.

Battelle Columbus Laboratories. 1973. Final Report of the Arizona Environmental and Economic Trade-Off Model. Phoenix: Arizona Office of Planning and Development.

Beale, Calvin L. 1976. "A Further Look at Nonmetropolitan Population Growth Since 1970". American Journal of Agricultural Economics 5 (5): 953-958.

Beckhelm, T. L., J. A. Chalmers, and W. M. Hannigan. 1975. A Description of the ATOM 3 and of the Research Related to Its Development. Washington, D.C.: Four Corners Regional Commission.

Bender, Lloyd D. 1980. "The Effect of Trends in Economic Structures on Population Change in Rural Areas", in New Directions in Urban-Rural Migration: The Population Turnaround in Nonmetropolitan America, eds., David L. Brown and John W. Wardwell, New York: Academic Press.

Bender, Lloyd D. 1975. Predicting Employment in Four Regions of the Western United States. USDA Tech. Bull. No. 1529. Washington, D.C.: Economic Research Service, U.S. Department of Agriculture, in cooperation with Agricultural Experiment Station, Montana State University.

Berkey, E., N. G. Carpenter, W. C. Metz, D. W. Myers, D. R. Porter, J. E. Singley, and R. K. Travis. 1977. Social Impact Assessment, Monitoring, and Management by the Electric Energy Industry: State-of-the-Practice. Washington, D.C.: Atomic Industrial Forum and Edison Electric Institute.

Berry, B. J. L. 1967. Geography of Market Centers and Retail Distribution. Englewood Cliffs, N.J.: Prentice Hall.

Berry, B. J. L. 1973. Growth Centers in the American Urban System. Cambridge, Mass.: Ballinger Publishing Company.

Berry, B. J. L., and W. L. Garrison. 1958. "Recent Development of Central Place Theory". Papers and Proceedings of the Regional Science Association 4: 107-121.

Betters, David R. 1979. The Harris Model and DYRAM: An Evaluation and Comparison. Denver: USDI Bureau of Land Management.

Bigler, C., R. Reeve, and R. Weaver. 1972. Report on the Development of the Utah Process: A Procedure for Planning Coordination Through Forecasting and Evaluating Alternative State Futures. Salt Lake City: Utah State Planning Coordinator.

Billings, R. B. 1969. "The Mathematical Identity of the Multipliers Derived From the Economic Base and the Input-Output Model". Journal of Regional Science 9: 471-473.

Bjornstad, D., Jr., C. H. Patrick, and K. P. Nelson. 1975. State Population Projections: A Comparative Review of National Series and Their Practical Usefulness. Oak Ridge, Tenn.: Oak Ridge National Laboratory.

Blalock, H. M. 1979. "Measurement and Conceptualization Problems". American Sociological Review 44 (6): 881-894.

Blumer, Herbert. 1980. "Social Behaviorism and Symbolic Interactionism". American Sociological Review 45 (3): 409-419.

Blumer, Herbert. 1969. Symbolic Interactionism: Perspective and Method. Englewood Cliffs, N.J.: Prentice Hall.

Bohm, R. A., and J. H. Lord. 1972. "Regional Economic Simulation Modeling -- The T.V.A. Experience". Paper presented at the Annual Meetings of the Northeast Regional Science Association, University Park, Pa., April 14-15.

Boisvert, R. N., and N. L. Bills. 1976. A Nonsurvey Technique for Regional I-O Models: Application to River Basin Planning. A.E. Res. 76-19. Ithaca, N.Y.: Cornell University.

Bogue, Donald J. 1974. Techniques for Making Population Projections: How to Make Age-Sex Projections by Electronic Computer. Chicago: University of Chicago Community and Family Study Center.

Bonner, E. R., and V. L. Fahle. 1967. Technique for Area Planning. Pittsburgh, Pa.: Regional Economic Development Institute.

Borchert, J. R., and R. B. Adams. 1963. Trade Centers and Trade Areas of the Upper Midwest. Urban Report No. 3.

260

Minneapolis: Upper Midwest Council.

Boster, R. S., and W. E. Martin. 1972. "The Value of Primary
    Versus Secondary Data in Interindustry Analysis: A Study
    in the Economics of Economic Models". The Annals of
    Regional Science 6 (2): 35-44.
Bowles, G. K., C. L. Beale, and E. S. Lee. 1975. Net Migration
    of the Population, 1960-70 by Age, Sex, and Color. Athens:
    University of Georgia Printing Department.
Bowles, G. K., and J. D. Tarver. 1965. Net Migration of the
    Population, 1950-60 by Age, Sex, and Color. Washington,
    D.C.: U.S. Government Printing Office.
Braschler, Curtis. 1972. "A Comparison of Least Squares Esti-
    mates of Regional Employment Multipliers with Other Meth-
    ods". Journal of Regional Science 12 (3): 457-468.
Briscoe, Maphis, Murray, Lamont, Inc. 1978. Action Handbook:
    Managing Growth in the Small Community. Washington, D.C.:
    U.S. Government Printing Office.
Brown, F. L., and L. B. Zink. 1977. New Mexico Economic and
    Demographic Model, Final Report. Albuquerque: University
    of New Mexico Institute for Applied Research Services.
Buchanan, S. C., and B. A. Weber. 1979. "The Impact of Popu-
    lation Growth on Residential and Nonresidential Property
    Taxes". Paper presented at 1979 Annual Meeting of Ameri-
    can Agricultural Economics Association, Pullman, Wash.,
    July 29-August 1.
Burchell, R. W., and D. Listokin. 1978. The Fiscal Impact
    Handbook. New Brunswick, N. J.: Rutgers Center for
    Urban Policy Research.
Carlson, J. F., and G. F. Doll with C. Phillips, J. Lofgren,
    and J. W. Brock. 1976. The North Platte River Basin
    Economic Simulation Model: A Technical Report. Laramie:
    University of Wyoming Water Resources Research Institute.
Carnes, S., and P. Friesma. 1974. Urbanization and the Northern
    Great Plains. Denver: Northern Great Plains Resources
    Program.
Carpenter, Edwin H. 1977. "Evaluation of Mail Questionnaires
    for Obtaining Data for More than One Respondent in a House-
    hold". Rural Sociology 42 (2): 250-259.
Carrothers, Gerald P. 1956. "An Historical Review of the Grav-
    ity and Potential Concepts of Human Interaction". Journal
    of the American Institute of Planners 22 (2): 94-99.
Catton, W. R., and R. E. Dunlap. 1978. "Environmental Sociolo-
    gy: A New Paradigm". The American Sociologist 13: 41-49.
Chalmers, J. A., and E. J. Anderson. 1977. Economic-Demographic
    Assessment Manual: Current Practices, Procedural Recommend-
    ations, and a Test Case. Denver: U.S. Bureau of Recla-
    mation.
Chalmers, J. A., E. J. Anderson, T. Beckhelm, and W. Hannigan.
    1977. "An Empirical Model of Spatial Interaction in
    Sparsely Populated Regions". Paper presented at 24th

Annual Meeting of Regional Science Association, Phila-
delphia, Pa., November 11-13.
Chenery, H. B. 1953. "Regional Analysis", in The Structure
and Growth of the Italian Economy, eds., Chenery, Clark,
and Cao-Pinna, Rome: U.S. Mutual Security Agency, pp.
97-116.
Christaller, W. 1933. Die Zentralen Orte in Suddeutchland.
Jena: Fischer (translated as Central Places in Southern
Germany by C. W. Baskin and published by Prentice-Hall,
Englewood Cliffs, N.J., 1966).
Christenson, J. A., and J. W. Robinson, Jr. 1980. Community
Development in America. Ames: Iowa State University Press.
Christenson, J. A. 1976. "Quality of Community Services: A
Macrodimensional Approach with Experimental Data". Rural
Sociology 41: 509-525.
Cluett, C., M. T. Mertaugh, and M. Micklin. 1977. "A Demo-
graphic Model for Assessing the Socioeconomic Impacts of
Large-Scale Industrial Development Projects". Paper
presented at 1977 Annual Meeting of the Southern Regional
Demographic Group, Virginia Beach, Va., October 21-22.
Coddington, D. C., and J. S. Gilmore. 1980. "A Review of the
State-of-the-Art in Local Impact Assessment". Paper
presented to GPC-8 Workshop on Modeling Local Impacts of
Energy Development, Denver, March 18-19.
Colony Development Operation. 1974. An Environmental Impact
Analysis for a Shale Oil Complex at Parachute Creek,
Colorado. Denver: Colony Development Operation.
Cooley, C. H. 1909. Social Organization. New York:
Scribner's and Son.
Conopask, J. V. 1978. A Data-Pooling Approach to Estimate
Employment Multipliers For Small Regional Economies.
USDA Tech. Bull. No. 1583. Washington, D.C.: U.S. Govern-
ment Printing Office.
Cortese, C., and B. Jones. 1977. "The Sociological Analysis of
Boom Towns". Western Sociological Review 8 (1): 76-90.
Coser, Lewis A. 1967. Continuities in the Study of Social
Conflict. New York: Free Press.
Council on Environmental Quality. 1978. "National Environ-
mental Policy Act". Federal Register 43 (June 9): 112.
Council on Environmental Quality. 1973. "Preparation of En-
vironmental Impact Statements: Guidelines". Federal
Register 38 (147): August 1.
Crow, R. T. 1973. "A Nationally Linked Regional Econometric
Model". Journal of Regional Science 13: 187-204.
Cummings, R. G., and W. D. Schulze. 1978. "Optimal Investment
Strategy for Boomtowns: A Theoretical Analysis". Ameri-
can Economic Review 68 (3): 374-385.
Dacey, M. F. 1966. "Population of Places in a Central Place
Hierarchy". Journal of Regional Science 6: 27-33.
Dahrendorf, Ralf. 1959. Class and Class Conflict in Industrial
Society. Stanford, Calif.: Stanford University Press.

Dalsted, N. L., A. G. Leholm, N. E Toman, R. C. Coon, T. A. Hertsgaard, and F. L. Leistritz. 1976. Economic Impacts of a Proposed Coal Gasification Plant In Dunn County, North Dakota. Fargo: North Dakota Agricultural Experiment Station.

Dalsted, N. L., F. L. Leistritz, and T. A. Hertsgaard. 1974. Economic Impact of Alternative Energy Development Patterns in North Dakota. Denver: Northern Great Plains Resources Program.

Davis, H. Craig. 1976. "Regional Sector Multipliers with Reduced Data Requirements". International Regional Science Review 1 (2): 18-29.

Davis, H. Craig. 1978. "A Synthesis of Two Methods of Estimating Regional Sector Multipliers". Growth and Change 9 (2): 9-13.

Deacon, R. T. 1978. "A Demand Model for the Local Public Sector". Review of Economics and Statistics 60 (2): 184-192.

Denver Research Institute. 1979. Socioeconomic Impact of Western Energy Resource Development. Washington, D.C.: Council on Environmental Quality.

Dillman, D. 1978. Mail and Telephone Surveys: The Total Design Method. New York: John Wiley and Sons, Inc.

Division of Business and Economic Research. 1975. The Socioeconomic Impact of the Proposed Laramie River Station. Laramie: University of Wyoming, Division of Business and Economic Research.

Doeksen, G. A., and D. F. Schreiner. 1974. Interindustry Models for Rural Development Research. Tech. Bull. T-139. Stillwater: Oklahoma Agricultural Experiment Station.

Drake, Ronald L. 1976. "A Short-Cut to Estimates of Regional Input-Output Multipliers: Methodology and Evaluation". International Regional Science Review 1 (2): 1-17.

Drake, R., S. Randall, and M. Skinner. 1973. Evaluation of Economic Impact of Forest Service Programs in Northern New Mexico: Development of Analytical Tools. Berkeley, Calif.: USDA Economic Research Service.

Duncan, O. D., and A. J. Reiss, Jr. 1956. Social Characteristics of Urban and Rural Communities, 1950. New York: John Wiley and Sons, Inc.

Duncan, O. D., and L. Schnore. 1959. "Culture, Behavioral, and Ecological Perspectives in the Study of Social Organization". American Journal of Sociology 65: 132-146.

Duncan, O. D., R. Scott, S. Lieberson, B. Duncan, and H. H. Winsborough. 1960. Metropolis and Region. Baltimore: Johns Hopkins University Press.

Duncan, O. D. 1964. "Social Organization and the Ecosystem". in Handbook of Modern Sociology, ed., Robert Faris, Chicago: Rand McNally and Co., pp. 36-82.

Durkheim, Emile. 1933. The Division of Labor in Society. New York: The Free Press.

Easterlin, R. A., M. L. Wachter, and S. M. Wachter. 1978. "Demographic Influences on Economic Stability: The United States Experience". Population and Development Review 4: 1-22.

Edwards, Jack D. 1980. "Local Impacts of Resource Development Projects". Paper presented to GPC-8 Workshop on Modeling Local Impacts of Energy Development, Denver, March 18-19.

Ellis, Robert H. 1974. The Planning and Management of Problem-Oriented, Interdisciplinary Research at Academic Institutions. Hartford: Connecticut Rensselaer Hartford Graduate Center.

Evans, M. K., and L. R. Klein. 1968. The Wharton Economic Forecasting Model. Philadelphia: University of Pennsylvania.

Federal Energy Administration. 1976. National Energy Outlook. Washington, D.C.: U.S. Government Printing Office.

Finsterbusch, K. 1977. Methods for Evaluating Nonmarket Impacts in Policy Decisions with Special Reference to Water Resources Development Projects. Fort Belvoir, Va.: U.S. Army Corps of Engineers.

Fitzsimmons, S. J., L. I. Stuart, and P. C. Wolf. 1975. Social Assessment Manual: A Guide to the Preparation of the Social Well-Being Account. Washington, D.C.: U.S. Bureau of Reclamation.

Ford, Andrew. 1976. User's Guide to the BOOM 1 Model. LA-6396-MS. Los Alamos, N.M.: Los Alamos Scientific Laboratory.

Forrester, Jay W. 1961. Industrial Dynamics. Cambridge, Mass.: The MIT Press.

Forrester, Jay W. 1968. Principles of Systems. Cambridge, Mass.: Wright-Allen Press, Inc.

Forrester, J. W. 1969. Urban Dynamics. Cambridge, Mass.: The MIT Press.

Freeman, D. M., J. M. Quint, K. E. Jones, and R. S. Frey. 1978. "Employing a Delphi Method for Estimating and Comparing Impacts of Proposed Natural Resource Management Alternatives: Effects of Participant Ideology and Alternative Complexity on Reliability". Paper presented at the Rural Sociological Society Annual Meetings, San Francisco, Calif., August 30-September 3.

Freudenburg, William R. 1980. "The Effects of Rapid Population Growth on the Social and Personal Well-Being of Local Residents". Paper presented at the Seminar on the Social and Economic Impacts of Rapid Growth, Scottsdale, Ariz., February, 26-27.

Freudenburg, William R. 1981. "Social Impact Assessment", in Rural Society: Research Issues for the 1980s, eds., Don Dillman and Darryll Hobbs: Boulder, Colo.: Westview Press.

264

Freudenburg, William R. 1979. "The Social Impact of Energy Boom Development on Rural Communities: A Review of Literature and Some Predictions". Paper presented at the Annual Meeting of the American Sociological Association, New York, August 31.

Fromm, G., W. L. Hamilton, and D. E. Hamilton. 1975. Federally Supported Mathematical Models: Survey and Analysis. Washington, D.C.: National Science Foundation.

Gabler, L. R. 1971. "Population Size as a Determinant of City Expenditures and Employment -- Some Further Evidence". Land Economics 47 (2): 130-138.

Garnick, D. H. 1970. "Differential Regional Multiplier Models". Journal of Regional Science 10: 35-47.

Gillies, L., and W. Grigsby. 1956. "Classification Errors in Base-Ratio Analysis". Journal of the American Institute of Planners 22: 17-23.

Gilmore, J. S. 1976. "Boom Towns May Hinder Energy Resource Development". Science 191: 535-540.

Gilmore, J. S., K. D. Moore, D. M. Hammond, and D. C. Coddington. 1976a. Analysis of Financing Problems in Coal and Oil Shale Boom Towns. Washington, D.C.: Federal Energy Administration.

Gilmore, J. S., K. D. Moore, and D. M. Hammond. 1976b. Synthesis and Evaluation of Initial Methodologies For Assessing Socioeconomic and Secondary Environmental Impacts of Western Energy Resource Development. Working Paper No. 2. Denver: Denver Research Institute.

Gilmore, J. S., and M. K. Duff. 1975. Boom Town Growth Management: A Case Study of Rock Springs -- Green River, Wyoming. Boulder, Colo.: Westview Press.

Gilmore, J. S., R. E. Giltner, D. C. Coddington, and M. K. Duff. 1975. Factors Influencing an Area's Ability to Absorb a Large-Scale Commercial Coal-Processing Complex. Washington, D.C.: Energy Research and Development Administration.

Glaser, B. G., and A. L. Strauss. 1967. The Discovery of Grounded Theory. Chicago: Aldine Publishing Company.

Glickman, N. J. 1977. Econometric Analysis of Regional Systems: Exploration of Model-Building and Policy Analysis. New York: Academic Press.

Goffman, Erving. 1961. Asylums: Essays on the Social Situation of Mental Patients and Other Inmates. New York: Doubleday and Company.

Gold, Raymond L. 1974. A Comparative Case Study of the Impacts of Coal Development on the Way of Life of People in the Coal Areas of Eastern Montana and Northeastern Wyoming. Denver: Northern Great Plains Resources Program.

Gold, Raymond L. 1958. "Roles in Sociological Field Observations". Social Forces 36: 217-23.

Goodman, N., and G. T. Marx. 1978. Society Today. Third Edition. New York: Random House.

Gray, J. R., L. Austin, W. Capener, L. Catlett, C. Eastman, B. Ives, M. Mathews, and R. Supalla. 1977. Socioeconomic Impacts of Coal Mining on Communities in Northwestern New Mexico. Bull. No. 652. Las Cruces: New Mexico Agricultural Experiment Station.

Greenberger, M., M. A. Crenson, and B. L. Crissey. 1976. Models in the Policy Process: Public Decision Making in the Computer Era. New York: Russell Sage Foundation.

Greenburg, M. R., D. A. Krueckeburg, and C. O. Michaelson. 1978. Local Population and Employment Projection Techniques. New Brunswick, N.J.: The Center for Urban Policy Research.

Greenhut, M. L. 1956. Plant Location in Theory and Practice. Chapel Hill: North Carolina University Press.

Greenwood, M. J. 1975. "Research on Internal Migration in the United States". Journal of Economic Literature 13 (2): 397-433.

Greytak, D. 1969. "A Statistical Analysis of Regional Export Estimating Techniques". Journal of Regional Science 9: 387-395.

Groves, H. M., and R. L. Bish. 1973. Financing Government. Seventh Edition. New York: Holt, Rinehart, and Winston, Inc.

Groves, R. M., and R. L. Kahn. 1979. Surveys by Telephone: A National Comparison with Personal Interviews. New York: Academic Press.

Haig, R. 1926. "Toward an Understanding of the Metropolis: Some Speculations Regarding the Economic Basis of Urban Concentration". Quarterly Journal of Economics 40: 179-208.

Hamilton, H. C., and J. Perry. 1962. "A Short Method for Projecting Population by Age From One Decennial Census to Another". Social Forces 41 (22): 163-70.

Hamilton, H. R., S. E. Goldstone, F. H. Cesario, D. C. Sweet, D. E. Boyce, and A. L. Pugh. 1966. A Dynamic Model of the Economy of the Susquehanna River-Basin. Columbus, Ohio: The Battelle Memorial Institute.

Hamilton, H. R., S. E. Goldstone, J. W. Milliman, A. L. Pugh, E. B. Roberts, and A. Zellner. 1969. Systems Simulation for Regional Analysis: An Application to River-Basin Planning. Cambridge, Mass.: MIT Press.

Hansen, W. L., and C. M. Tiebout. 1963. "An Intersectoral Flows Analysis of the California Economy". Review of Economics and Statistics 45: 409-416.

Hansen, W. L., R. T. Robson, and C. M. Tiebout. 1961. Markets for California Products. Sacramento: State of California Economic Development Agency.

Harmstrom, F. K., and R. E. Lund. 1967. Application of an Input-Output Framework to a Community Economic System.

University of Missouri Studies. Vol. 42. Columbia: University of Missouri Press.

Harris, C. C. 1973. The Urban Economies, 1985: A Multi-regional, Multi-Industry Forecasting Model. Lexington, Mass.: Lexington Books.

Harvey, Andrew S. 1973. "Spatial Variation of Export Employment Multipliers: A Cross-Section Analysis". Land Economics 49 (4): 469-474.

Hathaway, D. E., J. A. Beegle, and W. Bryant. 1968. People of Rural America. Washington, D.C.: U.S. Bureau of the Census.

Hawley, Amos H. 1950. Human Ecology: A Theory of Community Structure. New York: Ronald Press.

Hawley, W. D., and F. M. Wirt (eds.). 1974. The Search for Community Power. Second Edition. Englewood Cliffs, N.J.: Prentice Hall.

Hayen, R. L., and G. L. Watts. 1975. A Description of Potential Socioeconomic Impacts From Energy-Related Developments on Campbell County, Wyoming. Laramie, Wyo.: Resource Management Systems.

Heberlein, T. A., and R. Baumgartner. 1978. "Factors Affecting Response Rates to Mailed Questionnaires". American Sociological Review 43 (4): 447-462.

Henry, M. S., A. Leholm, G. Schaible, and J. Haskins. 1980. "A Semi-Survey Approach to Building Regional Input-Output Models: An Application to Western North Dakota". North Central Journal of Agricultural Economics 2 (1): 17-24.

Hertsgaard, T. A., R. C. Coon, F. L. Leistritz, and N. L. Dalsted. 1977. Developing Economic Impact Projection Models for the Fort Union Coal Region. EPA-908/4-77-009. Denver: U.S. Environmental Protection Agency.

Hertsgaard, T., S. Murdock, N. Toman, M. Henry, and R. Ludtke. 1978. REAP Economic-Demographic Model: Technical Description. Bismarck: North Dakota Regional Environmental Assessment Program.

Hill, K. O., and J. Fowles. 1975. "The Methodological Worth of the Delphi Forecasting Techniques". Technological Forecasting and Social Change 7: 179-192.

Hirsch, W. Z. 1964. "Fiscal Impact of Industrialization on Local Schools". Review of Economics and Statistics 46: 191-199.

Hirsch, W. Z. 1973. Urban Economic Analysis. New York: McGraw-Hill Book Company.

Hite, J. C., and E. A. Laurent. 1972. Environmental Planning: An Economic Analysis, Applications to the Coastal Zone. New York: Praeger Publishers.

Hoos, Ida R. 1972. Systems Analysis in Public Policy: A Critique. Berkeley: University of California Press.

Hoover, E. M. 1971. An Introduction to Regional Economics. New York: Alfred A. Knopf.

Hoover, E. M. 1948. The Location of Economic Activity. New
York: McGraw-Hill.

Hotelling, H. 1929. "Stability in Competition". Economic
Journal 39: 41-57.

House, P. W., and J. McLeod. 1977. Large-Scale Models for
Policy Evaluation. New York: John Wiley and Sons, Inc.

Hoyt, H. 1933. One Hundred Years of Land Values in Chicago.
Chicago: University of Chicago Press.

Huston, Michael. 1979. "The United States Steel Project --
A Comprehensive Approach to Socioeconomic Analysis", in
Boom Towns: Managing Growth, Proceedings of Mini-
Symposium, SME-AIME Annual Meeting, New Orleans, La.,
February.

Inkeles, Alex. 1975. "Emerging Social Structure in the World".
World Politics 27: 467-95.

Inman, R. P. 1979. "The Fiscal Performance of Local Govern-
ments: An Interpretative Review", in Current Issues in
Urban Economics, eds., P. Mieszkowski and M. Straszheim,
Baltimore: Johns Hopkins University Press.

Intermountain Planners and Wirth-Berger Associates. 1974.
Powder River Basin Capital Facilities Study. Cheyenne:
Wyoming Department of Economic Planning and Development.

Irwin, Richard. 1977. Guide for Local Area Population Projections. U.S. Bureau of the Census. Washington, D.C.:
U.S. Government Printing Office.

Isard, W., C. Choguill, J. Kissin, R. Seyfarth, and R. Tatlock.
1972. Ecologic-Economic Analysis for Regional Development.
New York: The Free Press.

Isard, W. 1951. "Interregional and Regional Input-Output
Analysis: A Model of a Space Economy". Review of Economics and Statistics 33: 318-328.

Isard, W. 1960. Methods of Regional Analysis: An Introduction to Regional Science. Cambridge, Mass.: The MIT
Press.

Isard, W., and R. E. Coughlin. 1957. Municipal Costs and
Revenues from Community Growth. Wellesley, Mass.:
Chandler-Davis Publishing Company.

Isard, W., and R. E. Kuenne. 1953. "The Impact of Steel Upon
the Greater New York-Philadelphia Urban Industrial Region".
Review of Economics and Statistics 35: 289-301.

Isserman, A. 1980. "Alternative Economic Base Bifurcation
Techniques: Theory, Implementation, and Results", in
Economic Impact Analysis: Methodology and Applications,
ed., S. Pleeter, Boston: Martinus Nijhoff Publishing.

Isserman, A. M. 1977a. "The Accuracy of Population Projections for Subcounty Areas". Journal of the American
Institute of Planners 43: 247-259.

Isserman, A. M. 1977b. "The Location Quotient Approach to
Estimating Regional Economic Impacts". Journal of the
American Institute of Planners 43 (1): 33-41.

Jones, L. L., and S. H. Murdock. 1978. "The Incremental
Nature of Public Service Delivery: Implications for Rural
Areas". American Journal of Agricultural Economics 60 (5):
955-960.

Kalter, R. J. 1969. An Interindustry Analysis of the Central
New York Region. Ag. Exp. Sta. Bull. 1025. Ithaca,
N.Y.: Cornell University.

Karp, H., and D. Kelly. 1971. Towards an Ecological Analysis
of Intermetropolitan Migration. Chicago: Markham.

Kee, W. S. 1968. "Industrial Development and Its Impact on
Local Finance". Quarterly Review of Economics and Business 8: 19-24.

Kendall, Mark C. 1977. "Labor-Market Models", in Population
Forecasting for Small Areas. Oak Ridge, Tenn.: Oak Ridge
Associated Universities, pp. 49-58.

Keyfitz, Nathan. 1972. "On Future Population". Journal of
the American Statistical Association 67 (338): 347-363.

Kirlin, J., and H. J. Brown. 1979. The Public Expenditure
Model: Technical Documentation. Cambridge, Mass.:
Harvard University Landscape Architecture Research Office.

Klein, L. R. 1969. "The Specification of Regional Econometric Models". Papers of the Regional Science Association
23: 105-115.

Klindt, T. H., G. L. Bradford, and B. R. Beattie. 1972. Per-
fecting Methods for Predicting the Course of Rural Area
Development. Res. Rpt. 13. Lexington, Mass.: Kentucky
Agricultural Experiment Station.

Kohrs, E. 1974. Social Consequences of Boom Growth in
Wyoming. Casper, Wyoming: Central Wyoming Counseling
Center.

Kraenzel, C. 1955. The Great Plains in Transition. Norman:
University of Oklahoma Press.

Krannich, Richard S. 1978. "A Comparative Analysis of Fac-
tors Influencing the Socioeconomic Impacts of Electric
Generating Facilities". Paper presented at the 71st
Annual Meeting of the Air Pollution Control Association,
Houston, Texas, June 25-30.

Krutilla, J. V., and A. C. Fisher, with R. E. Rice. 1978.
Economic and Fiscal Impacts of Coal Development: North-
ern Great Plains. Baltimore: Johns Hopkins University
Press.

Kuhn, Thomas S. 1970. The Structure of Scientific Revolu-
tions. Second Edition. Chicago: University of Chicago
Press.

Lamont, W. 1974. Tax Lead Time Study: The Colorado Oil
Shale Region. Denver: Colorado Geological Survey.

Lansford, Notie H. 1980. An Economic Analysis of Rural
Community Service Expenditures in Texas. Master's Thesis,
Department of Agricultural Economics. College Station:
Texas A&M University.

Lee, J. W., and W. B. Hong. 1972. Regional Demographic Projections: 1960-1985. Population, Labor Force, Migration and Households for Regions and States. Rpt. No. 72-R-1. Washington, D.C.: National Planning Association.

Leholm, A. G., F. L. Leistritz, and T. A. Hertsgaard. 1976a. "Fiscal Impact of a New Industry in a Rural Area: A Coal Gasification Plant in Western North Dakota". Regional Science Perspectives 60: 40-56.

Leholm, A. G., F. L. Leistritz, and J. S. Wieland. 1976b. Profile of North Dakota's Electric Power Plant Construction Work Force. Ag. Econ. Stat. Series No. 22. Fargo: North Dakota Agricultural Experiment Station.

Leholm, A. G., N. L. Dalsted, N. E. Toman, F. L. Leistritz, T. A. Hertsgaard, and R. C. Coon. 1976c. Economic Impacts of Construction and Operation of Coyote #1 Electrical Generation Plant and Expansion of Coal Handling Facilities at the Beulah Mine of Knife River Coal Company. Fargo: North Dakota Agricultural Experiment Station.

Leistritz, F. L., S. H. Murdock, and A. G. Leholm. 1980a. "The Effects of Rapid Population Growth on the Local Economy". Paper presented at Seminar on Social and Economic Impacts of Rapid Growth, Western Rural Development Center, Scottsdale, Ariz., February 26-27.

Leistritz, F. L., S. H. Murdock, D. M. Senechal, and T. A. Hertsgaard. 1980b. "Computerized Socioeconomic Impact Models: Usefulness and Limitations". Paper presented at Conference on Computer Models for Forecasting Socioeconomic Impacts of Growth and Development, Jasper Park, Alberta, April 20-23.

Leistritz, F. L., S. H. Murdock, N. E. Toman, and T. A. Hertsgaard. 1979a. "A Model For Projecting Localized Economic, Demographic, and Fiscal Impacts of Large-Scale Projects". Western Journal of Agricultural Economics 4 (2): 1-16.

Leistritz, F. L., S. H. Murdock, N. E. Toman, L. L. Jones, and J. de Montel. 1979b. "Alternative Energy Resource Taxation Systems: Implications for Local Governments". Paper presented at 1979 Annual Meeting of American Agricultural Economics Association, Pullman, Washington, July 29-August 1.

Leontief, W. 1941. The Structure of the United States Economy, 1919-1939. Cambridge, Mass.: Harvard University Press.

Leontief, W. 1936. "Quantitative Input and Output Relations in the Economic System of the United States". Review of Economics and Statistics 18: 105-125.

Levan, C. L. 1956. "Measuring the Economic Base". Papers of the Regional Science Association 2: 250-258.

Levan, C. L. 1961. "Regional Income and Product Accounts: Construction and Applications", in Design of Regional Accounts, ed., W. Hochwald, Baltimore: Johns Hopkins University Press, pp. 148-195.

270

Lewis, C., and S. Albrecht. 1977. "Attitudes Towards Acceler-
    ated Urban Development in Low Population Areas". Growth
    and Change 8: 22-27.
Lewis, W. Cris. 1976. "Export Base Theory and Multiplier
    Estimation: A Critique". Annals of Regional Science
    11 (3): 58-70.
Lofland, John. 1971. Analyzing Social Settings. Belmont,
    Calif.: Wadsworth Publishing Company, Inc.
Long, L. H., and K. A. Hansen. 1979. Reasons for Interstate
    Migration. Current Population Reports. No. P-23, 81.
    Washington, D.C.: U.S. Government Printing Office.
Lonsdale, R. E., and H. L. Seyler. 1979. Nonmetropolitan
    Industrialization. New York: John Wiley and Sons, Inc.
Lopreato, S. C., and M. Blisset. 1978. An Attitudinal Survey
    of Citizens in a Potential Gulf Coast Geopressured-
    Geothermal Test-Well Locality. Washington, D.C.: Energy
    Research and Development Administration.
Losch, A. 1940. Die raumliche Ordnung der Wirtschaft. Jena:
    Fischer (translated as The Economics of Locations by W.
    Woglom and W. Stopler and published by Yale University
    Press, New Haven, 1954).
Love, Ruth. 1978. Doing Social Effects Assessment: Two Cases
    from a Corps Field District. Fort Belvoir, Va.: U.S. Army
    Corps of Engineers.
Lovejoy, Stephen B. 1977. Local Perceptions of Energy Develop-
    ment: The Case of the Kaiparowitz Plateau. Lake Powell
    Research Project. Bull. No. 62. Logan: Utah State
    University.
Low, Laurent. 1980. "Computer Models and the Planning Revo-
    lution". Paper presented at Conference on Computer Models
    for Forecasting Socioeconomic Impacts of Growth and
    Development, Jasper, Alberta, April 20-23.
Ludtke, Richard L. 1978. Social Impacts of Energy Develop-
    ment: A Combined Report of Content Analysis and Survey
    Data for Southwestern North Dakota. Grand Forks: Uni-
    versity of North Dakota.
McConnell, C. R. 1969. Economics: Principles, Problems,
    and Policies. Fourth Edition. New York: McGraw-Hill.
McCoy, Clyde B. 1975. "The Impact of an Impact Study: Con-
    tributions of Sociology to Decision-Making in Govern-
    ment". Environment and Behavior 7 (3): 358-372.
McKee, Russell. 1974. The Last West: A History of the Great
    Plains of North America. Toronto: Fitzhenry and White-
    side.
McNulty, James E. 1977. "A Test of the Time Dimension in
    Economic Base Analysis". Land Economics 53 (3): 359-368.
Mace, R. L. 1961. Municipal Cost-Revenue Research in the
    United States. Chapel Hill: University of North Carolina.
Mace, R. L., and W. J. Wicker. 1968. Do Single Family Homes
    Pay Their Way?: A Comparative Analysis of Costs and

Revenues for Public Services. Research Monograph No. 15. Washington, D.C.: Urban Land Institute.

Mackey, R. B. 1977. Costs For Rural Community Services in Nevada: An Economic-Engineering Approach. Bull. T-21. Reno: Nevada Agricultural Experiment Station.

Malthus, T. R. 1798. Essay on the Principle of Population as It Affects the Future of Society. First Edition. London: Reeves and Turner.

Margolis, J. 1968. "The Demand For Urban Public Services", in Issues in Urban Economics, eds., H. S. Perloff and L. Wingo. Baltimore: Johns Hopkins University Press.

Markusen, A. R. 1978a. "Socioeconomic Impact Models For Boom Town Planning and Policy Evaluation". Paper presented at 1978 Annual Meeting of Western Regional Science Association, Sacramento, Calif., February 25.

Markusen, A. R. 1978b. "Federal Budget Simplification: Preventive Programs vs. Pallatives For Local Governments With Booming, Stable, and Declining Economies". National Tax Journal 30 (3): 249-258.

Massey, Garth. 1978. Building a Power Plant: Newcomers and Social Impact. Prepared for the Metro Center, National Institute of Mental Health, Rockville, Md.

Mathur, V., and H. Rosen. 1974. "Regional Employment Multiplier: A New Approach". Land Economics 50 (1): 93-96.

Matson, R. A., and J. B. Studer. 1975. "Simulating the Employment Impact of Coal Development in Wyoming". Regional Science Perspectives 5: 43-60.

Maxwell, James A. 1969. Financing State and Local Governments. Revised Edition. Washington, D.C.: The Brookings Institution.

Mead, George Herbert. 1934. Mind, Self, and Society. Chicago: University of Chicago Press.

Mehr, A. F., and R. G. Cummings. 1977. Time Series Profile of Urban Infrastructure Stocks in Selected Boomtowns in Rocky Mountain States. LA-6687-MS. Los Alamos, N. M.: Los Alamos Scientific Laboratory.

Merton, Robert K. 1968. Social Theory and Social Structure. New York: Free Press.

Micklin, Michael. 1973. Population, Environment, and Social Organization. Hinsdale, Illinois: Dryden Press.

Miernyk, W. H. 1976. "Comments on Recent Developments in Regional Input-Output Analysis". International Regional Science Review 1 (2): 47-55.

Miernyk, W. H. 1965. Elements of Input-Output Economics. New York: Random House.

Miernyk, W. H. 1968. "Long Range Forecasting with a Regional Input-Output Model". Western Economic Journal 6: 165-176.

Miller, David C. 1977. "Methods for Estimating Social Future", in Methodology of Social Impact Assessment, eds., K. Finsterbusch and C. P. Wolf, Stroudsburg, Pa.: Dowden, Hutchinson, and Ross, Inc., pp. 202-210.

Mishan, E. J. 1971. Cost-Benefit Analysis. London: Allen and Unwin.

Monarchi, D. E., and R. H. Taylor. 1977. An Introduction to Socioeconomic Model Building and the Colorado Population and Employment Model (CPEIO). Boulder: University of Colorado Business Research Division.

Monts, J. K. 1978. BOOMP User's Guide. Austin: University of Texas Center for Energy Studies.

Monts, J. K., and E. R. Bareiss. 1979. Community-Level Impacts Projection System (CLIPS). Austin: University of Texas Center for Energy Studies.

Morrison, P. A. 1971. Demographic Information for Cities: A Manual for Estimating and Projecting Local Population Characteristics. Rand Rpt. R-618-HUD. Santa Monica, Calif.: Rand Corporation.

Morrison, P. A. 1977. "Forecasting Population of Small Areas: An Overview", in Population Forecasting for Small Areas, Oak Ridge, Tenn.: Oak Ridge Associated Universities, pp. 3-13.

Morrison, W. I., and P. Smith. 1974. "Nonsurvey Input-Output Techniques at the Small Area Level: An Evaluation". Journal of Regional Science 14: 1-14.

Morse, G. W., and L. J. Hushak. 1979. Income and Fiscal Impacts of Manufacturing Plants in Southeast Ohio. Res. Bull. 1108. Wooster: Ohio Agricultural Research and Development Center.

Morse, G. W. 1980. With-Without Perspectives in Growth Impact Models. Special Circular 103. Wooster: Ohio Agricultural Research and Development Center.

Moses, L. N. 1958. "Location and the Theory of Production". Quarterly Journal of Economics 72: 259-272.

Mountain West Research, Inc. 1977. Bureau of Reclamation Construction Worker Survey. Denver: U.S. Bureau of Reclamation.

Mountain West Research, Inc. 1978. Bureau of Reclamation Economic Assessment Model (BREAM) Technical Description. Denver: U.S. Bureau of Reclamation.

Mountain West Research, Inc. 1975. Construction Worker Profile. Washington, D.C.: Old West Regional Commission.

Mountain West Research, Inc. 1979. A Guide to Methods for Impact Assessment of Western Coal/Energy Development. Omaha, Neb.: Missouri River Basin Commission.

Muller, T. 1975. Fiscal Impacts of Land Development: A Critique of Methods and Review of Issues. URI 98000. Washington, D.C.: The Urban Institute.

Murdock, S. H., and E. C. Schriner. 1979. "Community Service Satisfaction and Stages of Community Development: An Examination of Evidence From Impacted Communities". Journal of the Community Development Society 10 (1): 109-124.

Murdock, S. H., and E. C. Schriner. 1978. "Structural and
    Distributional Factors in Community Development". Rural
    Sociology 43 (3): 426-449.
Murdock, S. H., F. L. Leistritz, and E. C. Schriner. 1980a.
    "The Demographic Impacts of Rapid Economic Development".
    Paper presented at the Seminar on the Social and Economic
    Impacts of Rapid Growth, Scottsdale, Ariz., February 26-27.
Murdock, S. H., F. L. Leistritz, and E. C. Schriner. 1980b.
    "Migration and Energy Developments: Implications for
    Rural Areas in the Great Plains", in New Directions in
    Urban-Rural Migration, eds., D. Brown and J. Wardwell,
    New York: Academic Press.
Murdock, S. H., L. L. Jones, F. L. Leistritz, and D. R. Andrews.
    1980c. "The Texas Assessment Modeling System (TAMS): A
    Case Study in Model Adaptation". Paper presented at Con-
    ference on Computer Models For Forecasting Impacts of
    Growth and Development, Jasper, Alberta, April 20-23.
Murdock, S. H., F. L. Leistritz, and E. C. Schriner. 1976.
    "Methodological and Conceptual Issues Concerning Social
    and Economic Impact Assessment". Paper presented at Semi-
    nar on Economic and Social Components of Environmental
    Impact Statements, Kansas City, Mo., October 13-15.
Murdock, S. H., and F. L. Leistritz. 1979. Energy Development
    in the Western United States: Impact on Rural Areas.
    New York: Praeger Publishers.
Murdock, S. H., F. L. Leistritz, and L. L. Jones. 1979a.
    "Interfacing Economic and Demographic Models for Rural
    Areas: Design and Methodological Considerations". South-
    ern Journal of Agricultural Economics 11: 139-144.
Murdock, S. H., F. L. Leistritz, L. L. Jones, D. Fannin, D.
    Andrews, B. Wilson, and J. de Montel. 1979b. Texas
    Assessment Modeling System: User Manual. College Station,
    Texas: Texas Agricultural Experiment Station, Texas A&M
    University.
Murdock, S. H., F. L. Leistritz, L. L. Jones, D. Andrews, B.
    Wilson, D. Fannin, and J. de Montel. 1979c. The Texas
    Assessment Modeling System: Technical Description. Tech.
    Rpt. No. 79-3. College Station: Texas Agricultural
    Experiment Station.
Murdock, S. H., and F. L. Leistritz. 1980. "Selecting Socio-
    economic Assessment Models: A Discussion of Criteria and
    Selected Models". Journal of Environmental Management
    10 (1): 1-12.
Murdock, S. H., J. S. Wieland, and F. L. Leistritz. 1978.
    "An Assessment of the Validity of the Gravity Model for
    Predicting Community Settlement Patterns in Rural Energy-
    Impact Areas in the West". Land Economics 54 (4): 461-471.
Murdock, S. H. 1979. "The Potential Role of the Ecological
    Framework in Impact Analysis". Rural Sociology 44 (3):
    543-565.

Murdock, S. H., and T. K. Ostenson. 1976. Population Projections by Age and Sex, 1975-2000. Fargo: North Dakota Agricultural Experiment Station.

Murphy, J. K. 1975. "Socioeconomic Impact Assistance for Synthetic Fuels Commerical Demonstration Program", in Financing Energy Development: Proceedings of the First National Conference on Financial Requirements For Energy Development in the Western States Region, eds., H. Hughes and R. Zee, Sante Fe: New Mexico Energy Resources Board, pp. 112-118.

Murphy and Williams, Consultants. 1978. Socioeconomic Impact Assessment: A Methodology Applied to Synthetic Fuels. Washington, D.C.: U.S. Department of Energy.

Murray, James A. 1980. "The Effects of Rapid Population Growth on the Provision and Financing of Local Public Services". Paper presented at Seminar on Social and Economic Impacts of Rapid Growth, Western Rural Development Center, Scottsdale, Ariz., February 26-27.

National Biocentric, Inc. 1977. Antelope Valley Station: Analysis of the Human Environment. Bismarck, N.D.: Basin Electric Power Cooperative.

National Center for Health Statistics. 1975. U.S. Decennial Life Tables, State Life Tables: 1969-1971. 2:27-51. Rockville, Md.: U.S. Department of Health, Education, and Welfare.

National Environmental Policy Act. 1970. Public Law PL-190.

Niskanen, William. 1971. Bureaucracy and Representative Government. Chicago: Aldine-Atherton.

Obermiller, F. W., B. McCarl, D. Martella, and T. K. White. 1975. The Purdue Development Model: An Interactive Approach to Modeling Population Growth and Economic Development -- An Overview. Res. Bull. No. 926. West Lafayette, Ind.: Purdue University Agricultural Experiment Station.

Office of the State Oil Shale Coordinator. 1974. IMPACT -- An Assessment of the Impact of Oil Shale Development -- Colorado Planning and Management Region II. Denver: State of Colorado, Office of the State Oil Shale Coordinator.

Olsen, M. E., M. G. Curry, M. R. Greene, B. D. Melber, and D. J. Merwin. 1977a. A Social Impact Assessment and Management Methodology Using Social Indicators and Planning Strategies. Seattle, Washington: Battelle Human Affairs Research Centers.

Olsen, R. J., G. W. Westley, H. W. Herzog, Jr., C. R. Kerley, D. J. Bjornstad, D. P. Voyt, L. G. Bray, S. T. Grady, and R. A. Nakosteen. 1977b. MULTIREGION: A Simulation-Forecasting Model of BEA Economic Area Population and Employment. ORNL/RUS-25. Oak Ridge, Tenn.: Oak Ridge National Laboratory.

Olsen, R. J., G. W. Westley, C. R. Kerley, L. G. Bray, D. P. Vogt, H. H. Herzog, S. T. Grady, and R. A. Nakosteen.

1975. "MULTIREGION: A Simulation-Forecasting Model of Regional (BEA Economic Area) Population and Employment (For Regional Planning". Paper presented at Annual Meeting of Southeastern Income Conference, New Orleans, November 12.

Parr, J. B., K. G. Deinke, and G. Mulligan. 1975. "City-Size Models and the Economic Base: A Recent Controversy". Journal of Regional Science 15: 1-8.

Parsons, Talcott. 1951. The Social System. New York: The Free Press.

Perloff, H. S. 1961. "Relative Regional Economic Growth: An Approach to Regional Accounts", in Design of Regional Accounts, ed., W. Hochwald, Baltimore: Johns Hopkins Press.

Pfister, R. 1980. "The Minimum Requirements Technique of Estimating Exports: A Further Evaluation", in Economic Impact Analysis: Methodology and Applications, ed., S. Pleeter, Boston: Martinus Nijhoff Publishing.

Pfister, R. 1976. "On Improving Export Base Studies". Regional Science Perspectives 6: 104-116.

Pidot, G. B. 1969. "A Principal Components Analysis of the Determinants of Local Government Fiscal Patterns". Review of Economics and Statistics 51 (2): 176-188.

Pill, Juri. 1971. "The Delphi Method: Substance, Context, a Critique, and an Annotated Bibliography". Socioeconomic Planning Sciences 5: 57-71.

Pindyck, R. S., and D. L. Rubinfeld. 1976. Econometric Models and Economic Forecasts. New York: McGraw-Hill.

Pittenger, Donald. 1976. Projecting State and Local Populations. Cambridge, Mass.: Ballinger Publishing Company.

Pittenger, Donald. 1974. "A Typology of Age-Specific Net Migration Rate Distributions". Journal of the American Institute of Planners 40 (4): 278-83.

Pleeter, Saul. 1980. "Methodologies of Economic Impact Analysis: An Overview", in Economic Impact Analysis: Methodology and Applications, ed., S. Pleeter, Boston: Martinus Nijhoff Publishing.

Polenske, K. R. 1969. A Multiregional Input-Output Model -- Concept and Results. Cambridge, Mass.: Harvard Economic Research Project.

Popenoe, David. 1980. Sociology. Fourth Edition. Englewood Cliffs, N.J.: Prentice-Hall.

Portland State University, Center for Population Research and Census. 1975. Population Projections to the Year 2000: Oregon Administration District 2. Portland, Ore.: Comprehensive Health Planning Association for the Metropolitan Portland Area.

Price, N. O., and M. M. Sikes. 1975. Rural-Urban Migration Research in The United States. Bethesda, Md.: U.S. Department of Health, Education, and Welfare.

Purdy, B. J., E. Peele, B. H. Bronfman, and D. J. Bjornstad. 1977. A Post Licensing Study of Community Effects of Two Operating Nuclear Power Plants. Oak Ridge, Tenn.: Oak Ridge National Laboratory.

Rapp, D. A. 1976. Western Boom Towns: A Comparative Analysis of State Actions. Denver: Western Governor's Regional Energy Policy Office.

Rau, William C. 1980. "The Tacit Conventions of the Modernity School". American Sociological Review 45 (2): 244-260.

Real Estate Research Corporation. 1976. The Costs of Sprawl. Washington, D.C.: Council on Environmental Quality.

Reeve, R., R. Weaver, and E. Natwig. 1976. The Navaho Economic-Demographic Model: A Method for Forecasting and Evaluating Alternative Navaho Economic Futures. Salt Lake City: Utah State Planning Coordinator.

Reeve, R., and R. Weaver. 1974. Report on the Development and Implementation of the Utah Land Use and Tax Base Model (UPLAND). Salt Lake City: Utah State Planning Coordinator.

Richardson, H. W. 1969. Elements of Regional Economics. New York: Penguin Books.

Richardson, H. W. 1972. Input-Output and Regional Economics. New York: Halsted Press.

Richardson, H. W. 1978. Regional and Urban Economics. New York: Penguin Books.

Rink, R., and A. Ford. 1978. A Simulation Model for Boom Town Housing. LA-7324-MS. Los Alamos, N.M.: Los Alamos Scientific Laboratory.

Ritchey, P. Neal. 1976. "Explanations of Migration". The Annual Review of Sociology II. Palo Alto, Calif.: Annual Review, Inc.

Roesler, T. W., F. C. Lamphear, and M. D. Beveridge. 1968. The Economic Impact of Irrigated Agriculture on the Economy of Nebraska. Lincoln: University of Nebraska Bureau of Business Research.

Romanoff, E. 1974. "The Economic Base Model: A Very Special Case of Input-Output Analysis". Journal of Regional Science 14: 121-129.

Rossini, F. A., A. L. Porter, P. Kelly, and D. E. Chubin. 1978. Frameworks and Factors Affecting Integration Within Technology Assessments. Atlanta: Georgia Institute of Technology.

Ross, P. J., H. Bluestone, and F. K. Hines. 1979. Indicators of Social Well-Being for U.S. Counties. Rural Development Research. Rpt. No. 10. Washington, D.C.: U.S. Department of Agriculture.

Sanderson, W. C. 1978. Economic-Demographic Models: A Review of Their Usefulness for Policy Analysis. Tech. paper 4. Rome: Food and Agriculture Organization of the United Nations.

San Diego Comprehensive Planning Organization. 1977. IPEF 77, Interactive Population, Employment Forecasting Model, Technical Users' Manual. San Diego: San Diego Comprehensive Planning Organization.

San Diego Comprehensive Planning Organization. 1972. Technical User's Manual for the Interactive Population/Employment Forecasting Model. San Diego: San Diego Comprehensive Planning Organization.

Schaffer, W. A., and K. Chu. 1969. "Nonsurvey Techniques for Constructing Regional Inter-industry Models". Papers of the Regional Science Association 23: 83-101.

Schmidt, J. R., R. L. Oehrtman, and C. A. Doeksen. 1978. "Planning Ambulance Services for a Rural Emergency Medical Service District". Southern Journal of Agricultural Economics 10: 127-132.

Schriner, E. C., J. N. Query, T. D. McDonald, F. Keogh, and T. Gallagher. 1976. An Assessment of the Social Impacts Associated with a Coal Gasification Complex Proposed for Dunn County, North Dakota. Fargo: North Dakota State University.

Schuman, H., and M. P. Johnson. 1976. "Attitudes and Behavior", in Annual Review of Sociology 2, ed., Alex Inkeles, Palo Alto, Calif.: Annual Reviews, pp. 161-202.

Schwartz, D. F. 1977. Reservation Manpower Survey. Bismarck, North Dakota: United Tribes Educational Technical Center.

Scott, C. D. V. 1972. Forecasting Local Government Spending. Washington, D.C.: The Urban Institute.

Scott, D. F., and C. Braschler. 1975. Estimation of Industry Labor Income Multipliers for County Groupings in Missouri. Res. Bull. 998. Columbia: Missouri Agricultural Experiment Station.

Selbyg, Arne. 1978. Residents' Perceptions and Attitudes. Bismarck: North Dakota Regional Environmental Assessment Program.

Selltiz, C., M. Jahoda, M. Deutsch, and S. W. Cook. 1959. Research Methods in Social Relations. New York: Holt, Rinehart, and Winston.

Senechal, D. M. 1971. Analysis of Validity of North Dakota Input-Output Models. Master's Thesis. Fargo: North Dakota State University.

Shaffer, R. E. 1979. "Estimating Local Income Multipliers: A Review and Evaluation of the Techniques for Ex Ante Use". Paper presented to North Central Interest Network on Ex Ante Growth Impact Models, Columbus, Ohio, March 6-7.

Shaffer, R. E., and L. G. Tweeten. 1974. Economic Changes From Industrial Development in Eastern Oklahoma: Bull. B-175. Stillwater: Oklahoma Agricultural Experiment Station.

Shapiro, Harold T. 1973. "Is Verification Possible? The Evaluation of Large Econometric Models". American Journal of Agricultural Economics 55 (2): 250-258.

278

Shapiro, Harvey. 1963. "Economies of Scale and Local Government Finance". Land Economics 35 (2): 175-186.

Sherafat, N., A. Pagoulatos, and K. R. Anschel. 1978. "The
Exploitation of Coal as an Engine for Growth in Eastern
Kentucky -- An Input-Output Study". Southern Journal of
Agricultural Economics 10 (2): 81-86.

Shields, M. A., J. T. Cowan, and D. J. Bjornstad. 1979. Soc-
ioeconomic Impacts of Nuclear Power Plants: A Paired
Comparison of Operating Facilities. Oak Ridge, Tenn.:
Oak Ridge National Laboratory.

Shryock, H. S., and J. S. Siegel. 1973. The Methods and
Materials of Demography. Washington, D.C.: U.S. Bureau
of the Census. U.S. Government Printing Office.

Sjaastad, L. A. 1962. "The Costs and Returns of Human Migration". Journal of Political Economy 70: 580-593.

Smith, David M. 1971. Industrial Location: An Economic Geographical Analysis. New York: John Wiley and Sons, Inc.

Smith, P., and W. I. Morrison. 1974. Simulating the Urban
Economy: Experiments with Input-Output Techniques.
London: Pion Limited.

Stanford Research Institute. 1975. Manpower, Materials,
Equipment, and Utilities Required to Operate and Maintain
Energy Facilities. Menlo Park, Calif.: Stanford Research
Institute.

Stenehjem, Erik J., and J. E. Metzger. 1976. A Framework for
Projecting Employment and Population Changes Accompanying
Energy Development. Argonne, Ill.: Argonne National
Laboratory.

Stenehjem, Erik J. 1978. Summary Description of SEAM: The
Social and Economic Assessment Model. Argonne, Ill.:
Argonne National Laboratory.

Stevens, B. H., and G. A. Trainer. 1980. "Error Generation in
Regional Input-Output Analysis and Its Implications for
Nonsurvey Models", in Economic Impact Analysis: Method-
ology and Applications, ed., S. Pleeter, Boston: Martinus
Nijhoff Publishing.

Stinson, Thomas F. 1978a. "The Dynamics of the Adjustment
Period in Rapid Growth Communities". Paper presented at
Western Agricultural Economics Association Annual Meeting,
Bozeman, Mont., July 24-25.

Stinson, T. F. 1978b. State Taxation of Mineral Deposits and
Production. USDA Rural Development Res. Rpt. No. 2.
Washington, D.C.: U.S. Government Printing Office.

Stinson, T. F., and S. W. Voelker. 1978. Coal Development in
the Northern Great Plains: The Impact on Revenues of
State and Local Governments. USDA Ag. Econ. Rpt. No. 394.
Washington, D.C.: U.S. Government Printing Office.

Stone, R. 1961. Input-Output and National Accounts. Paris:
Organization for European Economic Cooperation.

Summers, G. F., S. D. Evans, F. Clemente, E. M. Beck, and

J. Minkoff. 1976. Industrial Invasion of Nonmetropolitan America: A Quarter Century of Experience. New York: Praeger Publishers.

Swanson, E. R. 1979. "Working with Other Disciplines". American Journal of Agricultural Economics 61 (5): 849-859.

Tarver, J. D., and T. R. Black. 1966. Making County Population Projections: A Detailed Explanation of a Three-Component Method, Illustrated by Reference to Utah Counties. Logan: Utah Agricultural Experiment Station.

TERA Corporation. 1976. Fayette Power Project: Socioeconomic Study. Austin, Texas: Lower Colorado River Authority.

Thompson, J. G., A. L. Blevins, and G. L. Watts. 1978. Socioeconomic Longitudinal Monitoring Report. Washington, D.C.: Old West Regional Commission.

Tiebout, C. M. 1962. The Community Economic Base Study. Supplementary Paper No. 16. New York: Committee for Economic Development.

Toman, N. E., A. G. Leholm, N. L. Dalsted, and F. L. Leistritz. 1977. "A Fiscal Impact Model For Rural Industrialization". Western Journal of Agricultural Economics 1: 242-247.

Toman, N. E., N. L. Dalsted, A. G. Leholm, R. C. Coon, and F. L. Leistritz. 1976. Economic Impacts of the Construction and Operation of the Coal Creek Electrical Generation Complex and Related Mine. Fargo: North Dakota Agricultural Experiment Station.

Toman, N. E., N. L. Dalsted, J. S. Wieland, and F. L. Leistritz. 1978. Water as a Parameter for Development of Energy Resources in the Upper Great Plains -- Socioeconomic Effects of Alternative Patterns of Coal-Based Energy Development. Res. Rpt. No. 70. Fargo: North Dakota Agricultural Experiment Station.

Toman, N. E., S. H. Murdock, and T. A. Hertsgaard. 1979. REAP Economic Demographic Model Version II: Technical Description. Bismarck: North Dakota Regional Environmental Assessment Program.

Tweeten, L., and G. L. Brinkman. 1976. Micropolitan Development. Ames: Iowa State University Press.

Ullman, E. L., and M. F. Dacey. 1960. "The Minimum Requirements Approach to the Urban Economic Base". Papers of the Regional Science Association 6: 175-194.

U.S. Bureau of the Census. 1953. Current Population Reports. Series P-25, No. 56. Washington, D.C.: U.S. Government Printing Office.

U.S. Bureau of the Census. 1976. Computer Programs for Demographic Analysis. Washington, D.C.: U.S. Government Printing Office.

U.S. Bureau of the Census. 1977. "Gross Migration by County: 1965 to 1970". Current Population Reports. Series P-25, No. 701. Washington, D.C.: U.S. Government Printing Office.

U. S. Bureau of the Census. 1979a. "Illustrative Projections of State Populations by Age, Race, and Sex: 1975 to 2000". Current Population Reports. Series P-25, No. 796. Washington, D.C.: U.S. Government Printing Office.

U.S. Bureau of the Census. 1979b. "School Enrollment-Social and Economic Characteristics of Students: October 1978". Current Population Reports. Series P-20, No. 346. Washington D.C.: U.S. Government Printing Office.

U.S. Bureau of Economic Analysis, Department of Commerce. 1974. 1972 OBERS Projections, Regional Economic Activity in the U.S., Series E. Population. (7 Volumes). With the Economic Research Service, Department of Agriculture, for the U.S. Water Resources Council. Washington, D.C.: U.S. Government Printing Office.

U.S. Department of Commerce, Bureau of Economic Analysis. 1977. Industry-Specific Gross Output Multipliers for BEA Economic Areas. Washington, D.C.: U.S. Government Printing Office.

U.S. Department of Health, Education, and Welfare. 1979. Health United States, 1977. Rockville, Md.: National Center for Health Statistics.

U.S. Department of the Interior. 1978. Projects to Expand Energy Sources in the Western States. Bureau of Mines Info. Circ. 8772. Washington, D.C.: U.S. Government Printing Office.

Vidich, A. J., and J. Bensman. 1958. Small Town in Mass Society. Princeton, N.J.: Princeton University Press.

Vlachos, Evan. 1977. "The Use of Scenarios for Social Impact Assessment", in Methodology of Social Impact Assessment, eds., K. Finsterbusch and C. P. Wolf, Stroudsburg, Pa.: Dowden, Hutchinson, and Ross, Inc., pp. 211-233.

Voelker, S. W., D. L. Helgeson, and H. G. Vreugdenhil. 1978. A Functional Classification of Agricultural Trade Centers in North Dakota. Ag. Econ. Rpt. No. 125. Fargo: North Dakota Agricultural Experiment Station.

Watson, K. S. 1977. "Measuring and Mitigating Socioeconomic Environmental Impacts of Constructing Energy Projects: An Emerging Regulatory Issue". Natural Resources Lawyer 10: 393-403.

Webb, Walter Prescott. 1931. The Great Plains. New York: Grosset and Dunlap.

Weber, A. 1929. Theory of the Location of Industries. Chicago: University of Chicago Press.

Weber, B., and G. Goldman. 1979. Evaluating Fiscal Impact Studies: Community Guidelines. WREP16. Corvallis, Ore.: Western Rural Development Center.

Weber, B. 1979. "User Charges, Property Taxes, and Population Growth: The Distributional Implications of Alternative Municipal Financing Strategies". Technical Paper 5032. Corvallis: Oregon Agricultural Experiment Station.

Weiss, S. J., and E. C. Gooding. 1968. "Estimation of Differential Employment Multipliers in a Small Regional Economy". Land Economics 44 (2): 235-244.

Whittlesey, N. K. 1978. Agricultural Impact of Oil Shale Development. NRED Working Paper No. 46. Washington, D.C.: U.S. Department of Agriculture.

Wieland, J. S., F. L. Leistritz, and S. H. Murdock. 1979. "Characteristics and Residential Patterns of Energy-Related Work Forces in the Northern Great Plains". Western Journal of Agricultural Economics 4 (1): 57-68.

Wieland, J. S., F. L. Leistritz, and S. H. Murdock. 1977. Characteristics and Settlement Patterns of Energy-Related Operational Workers in the Northern Great Plains. Ag. Econ. Rpt. No. 123. Fargo: North Dakota Agricultural Experiment Station.

Wilson, B. R., L. L. Jones, and R. Floyd. 1979. "A User Oriented Computerized Industrial Impact Model". Paper presented at 11th Annual Meeting of Mid-Continent Regional Science Association, Minneapolis, Minn., May 31-June 2.

Wirth, L. 1938. "Urbanism as a Way of Life". American Journal of Sociology 44: 8-20.

Index

See Service standards.
See also Service assess-
ment methods -- impact
Service assessment methods --
impact, 120
Service categories, 108
education, 108, 109
fire protection, 108, 109
housing, 108, 109
law enforcement, 108, 109
libraries, 108, 110
medical and mental health,
108, 109
recreation, 108, 110
social welfare, 108-110
solid waste disposal, 108, 110
transportation, 108, 110
water supplies, 108, 109
water treatment, 108, 109
Service characteristics, 111-114
delivery system, 113
distribution of, 112
predevelopment levels, 111
quality of, 112
satisfaction with, 113
Service costs, 8-10, 13-14, 129-
131, 135-139
defined, 129-130.
See also Fiscal assessment
methods
Service standards, 107, 116
comparable area, 116, 117
general and engineering, 116,
117
predevelopment, 116
Services, 105, 120
factors affecting, 111-114.
See also Service assessment
methods; Service categories
Settlement patterns, 8-10, 96
SIMPACT Model, 212, 219, 226-231
Social assessment methods --
baseline, 161-170
participant observation, 167
secondary data, 162
survey, 162-167
unobtrusive research design,
167-168.
See also Content analysis;
Survey methods

Social assessment methods --
impact, 178, 182
delphi surveys, 178, 179-180
scenario forecasting, 178,
181-181
social change and development, 178-181
trend extrapolation, 178-179
value forecasting, 178, 180
Social assessment perspectives,
158-161
conflict, 159-160
functionalism, 159-160
human ecology, 159, 160-161
symbolic interactionism, 159
Social impact assessment process.
See Social impacts
Social impacts, 8-10, 14-15,
155
definition of, 156-157
factors affecting, 168-172
types of, 156-158.
See also Social assessment
methods; Social assessment
perspectives
Socioeconomic impact assessment,
6-15, 204, 234-237
factors affecting, 6-15
functions of, 234-236
requirements for, 2-4
state-of-the-art in, 247-252
users of, 2-4, 236-237
uses of, 2-4, 234-236
Socioeconomic impacts, 5, 6-15
definition of, 5
factors affecting, 6-15
interrelationships of dimensions, 6-15
Special populations, 74, 85
Study area delineation, 51-59,
91
local impact area, 52, 91
regional impact area, 52
Survey methods, 162-167
delphi-expert opinion, 166
sample survey, 166
steps in, 163-166
Survival rate (mortality rate),
77-78
Susquehanna River Basin Model,
209-211